JASON AARON
WRITER

ISSUES #1-5

ED McGUINNESS
PENCILER

DEXTER VINES
INKER

MARTE GRACIA
COLORIST

ISSUE #6

CAMERON STEWART
ARTIST

RACHELLE ROSENBERG
COLORIST

LETTERER: JOE CARAMAGNA
COVER ART: ED McGUINNESS, DEXTER VINES & MARTE GRACIA
ASSISTANT EDITORS: XANDER JAROWEY & FRANKIE JOHNSON
ASSOCIATE EDITOR: JORDAN D. WHITE
EDITORS: NICK LOWE & MIKE MARTS

COLLECTION EDITOR: JENNIFER GRÜNWALD ASSISTANT EDITOR: SARAH BRUNSTAD
ASSOCIATE MANAGING EDITOR: ALEX STARBUCK EDITOR, SPECIAL PROJECTS: MARK D. BEAZLEY
SENIOR EDITOR, SPECIAL PROJECTS: JEFF YOUNGQUIST SVP PRINT, SALES & MARKETING: DAVID GABRIEL
BOOK DESIGN: JEFF POWELL

EDITOR IN CHIEF: AXEL ALONSO CHIEF CREATIVE OFFICER: JOE QUESADA
PUBLISHER: DAN BUCKLEY EXECUTIVE PRODUCER: ALAN FINE

AMAZING X-MEN VOL. 1: THE QUEST FOR NIGHTCRAWLER. Contains material originally published in magazine form as AMAZING X-MEN #1-6. First printing 2014. ISBN# 978-0-7851-8821-6. Published by MARVEL WORLDWIDE, INC., a subsidiary of MARVEL ENTERTAINMENT, LLC. OFFICE OF PUBLICATION: 135 West 50th Street, New York, NY 10020. Copyright © 2013 and 2014 Marvel Characters, Inc. All rights reserved. All characters featured in this issue and the distinctive names and likenesses thereof, and all related indicia are trademarks of Marvel Characters, Inc. No similarity between any of the names, characters, persons, and/or institutions in this magazine with those of any living or dead person or institution is intended, and any such similarity which may exist is purely coincidental. Printed in Canada. ALAN FINE, EVP - Office of the President, Marvel Worldwide, Inc. and EVP & CMO Marvel Characters B.V.; DAN BUCKLEY, Publisher & President - Print, Animation & Digital Divisions; JOE QUESADA, Chief Creative Officer; TOM BREVOORT, SVP of Publishing; DAVID BOGART, SVP of Operations & Procurement, Publishing; C.B. CEBULSKI, SVP of Creator & Content Development; DAVID GABRIEL, SVP Print, Sales & Marketing; JIM O'KEEFE, VP of Operations & Logistics; DAN CARR, Executive Director of Publishing Technology; SUSAN CRESPI, Editorial Operations Manager; ALEX MORALES, Publishing Operations Manager; STAN LEE, Chairman Emeritus. For information regarding advertising in Marvel Comics or on Marvel.com, please contact Niza Disla, Director of Marvel Partnerships, at ndisla@marvel.com. For Marvel subscription inquiries, please call 800-217-9158. Manufactured between 4/25/2014 and 6/2/2014 by SOLISCO PRINTERS, SCOTT, QC, CANADA.
10 9 8 7 6 5 4 3 2 1

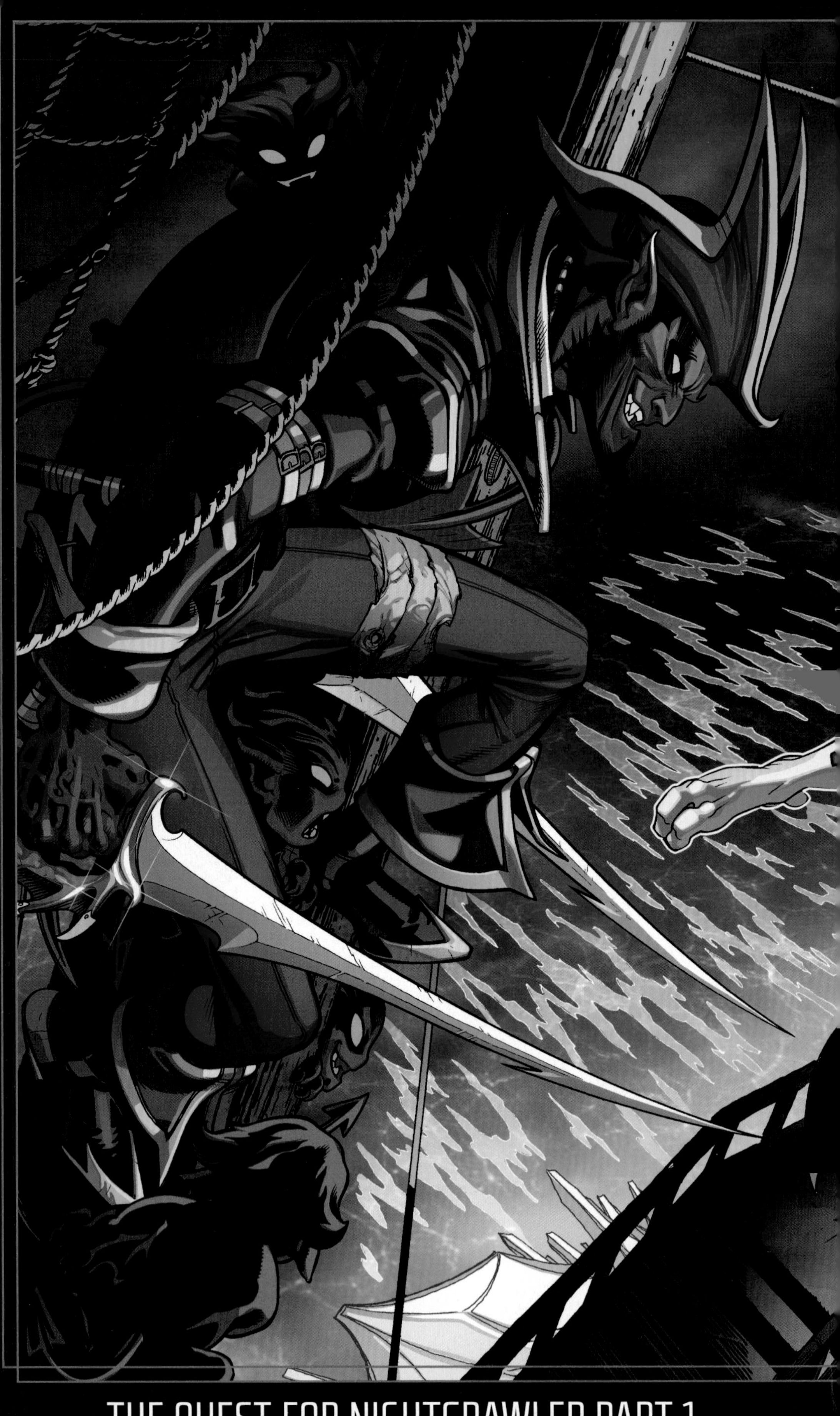

THE QUEST FOR NIGHTCRAWLER PART 1

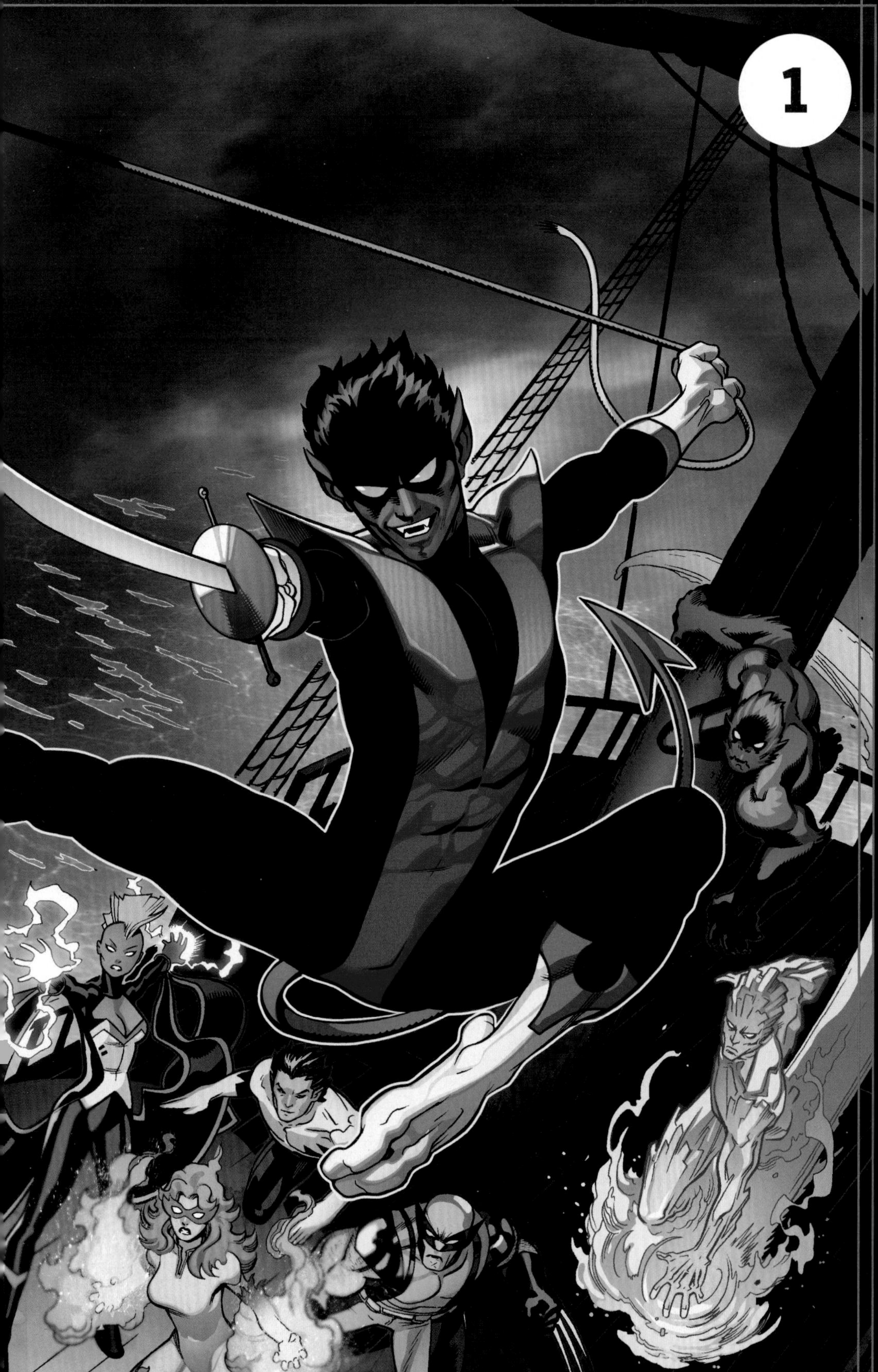
1

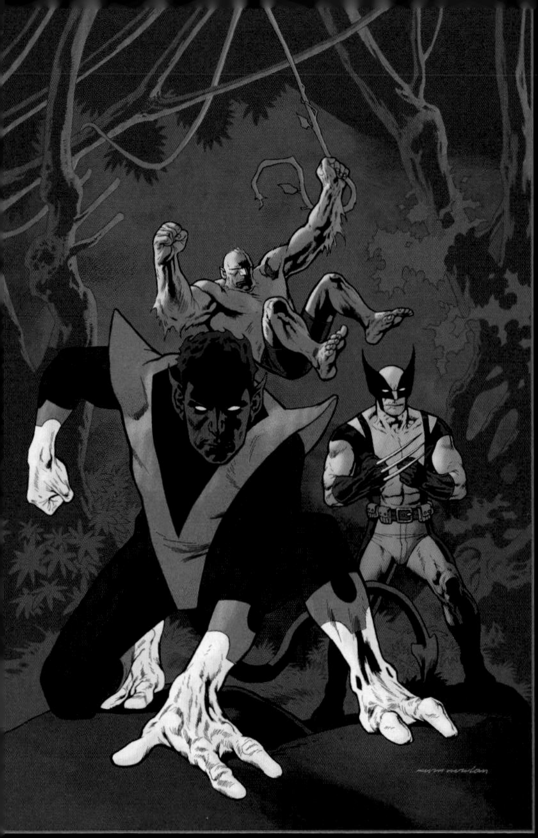

AMAZING X-MEN #1 VARIANT
BY KEVIN NOWLAN

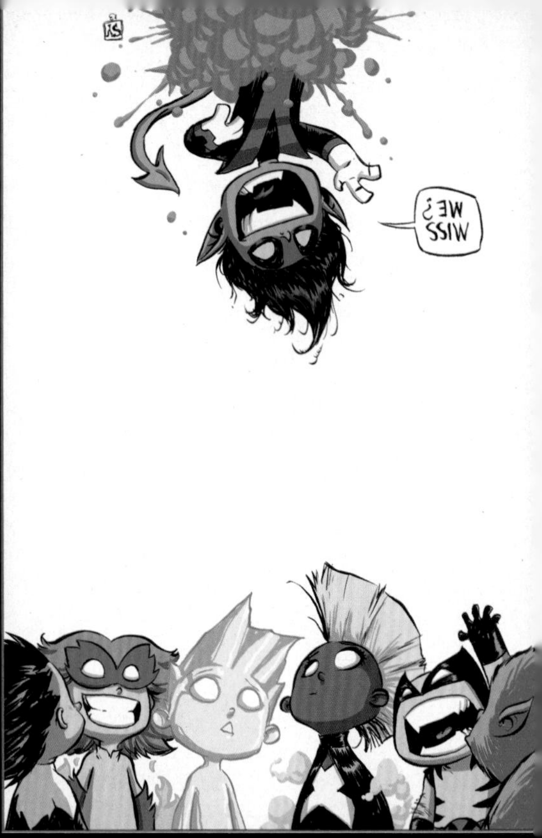
MISS ME?

AMAZING X-MEN #1 VARIANT
BY SKOTTIE YOUNG

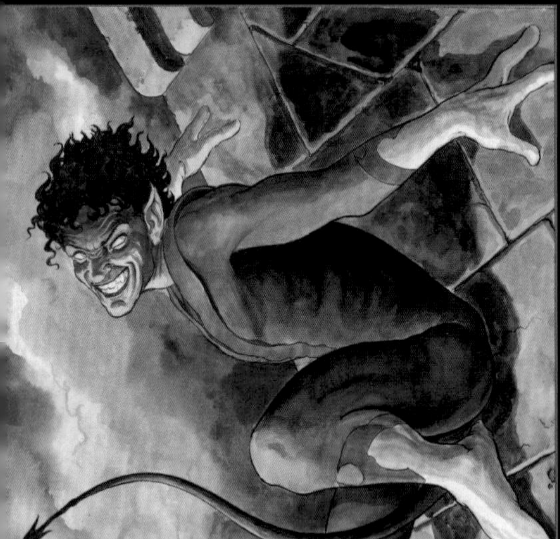

AMAZING X-MEN #1 VARIANT

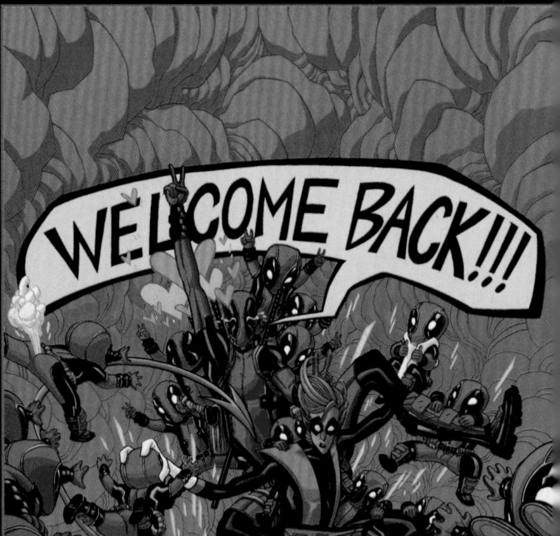
WELCOME BACK!!!

AMAZING X-MEN #1 DEADPOOL VARIANT

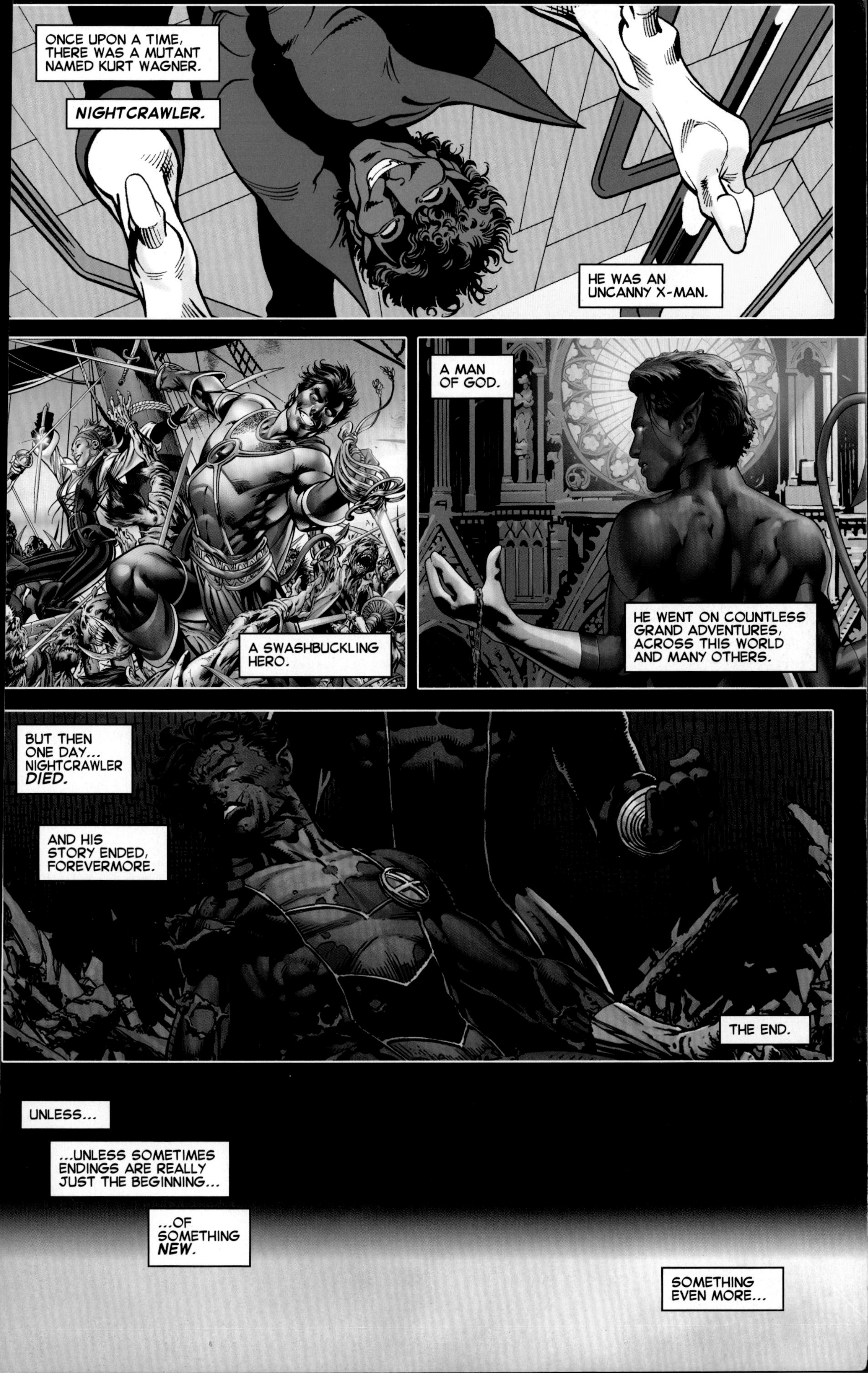
ONCE UPON A TIME, THERE WAS A MUTANT NAMED KURT WAGNER.
NIGHTCRAWLER.
HE WAS AN UNCANNY X-MAN.
A SWASHBUCKLING HERO.
A MAN OF GOD.
HE WENT ON COUNTLESS GRAND ADVENTURES, ACROSS THIS WORLD AND MANY OTHERS.
BUT THEN ONE DAY... NIGHTCRAWLER *DIED.*
AND HIS STORY ENDED, FOREVERMORE.
THE END.
UNLESS...
...UNLESS SOMETIMES ENDINGS ARE REALLY JUST THE BEGINNING...
...OF SOMETHING *NEW.*
SOMETHING EVEN MORE...

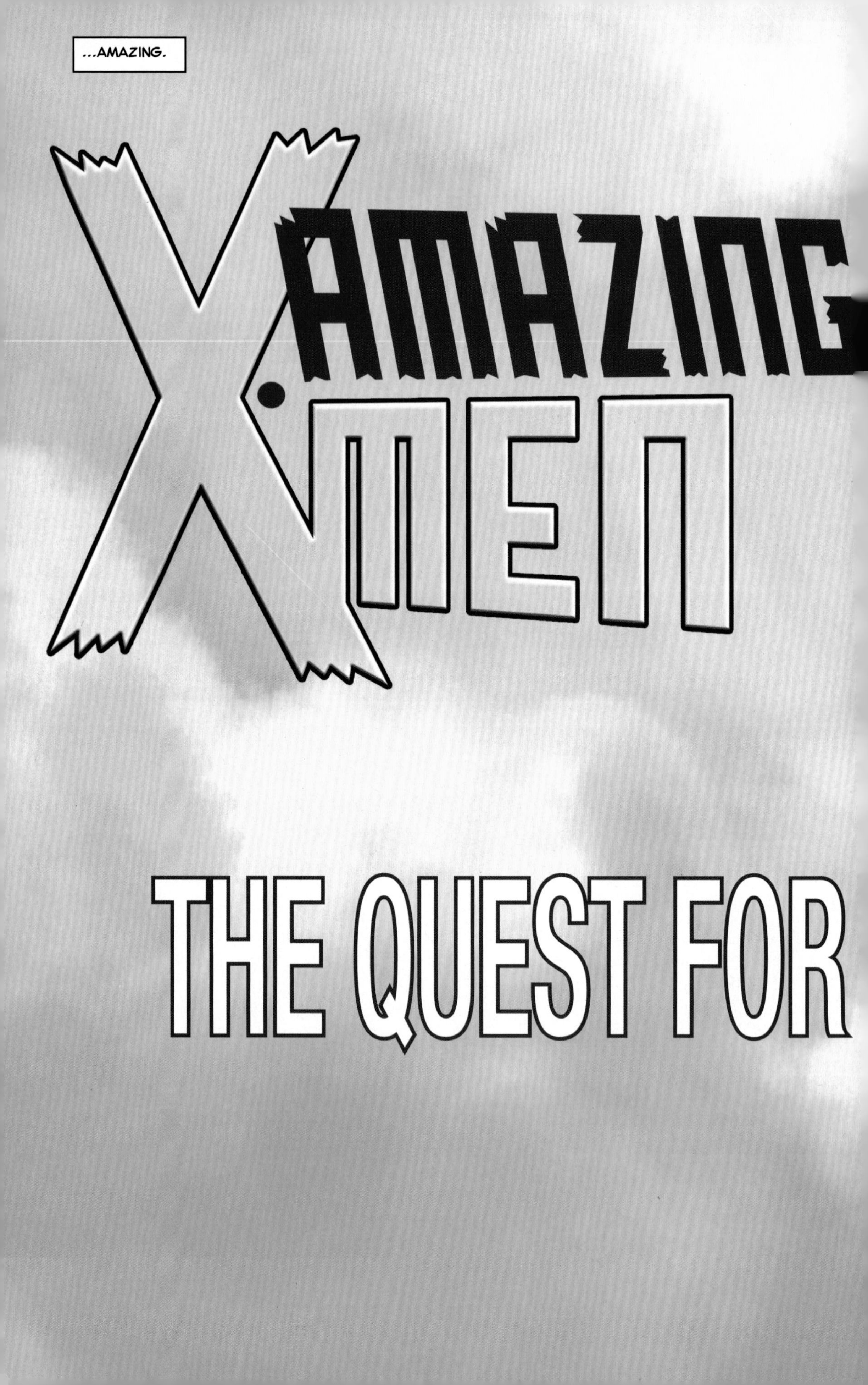
...AMAZING.
AMAZING X-MEN
THE QUEST FOR

NIGHTCRAWLER

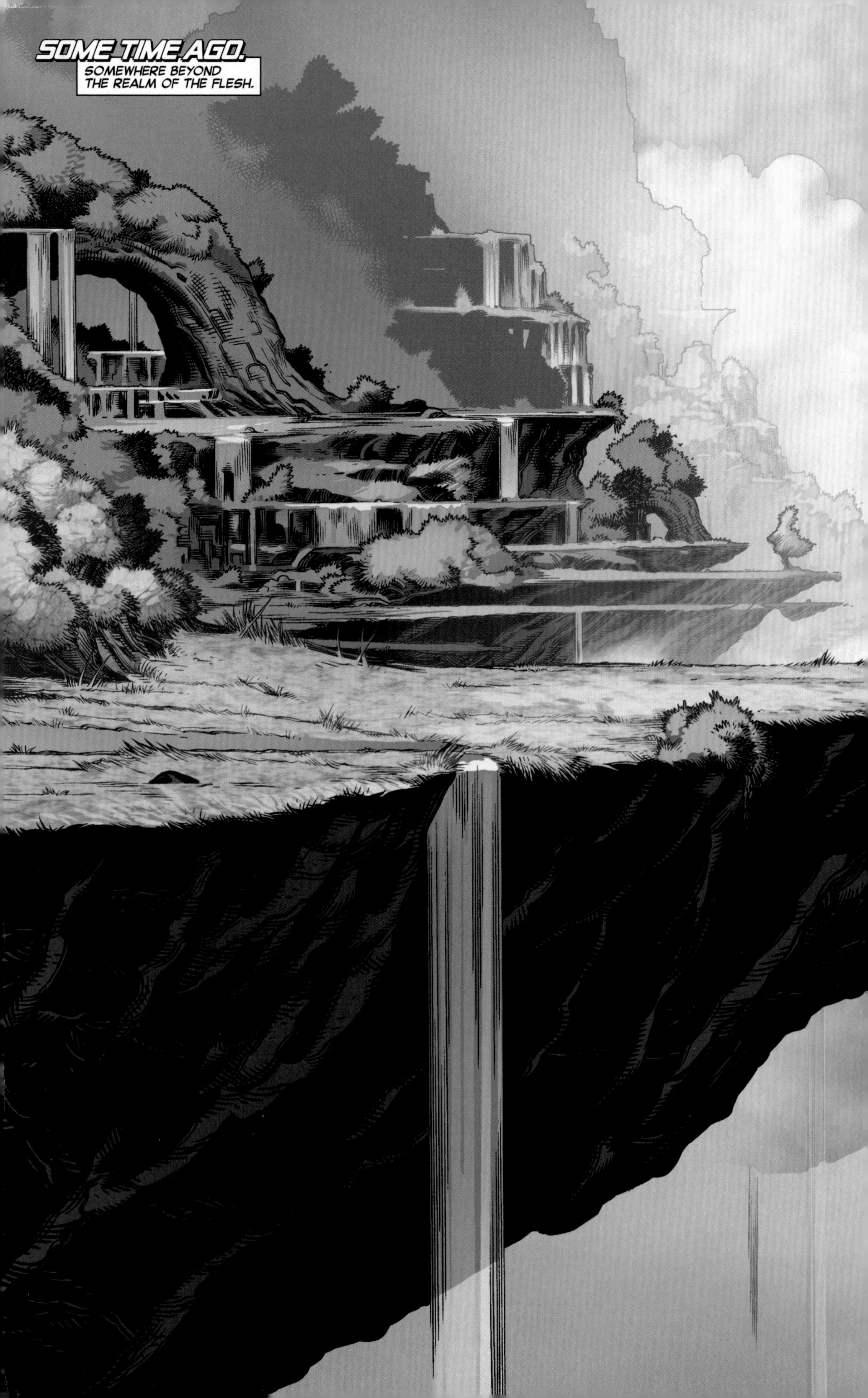
SOME TIME AGO.
SOMEWHERE BEYOND THE REALM OF THE FLESH.

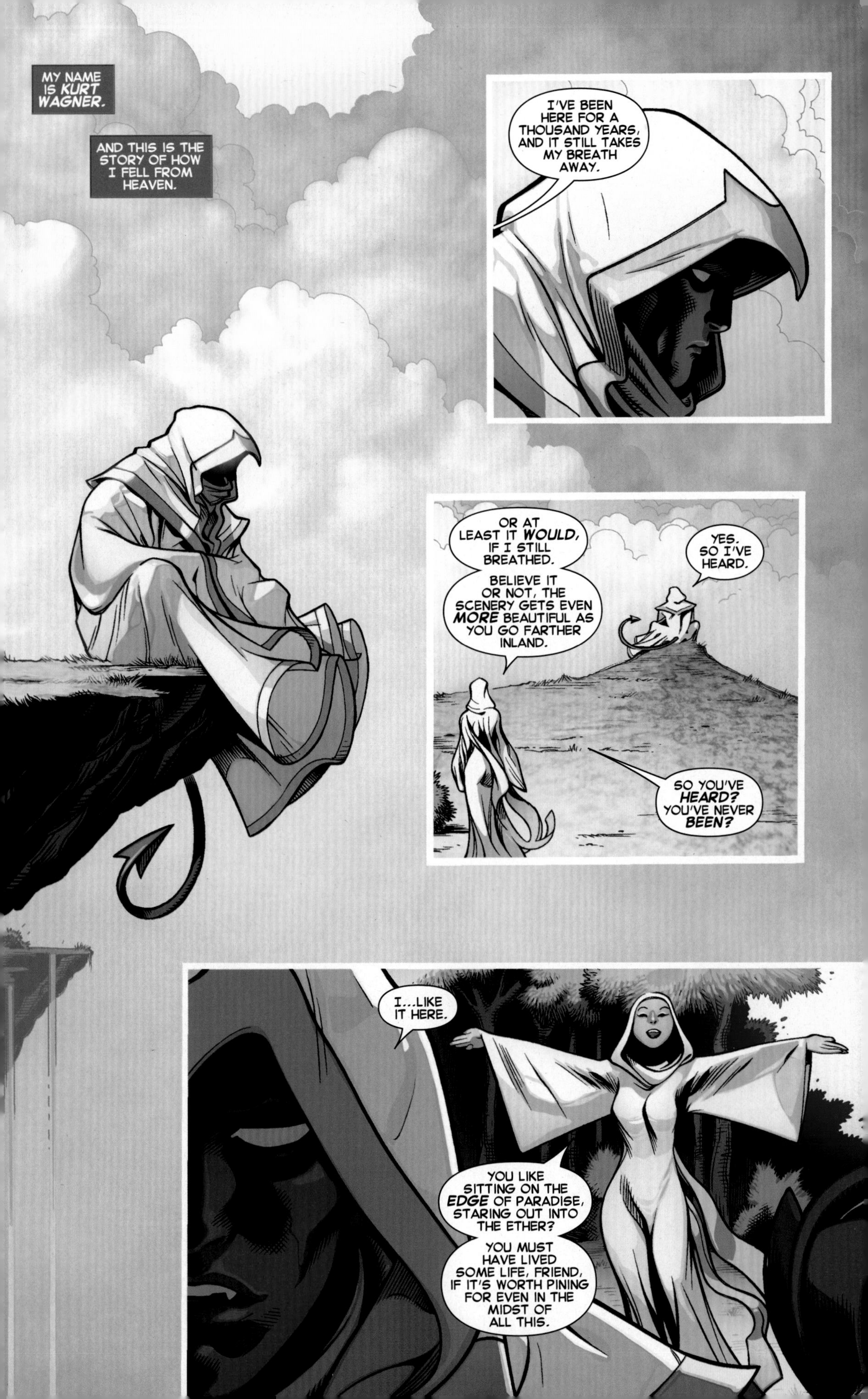
MY NAME IS KURT WAGNER.
AND THIS IS THE STORY OF HOW I FELL FROM HEAVEN.
I'VE BEEN HERE FOR A THOUSAND YEARS, AND IT STILL TAKES MY BREATH AWAY.
OR AT LEAST IT WOULD, IF I STILL BREATHED.
BELIEVE IT OR NOT, THE SCENERY GETS EVEN MORE BEAUTIFUL AS YOU GO FARTHER INLAND.
YES. SO I'VE HEARD.
SO YOU'VE HEARD? YOU'VE NEVER BEEN?
I...LIKE IT HERE.
YOU LIKE SITTING ON THE EDGE OF PARADISE, STARING OUT INTO THE ETHER?
YOU MUST HAVE LIVED SOME LIFE, FRIEND, IF IT'S WORTH PINING FOR EVEN IN THE MIDST OF ALL THIS.

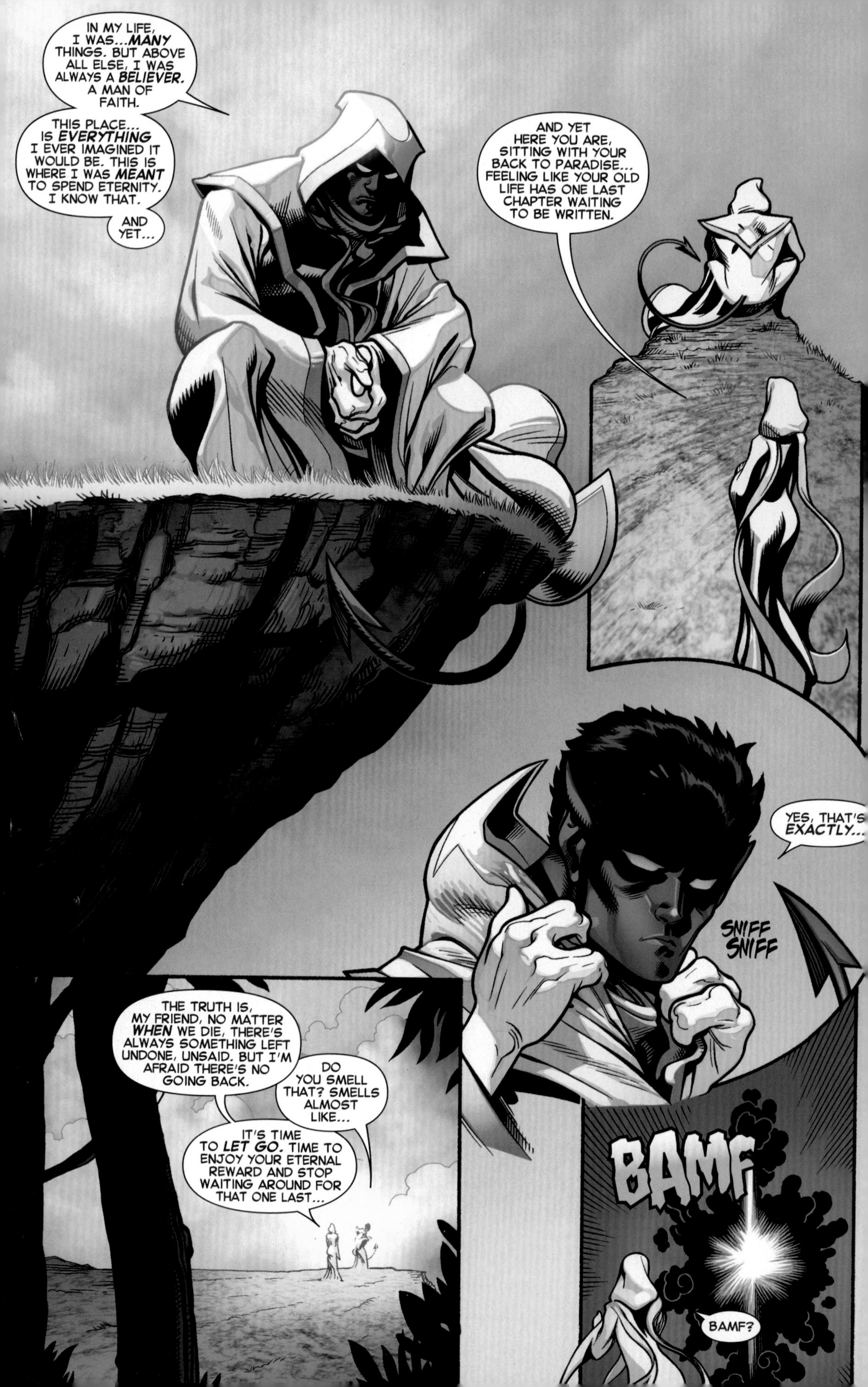
IN MY LIFE, I WAS...MANY THINGS. BUT ABOVE ALL ELSE, I WAS ALWAYS A BELIEVER. A MAN OF FAITH.
THIS PLACE... IS EVERYTHING I EVER IMAGINED IT WOULD BE. THIS IS WHERE I WAS MEANT TO SPEND ETERNITY. I KNOW THAT.
AND YET...
AND YET HERE YOU ARE, SITTING WITH YOUR BACK TO PARADISE... FEELING LIKE YOUR OLD LIFE HAS ONE LAST CHAPTER WAITING TO BE WRITTEN.
YES, THAT'S EXACTLY...
SNIFF SNIFF
THE TRUTH IS, MY FRIEND, NO MATTER WHEN WE DIE, THERE'S ALWAYS SOMETHING LEFT UNDONE, UNSAID. BUT I'M AFRAID THERE'S NO GOING BACK.
DO YOU SMELL THAT? SMELLS ALMOST LIKE...
IT'S TIME TO LET GO. TIME TO ENJOY YOUR ETERNAL REWARD AND STOP WAITING AROUND FOR THAT ONE LAST...
BAMF
BAMF?

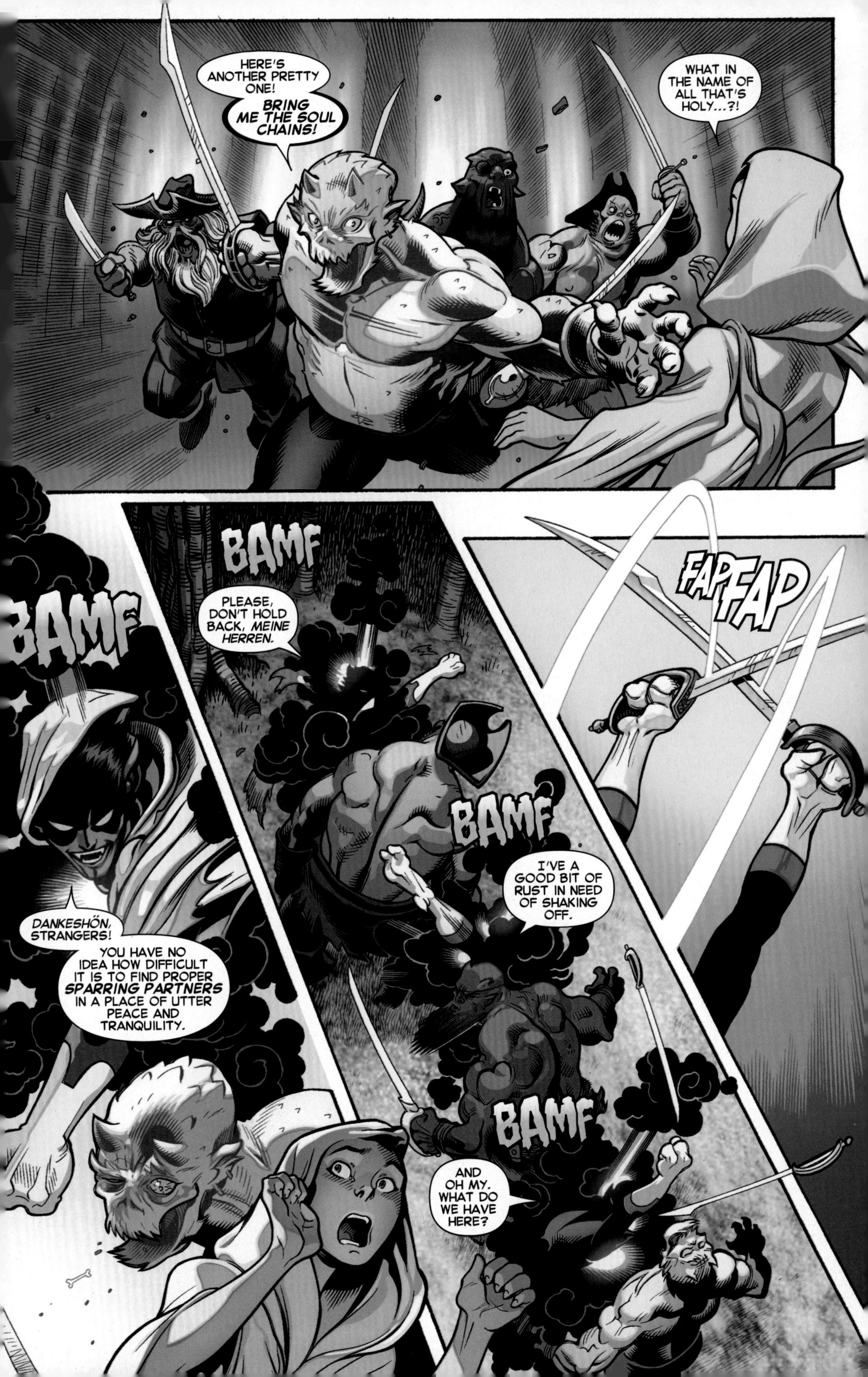
HERE'S ANOTHER PRETTY ONE!
BRING ME THE SOUL CHAINS!
WHAT IN THE NAME OF ALL THAT'S HOLY...?!
BAMF
DANKESHÖN, STRANGERS!
YOU HAVE NO IDEA HOW DIFFICULT IT IS TO FIND PROPER SPARRING PARTNERS IN A PLACE OF UTTER PEACE AND TRANQUILITY.
BAMF
PLEASE, DON'T HOLD BACK, MEINE HERREN.
BAMF
I'VE A GOOD BIT OF RUST IN NEED OF SHAKING OFF.
BAMF
AND OH MY. WHAT DO WE HAVE HERE?
FAP FAP

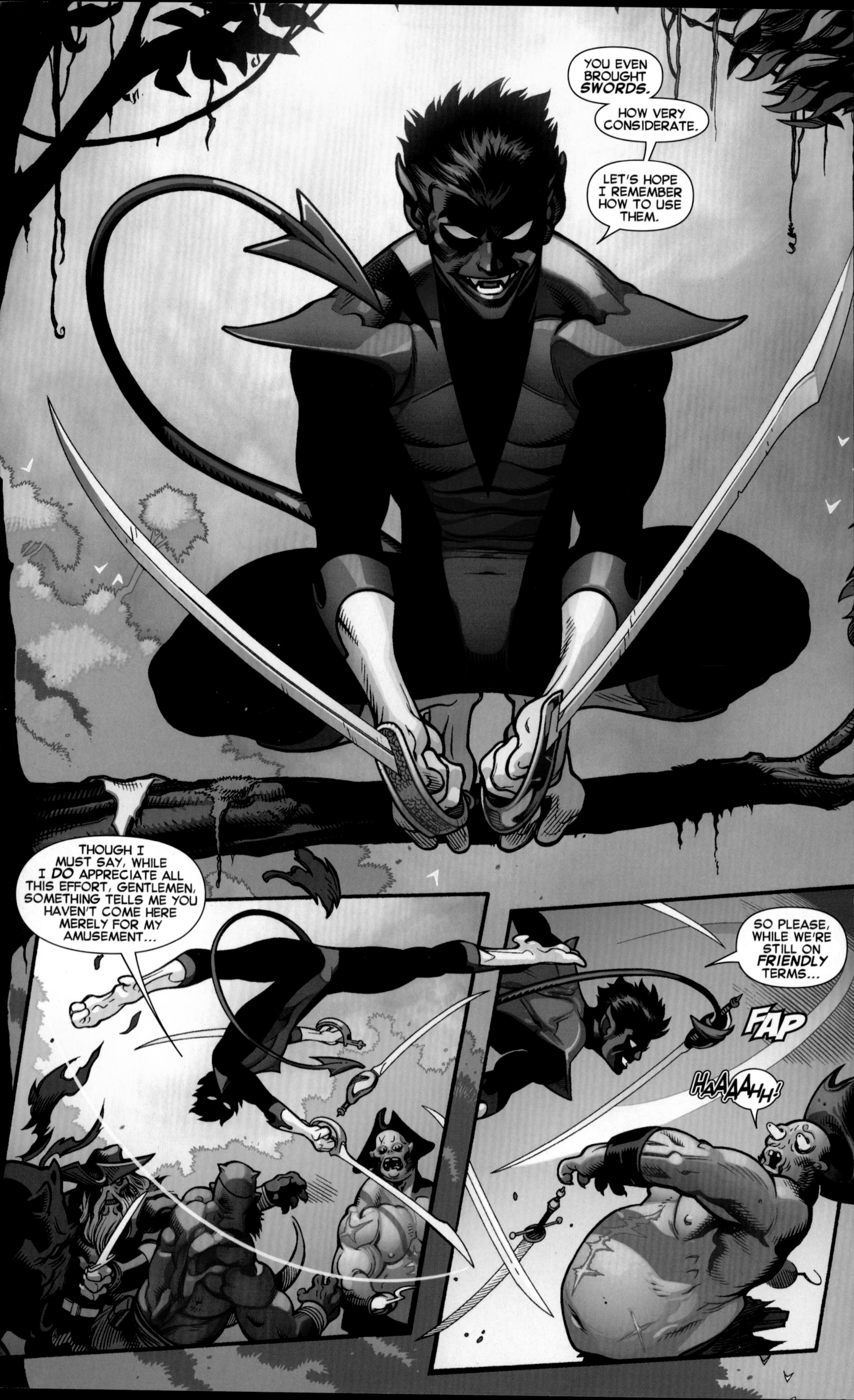
YOU EVEN BROUGHT SWORDS.
HOW VERY CONSIDERATE.
LET'S HOPE I REMEMBER HOW TO USE THEM.
THOUGH I MUST SAY, WHILE I DO APPRECIATE ALL THIS EFFORT, GENTLEMEN, SOMETHING TELLS ME YOU HAVEN'T COME HERE MERELY FOR MY AMUSEMENT...
SO PLEASE, WHILE WE'RE STILL ON FRIENDLY TERMS...
FAP
HAAAAHH!

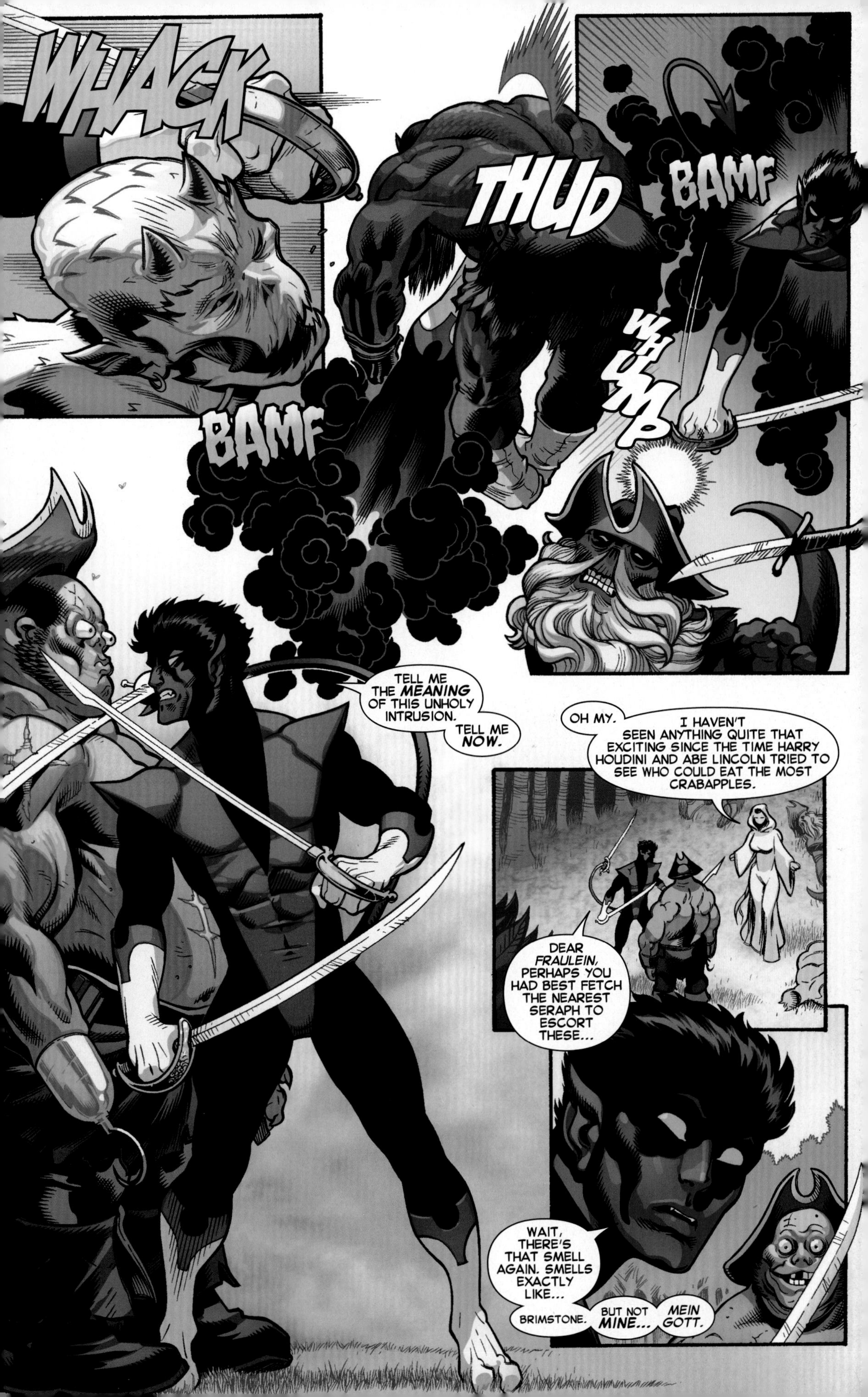
WHACK
THUD
BAMF
WHUMP
BAMF
TELL ME THE MEANING OF THIS UNHOLY INTRUSION.
TELL ME NOW.
OH MY.
I HAVEN'T SEEN ANYTHING QUITE THAT EXCITING SINCE THE TIME HARRY HOUDINI AND ABE LINCOLN TRIED TO SEE WHO COULD EAT THE MOST CRABAPPLES.
DEAR FRAULEIN, PERHAPS YOU HAD BEST FETCH THE NEAREST SERAPH TO ESCORT THESE...
WAIT, THERE'S THAT SMELL AGAIN. SMELLS EXACTLY LIKE...
BRIMSTONE.
BUT NOT MINE...
MEIN GOTT.

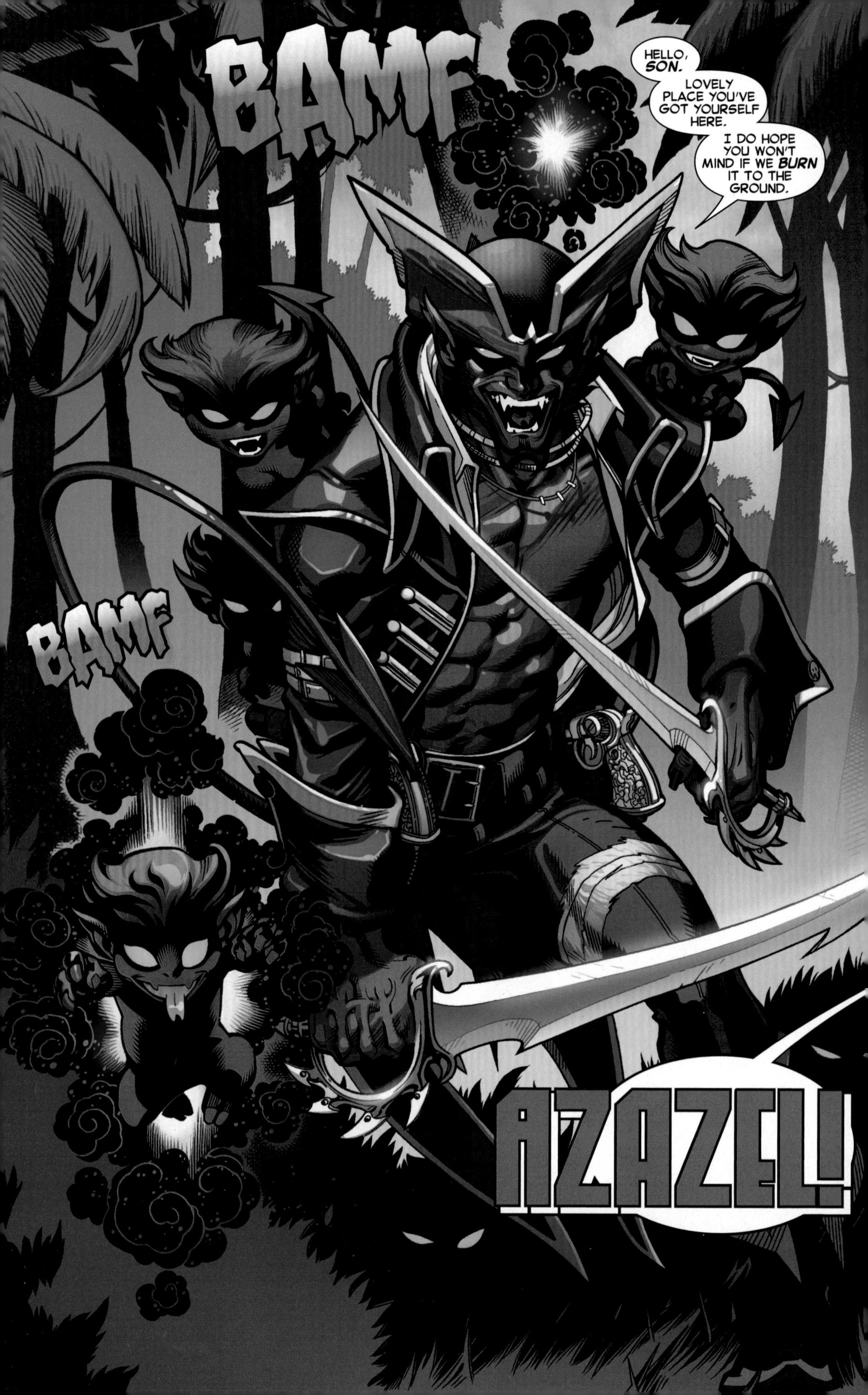
BAMF
HELLO, SON.
LOVELY PLACE YOU'VE GOT YOURSELF HERE.
I DO HOPE YOU WON'T MIND IF WE BURN IT TO THE GROUND.
BAMF
AZAZEL!

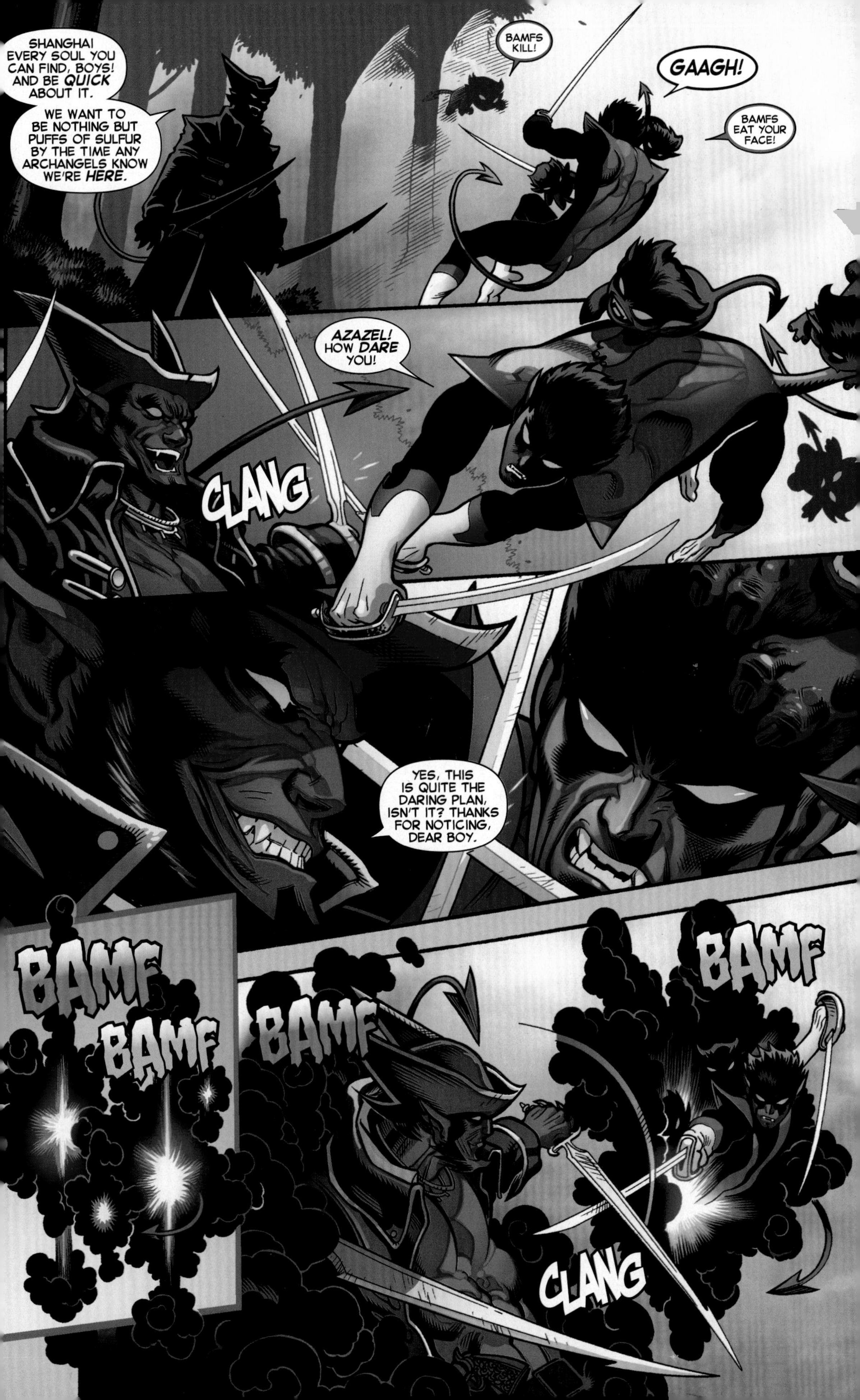
SHANGHAI EVERY SOUL YOU CAN FIND, BOYS! AND BE QUICK ABOUT IT.
WE WANT TO BE NOTHING BUT PUFFS OF SULFUR BY THE TIME ANY ARCHANGELS KNOW WE'RE HERE.
BAMFS KILL!
GAAGH!
BAMFS EAT YOUR FACE!
AZAZEL! HOW DARE YOU!
CLANG
YES, THIS IS QUITE THE DARING PLAN, ISN'T IT? THANKS FOR NOTICING, DEAR BOY.
BAMF
BAMF
BAMF
BAMF
CLANG

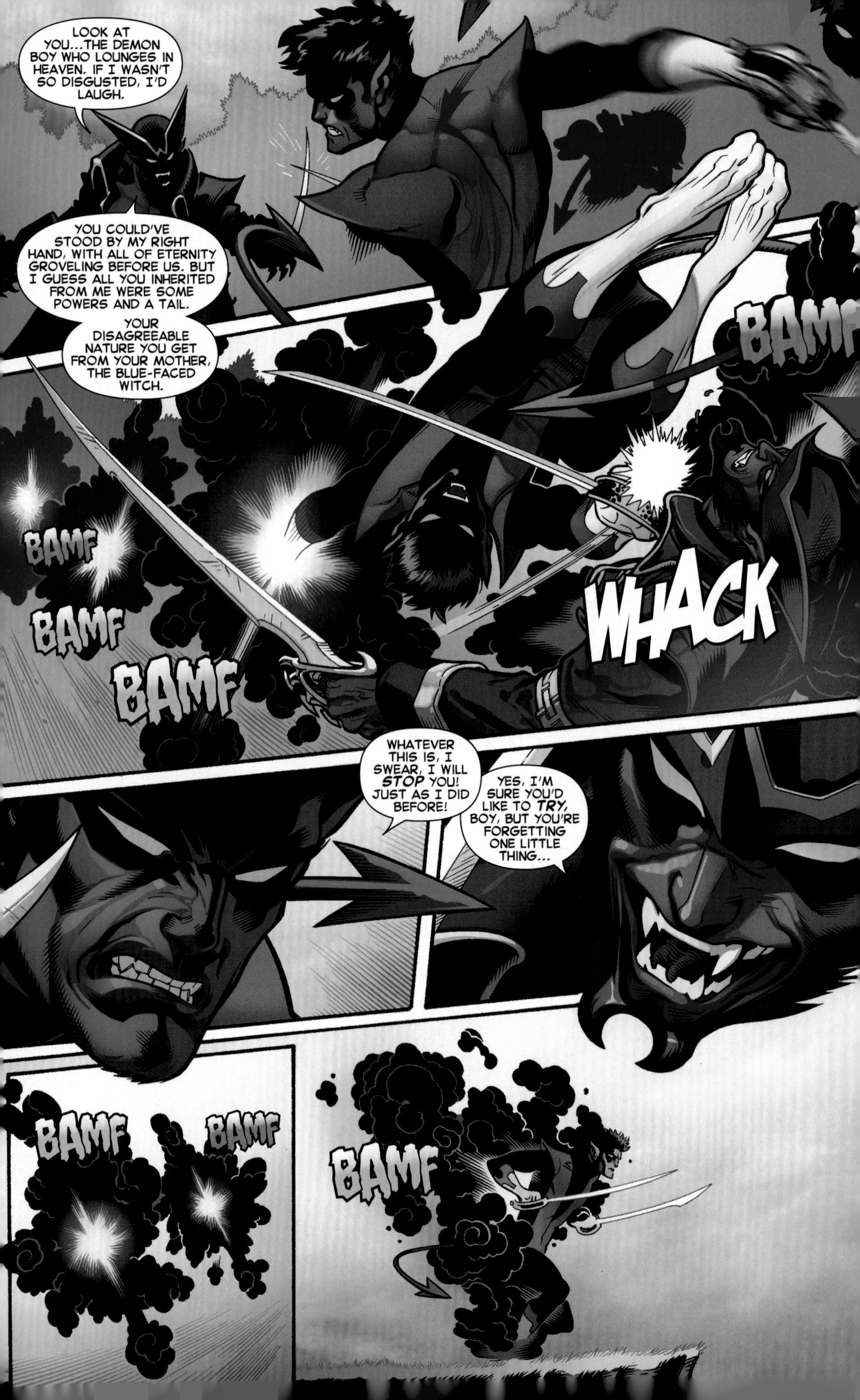

LOOK AT YOU...THE DEMON BOY WHO LOUNGES IN HEAVEN. IF I WASN'T SO DISGUSTED, I'D LAUGH.
YOU COULD'VE STOOD BY MY RIGHT HAND, WITH ALL OF ETERNITY GROVELING BEFORE US. BUT I GUESS ALL YOU INHERITED FROM ME WERE SOME POWERS AND A TAIL.
YOUR DISAGREEABLE NATURE YOU GET FROM YOUR MOTHER, THE BLUE-FACED WITCH.
BAMF
BAMF
BAMF
BAMF
WHACK
WHATEVER THIS IS, I SWEAR, I WILL *STOP* YOU! JUST AS I DID BEFORE!
YES, I'M SURE YOU'D LIKE TO *TRY*, BOY, BUT YOU'RE FORGETTING ONE LITTLE THING...
BAMF
BAMF
BAMF

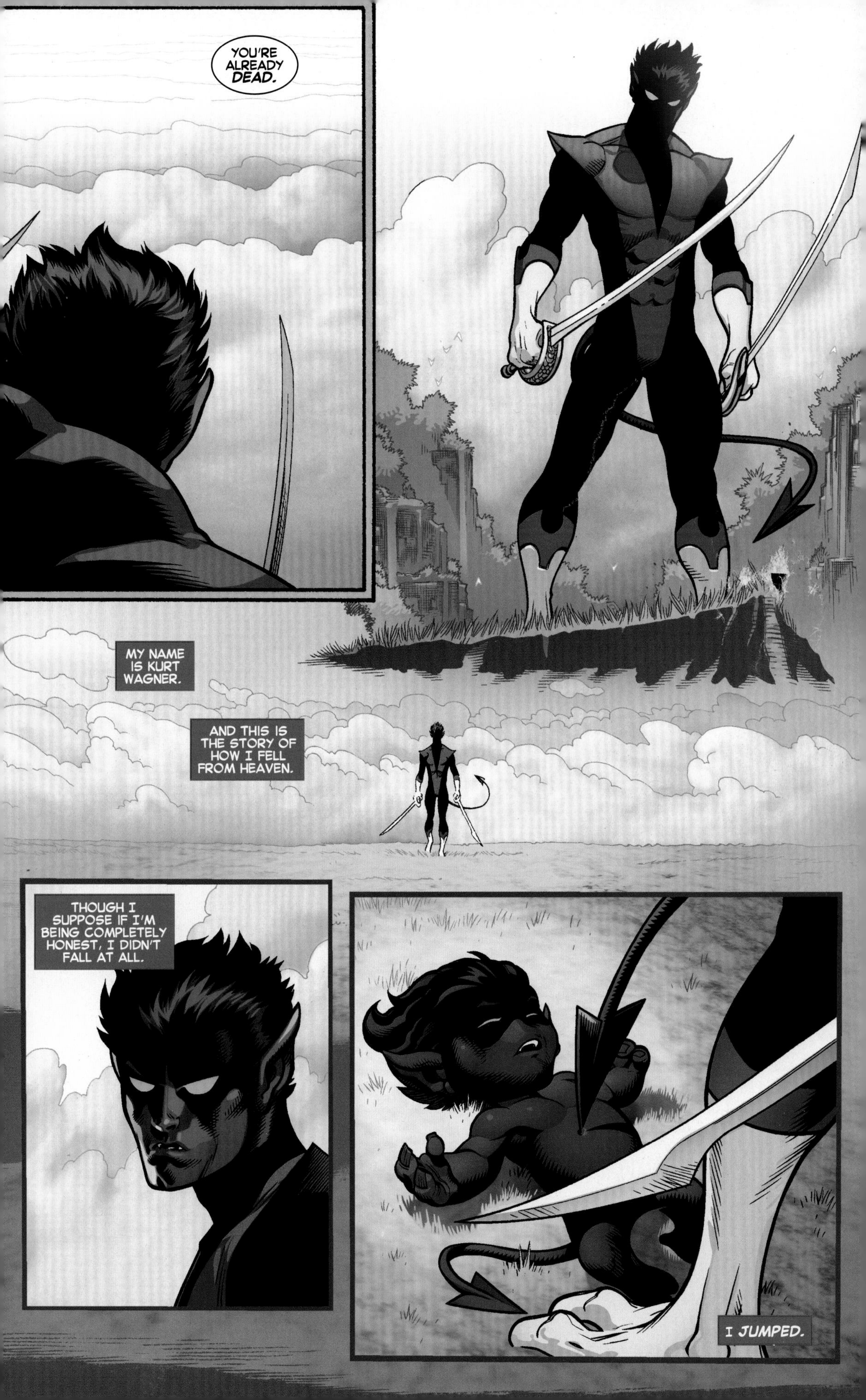
YOU'RE ALREADY DEAD.
MY NAME IS KURT WAGNER.
AND THIS IS THE STORY OF HOW I FELL FROM HEAVEN.
THOUGH I SUPPOSE IF I'M BEING COMPLETELY HONEST, I DIDN'T FALL AT ALL.
I JUMPED.

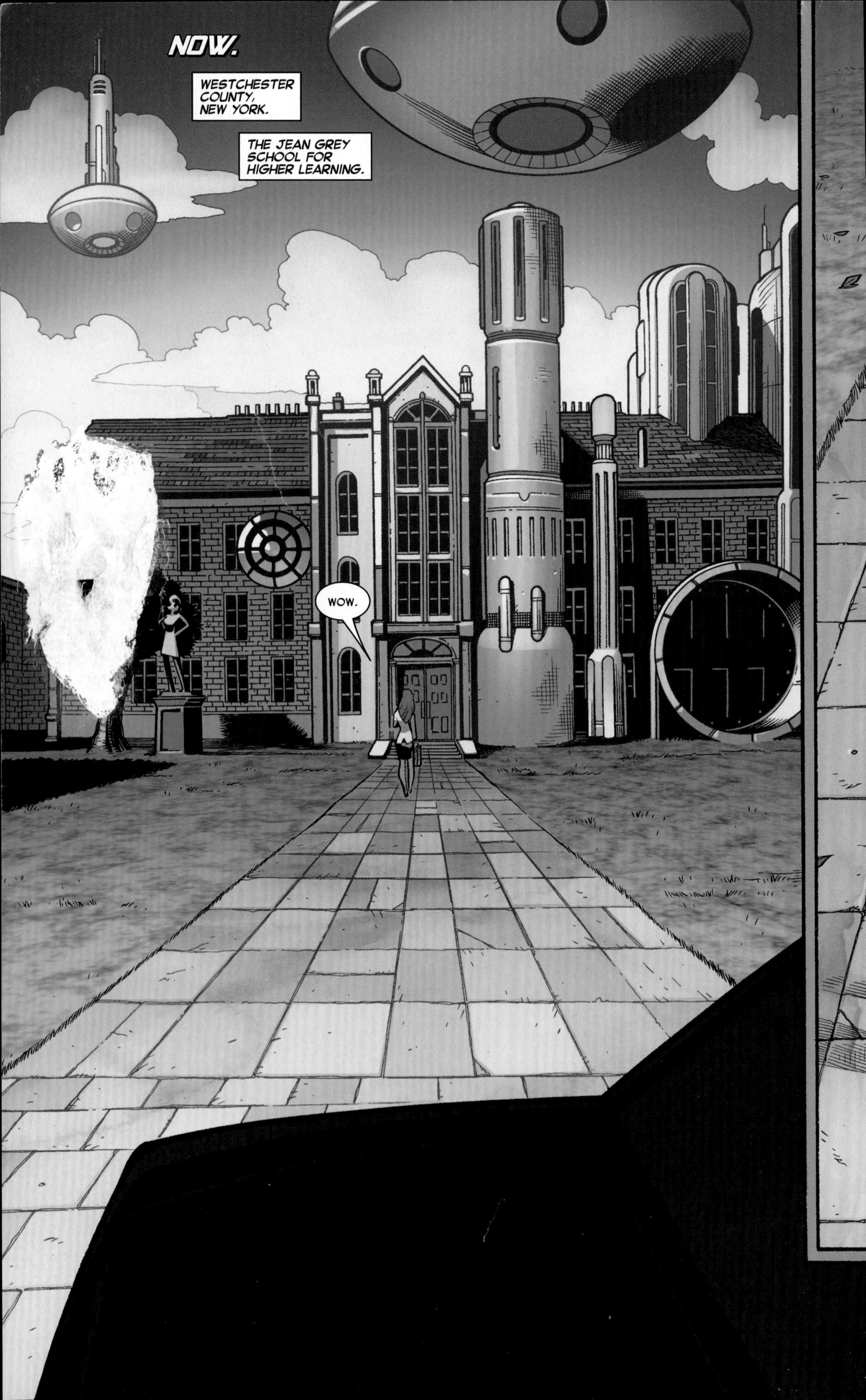
NOW.
WESTCHESTER COUNTY, NEW YORK.
THE JEAN GREY SCHOOL FOR HIGHER LEARNING.
WOW.

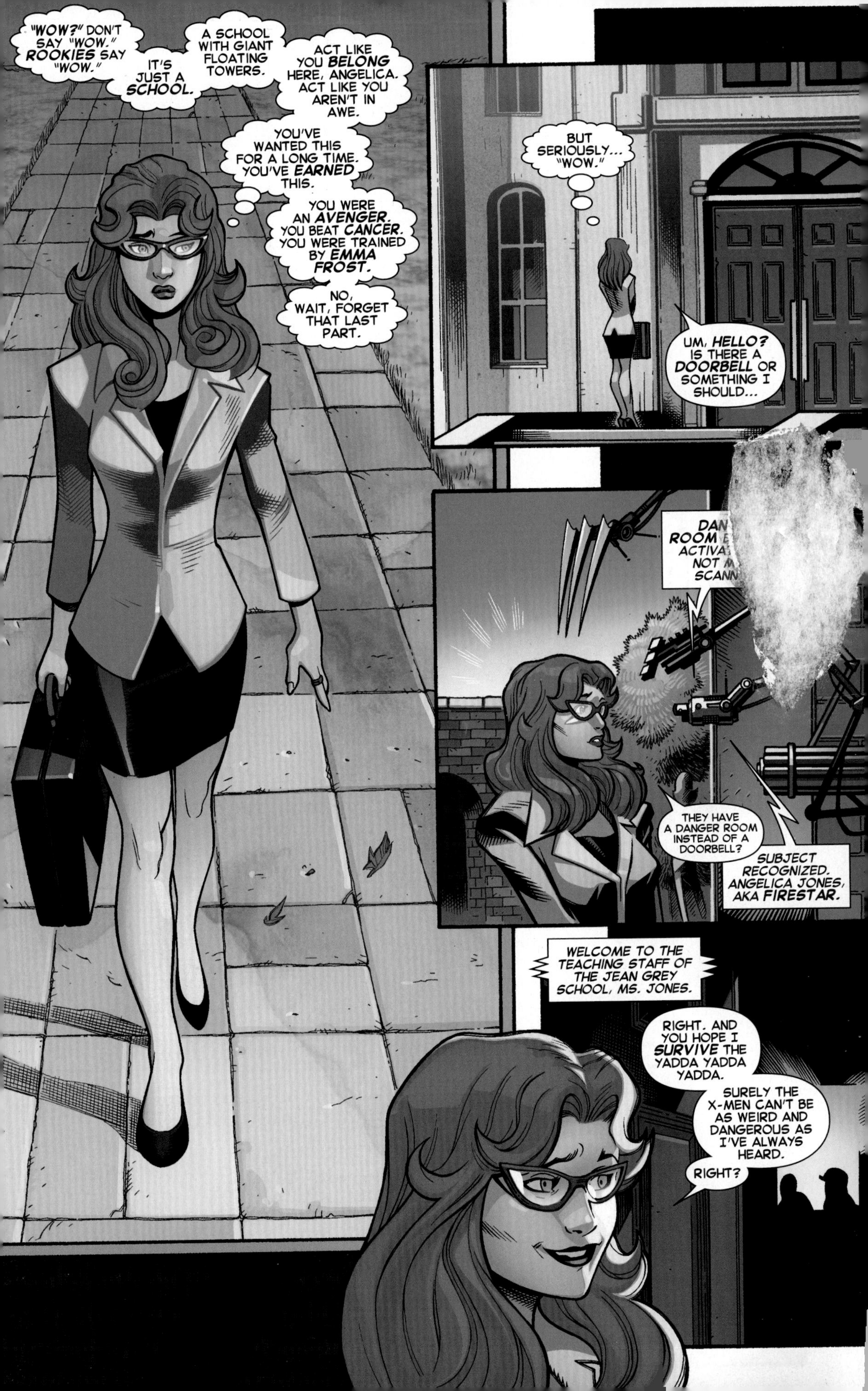

"WOW?" DON'T SAY "WOW." ROOKIES SAY "WOW."
IT'S JUST A SCHOOL.
A SCHOOL WITH GIANT FLOATING TOWERS.
ACT LIKE YOU BELONG HERE, ANGELICA. ACT LIKE YOU AREN'T IN AWE.
YOU'VE WANTED THIS FOR A LONG TIME. YOU'VE EARNED THIS.
YOU WERE AN AVENGER. YOU BEAT CANCER. YOU WERE TRAINED BY EMMA FROST.
NO, WAIT, FORGET THAT LAST PART.
BUT SERIOUSLY... "WOW."
UM, HELLO? IS THERE A DOORBELL OR SOMETHING I SHOULD...
THEY HAVE A DANGER ROOM INSTEAD OF A DOORBELL?
SUBJECT RECOGNIZED. ANGELICA JONES, AKA FIRESTAR.
WELCOME TO THE TEACHING STAFF OF THE JEAN GREY SCHOOL, MS. JONES.
RIGHT. AND YOU HOPE I SURVIVE THE YADDA YADDA YADDA.
SURELY THE X-MEN CAN'T BE AS WEIRD AND DANGEROUS AS I'VE ALWAYS HEARD.
RIGHT?

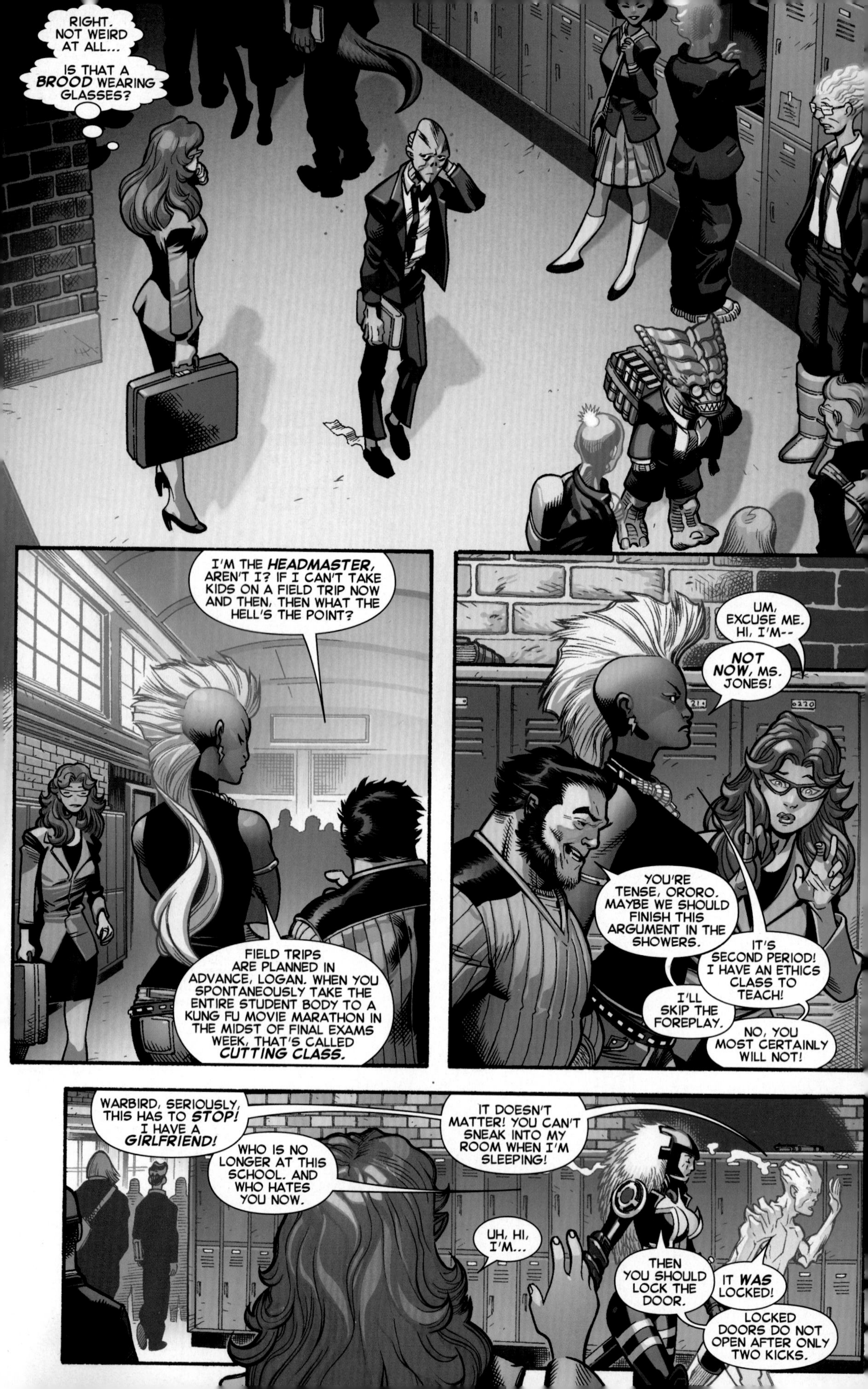
RIGHT. NOT WEIRD AT ALL... IS THAT A BROOD WEARING GLASSES?
I'M THE HEADMASTER, AREN'T I? IF I CAN'T TAKE KIDS ON A FIELD TRIP NOW AND THEN, THEN WHAT THE HELL'S THE POINT?
FIELD TRIPS ARE PLANNED IN ADVANCE, LOGAN. WHEN YOU SPONTANEOUSLY TAKE THE ENTIRE STUDENT BODY TO A KUNG FU MOVIE MARATHON IN THE MIDST OF FINAL EXAMS WEEK, THAT'S CALLED CUTTING CLASS.
UM, EXCUSE ME. HI, I'M--
NOT NOW, MS. JONES!
YOU'RE TENSE, ORORO. MAYBE WE SHOULD FINISH THIS ARGUMENT IN THE SHOWERS.
IT'S SECOND PERIOD! I HAVE AN ETHICS CLASS TO TEACH!
I'LL SKIP THE FOREPLAY.
NO, YOU MOST CERTAINLY WILL NOT!
WARBIRD, SERIOUSLY, THIS HAS TO STOP! I HAVE A GIRLFRIEND!
WHO IS NO LONGER AT THIS SCHOOL. AND WHO HATES YOU NOW.
IT DOESN'T MATTER! YOU CAN'T SNEAK INTO MY ROOM WHEN I'M SLEEPING!
UH, HI, I'M...
THEN YOU SHOULD LOCK THE DOOR.
IT WAS LOCKED!
LOCKED DOORS DO NOT OPEN AFTER ONLY TWO KICKS.

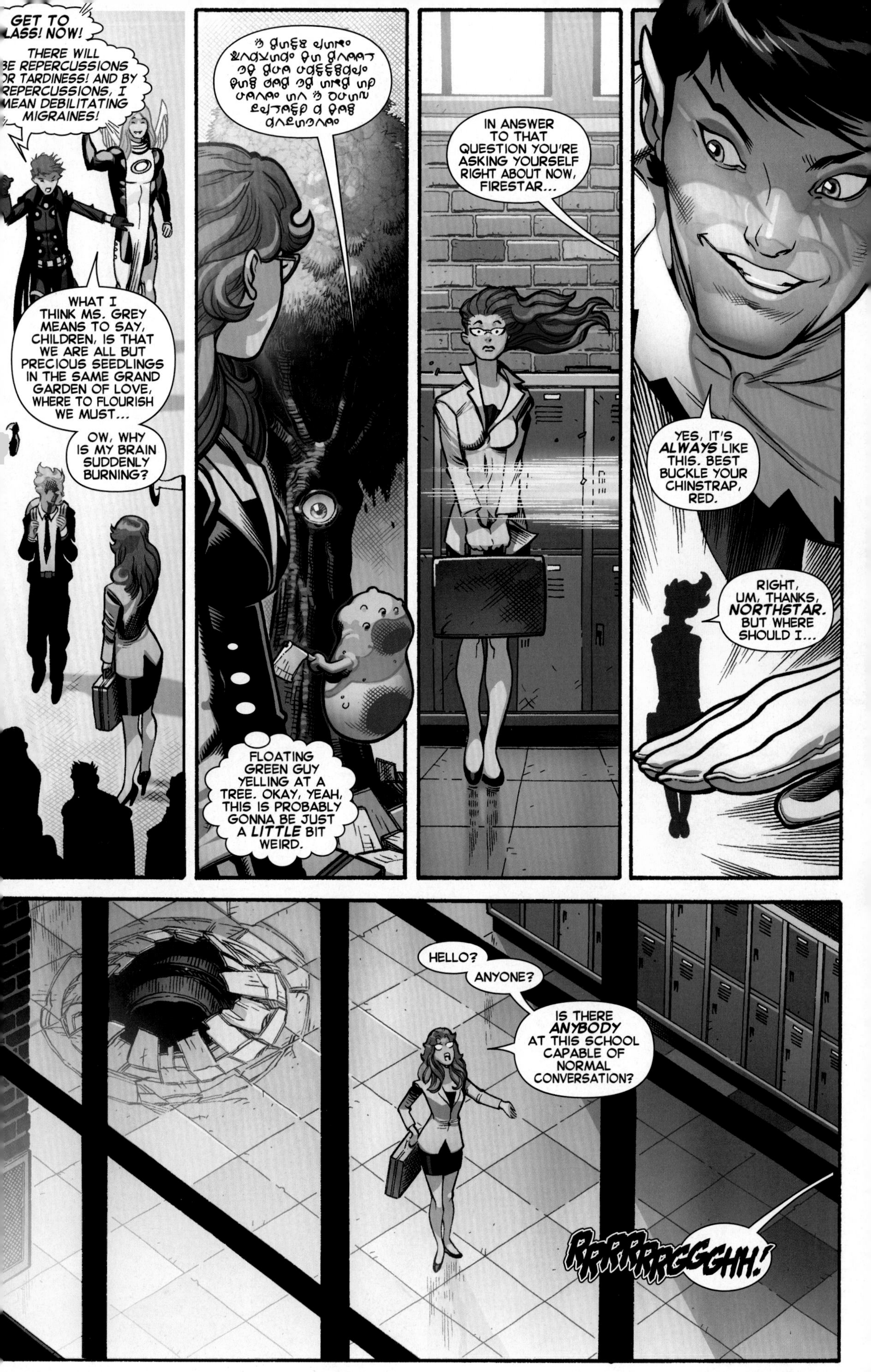

GET TO CLASS! NOW!
THERE WILL BE REPERCUSSIONS FOR TARDINESS! AND BY REPERCUSSIONS, I MEAN DEBILITATING MIGRAINES!
WHAT I THINK MS. GREY MEANS TO SAY, CHILDREN, IS THAT WE ARE ALL BUT PRECIOUS SEEDLINGS IN THE SAME GRAND GARDEN OF LOVE, WHERE TO FLOURISH WE MUST...
OW, WHY IS MY BRAIN SUDDENLY BURNING?
FLOATING GREEN GUY YELLING AT A TREE. OKAY, YEAH, THIS IS PROBABLY GONNA BE JUST A LITTLE BIT WEIRD.
IN ANSWER TO THAT QUESTION YOU'RE ASKING YOURSELF RIGHT ABOUT NOW, FIRESTAR...
YES, IT'S ALWAYS LIKE THIS. BEST BUCKLE YOUR CHINSTRAP, RED.
RIGHT, UM, THANKS, NORTHSTAR. BUT WHERE SHOULD I...
HELLO?
ANYONE?
IS THERE ANYBODY AT THIS SCHOOL CAPABLE OF NORMAL CONVERSATION?
RRRRRRRGGGHH!

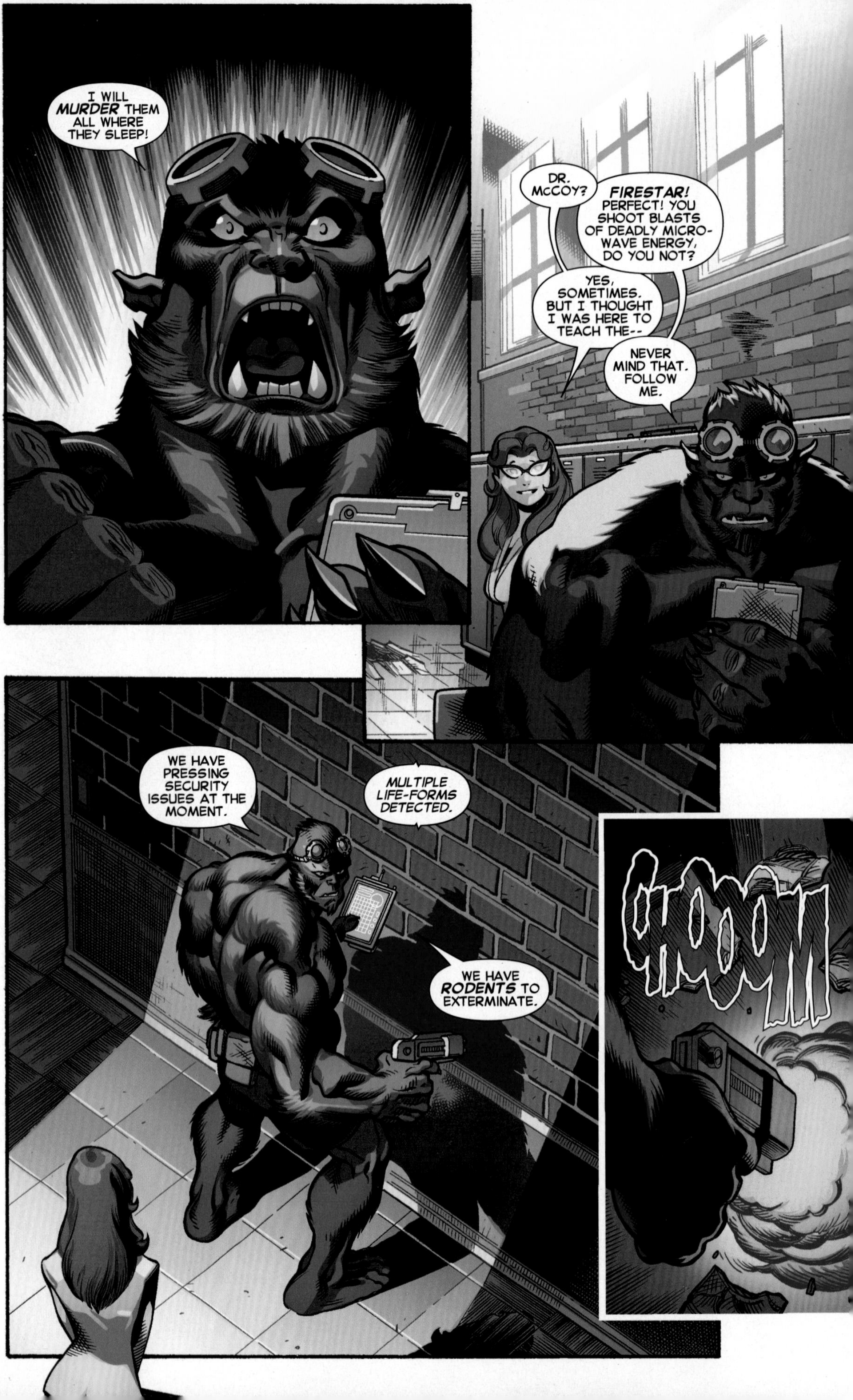
I WILL MURDER THEM ALL WHERE THEY SLEEP!
DR. McCOY?
FIRESTAR! PERFECT! YOU SHOOT BLASTS OF DEADLY MICRO-WAVE ENERGY, DO YOU NOT?
YES, SOMETIMES. BUT I THOUGHT I WAS HERE TO TEACH THE--
NEVER MIND THAT. FOLLOW ME.
WE HAVE PRESSING SECURITY ISSUES AT THE MOMENT.
MULTIPLE LIFE-FORMS DETECTED.
WE HAVE RODENTS TO EXTERMINATE.
CHOOOM

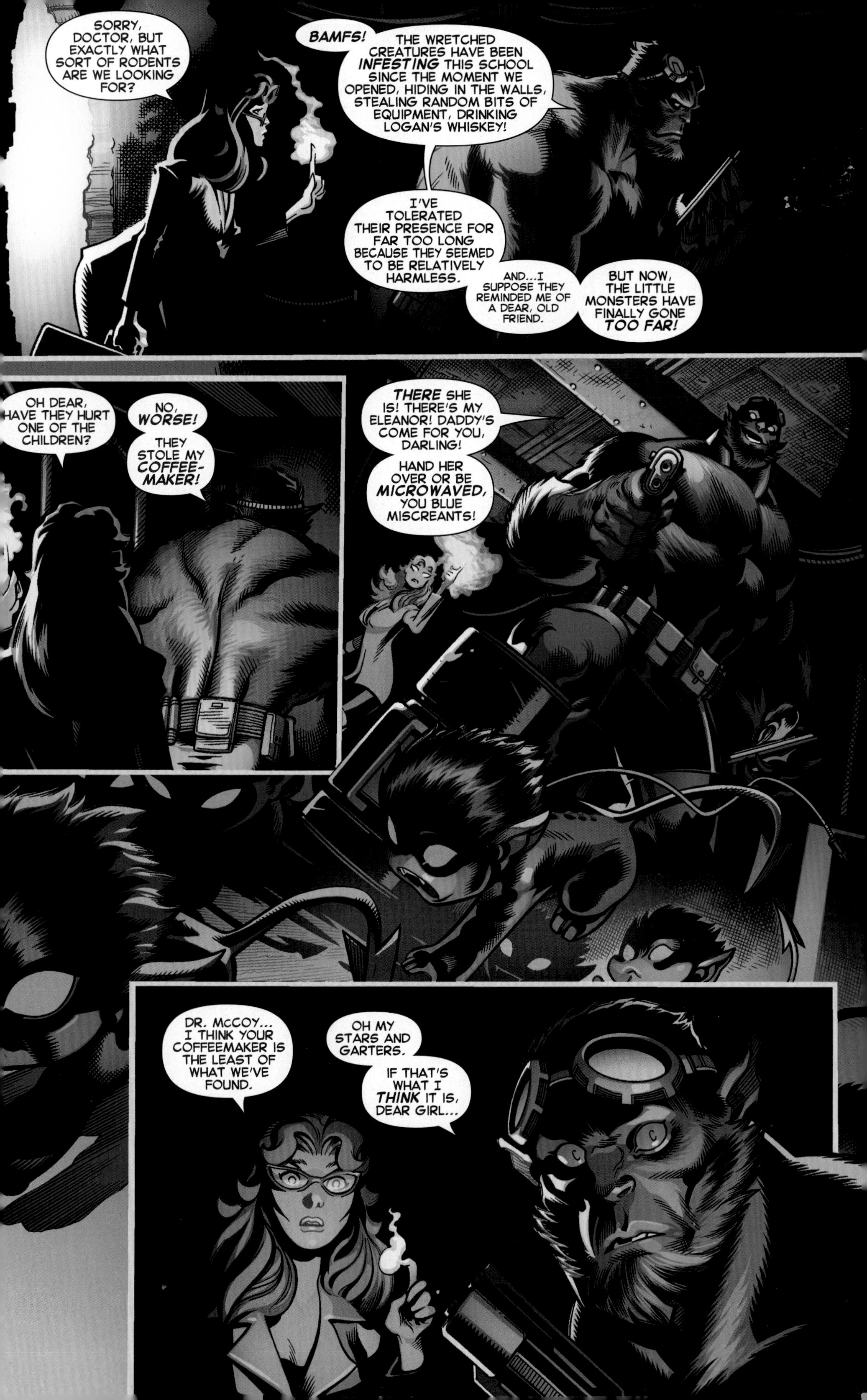

SORRY, DOCTOR, BUT EXACTLY WHAT SORT OF RODENTS ARE WE LOOKING FOR?
BAMFS! THE WRETCHED CREATURES HAVE BEEN INFESTING THIS SCHOOL SINCE THE MOMENT WE OPENED, HIDING IN THE WALLS, STEALING RANDOM BITS OF EQUIPMENT, DRINKING LOGAN'S WHISKEY!
I'VE TOLERATED THEIR PRESENCE FOR FAR TOO LONG BECAUSE THEY SEEMED TO BE RELATIVELY HARMLESS.
AND...I SUPPOSE THEY REMINDED ME OF A DEAR, OLD FRIEND.
BUT NOW, THE LITTLE MONSTERS HAVE FINALLY GONE TOO FAR!
OH DEAR, HAVE THEY HURT ONE OF THE CHILDREN?
NO, WORSE!
THEY STOLE MY COFFEE-MAKER!
THERE SHE IS! THERE'S MY ELEANOR! DADDY'S COME FOR YOU, DARLING!
HAND HER OVER OR BE MICROWAVED, YOU BLUE MISCREANTS!
DR. McCOY... I THINK YOUR COFFEEMAKER IS THE LEAST OF WHAT WE'VE FOUND.
OH MY STARS AND GARTERS.
IF THAT'S WHAT I THINK IT IS, DEAR GIRL...

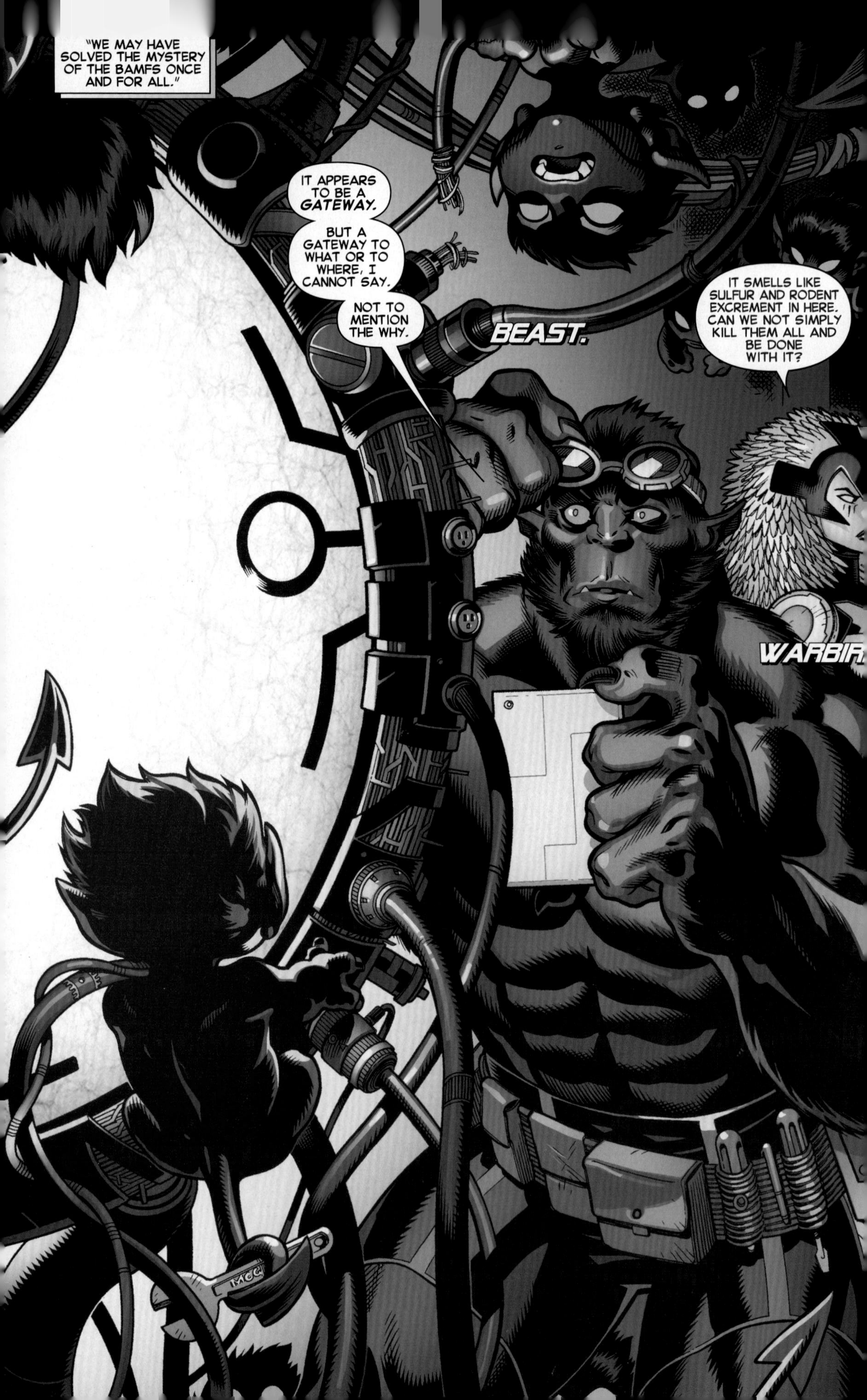
"WE MAY HAVE SOLVED THE MYSTERY OF THE BAMFS ONCE AND FOR ALL."
IT APPEARS TO BE A GATEWAY.
BUT A GATEWAY TO WHAT OR TO WHERE, I CANNOT SAY.
NOT TO MENTION THE WHY.
BEAST.
IT SMELLS LIKE SULFUR AND RODENT EXCREMENT IN HERE. CAN WE NOT SIMPLY KILL THEM ALL AND BE DONE WITH IT?
WARBIR

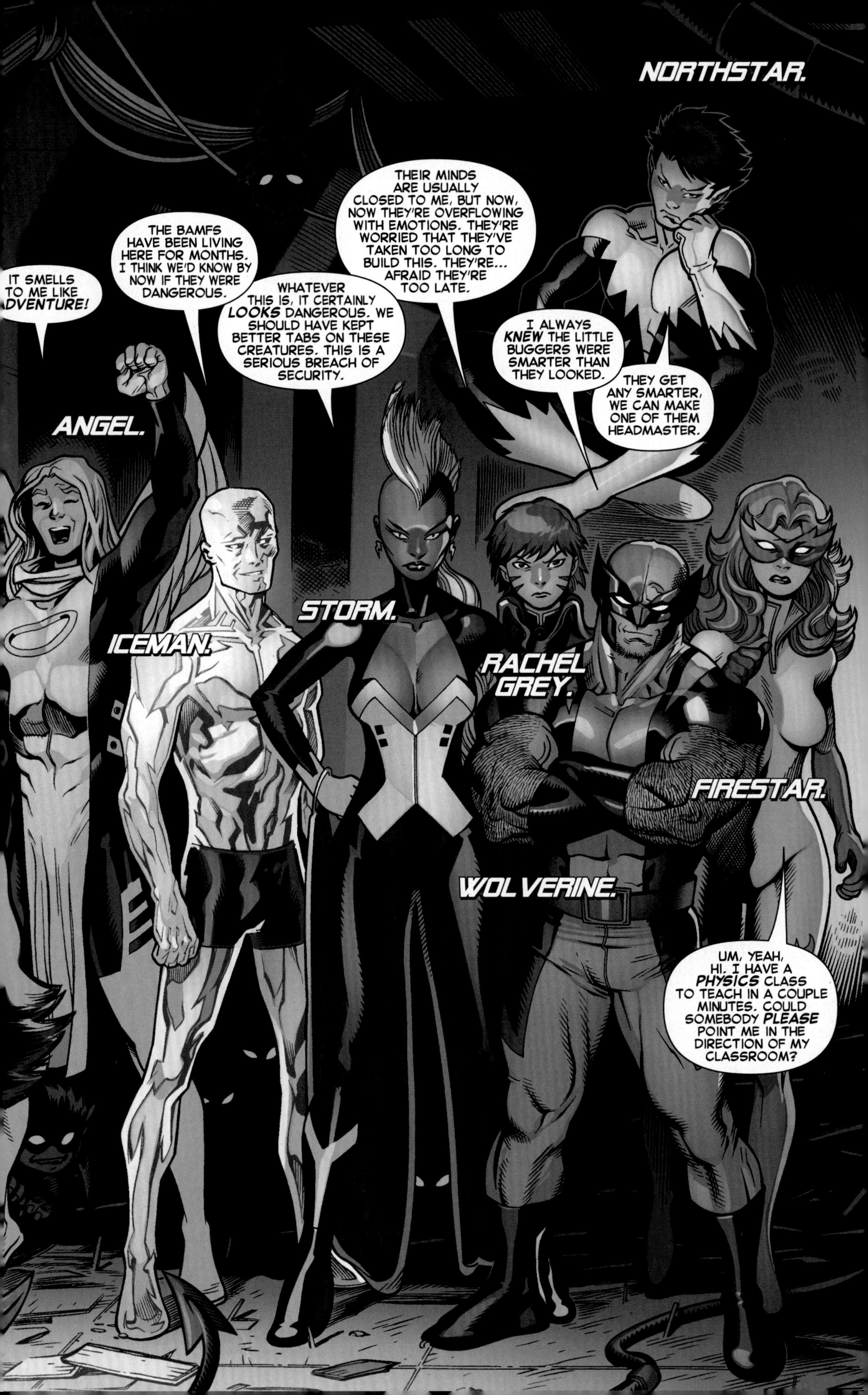
NORTHSTAR.
IT SMELLS TO ME LIKE ADVENTURE!
THE BAMFS HAVE BEEN LIVING HERE FOR MONTHS. I THINK WE'D KNOW BY NOW IF THEY WERE DANGEROUS.
WHATEVER THIS IS, IT CERTAINLY LOOKS DANGEROUS. WE SHOULD HAVE KEPT BETTER TABS ON THESE CREATURES. THIS IS A SERIOUS BREACH OF SECURITY.
THEIR MINDS ARE USUALLY CLOSED TO ME, BUT NOW, NOW THEY'RE OVERFLOWING WITH EMOTIONS. THEY'RE WORRIED THAT THEY'VE TAKEN TOO LONG TO BUILD THIS. THEY'RE... AFRAID THEY'RE TOO LATE.
I ALWAYS KNEW THE LITTLE BUGGERS WERE SMARTER THAN THEY LOOKED.
THEY GET ANY SMARTER, WE CAN MAKE ONE OF THEM HEADMASTER.
ANGEL.
ICEMAN.
STORM.
RACHEL GREY.
FIRESTAR.
WOLVERINE.
UM, YEAH, HI. I HAVE A PHYSICS CLASS TO TEACH IN A COUPLE MINUTES. COULD SOMEBODY PLEASE POINT ME IN THE DIRECTION OF MY CLASSROOM?

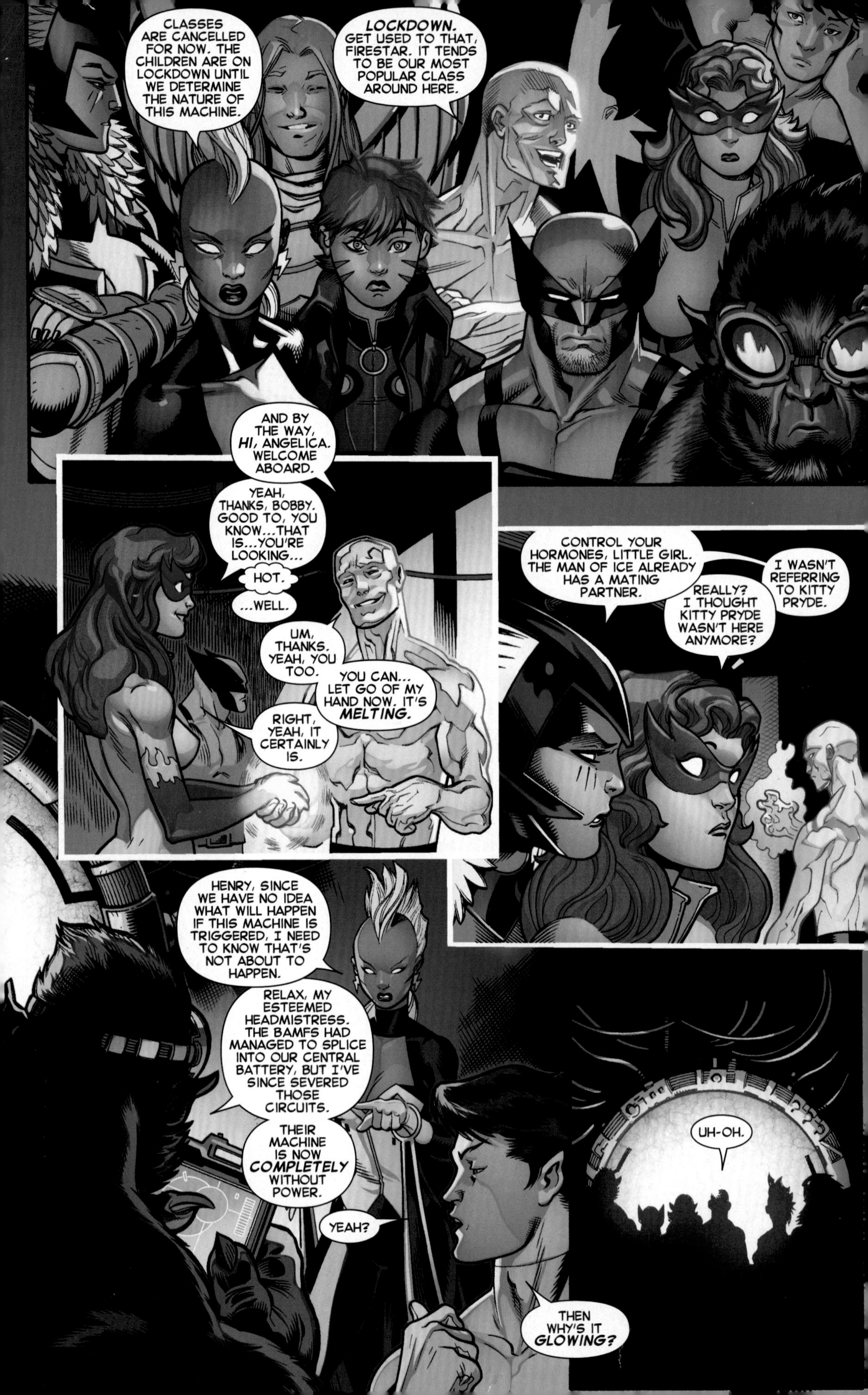
CLASSES ARE CANCELLED FOR NOW. THE CHILDREN ARE ON LOCKDOWN UNTIL WE DETERMINE THE NATURE OF THIS MACHINE.
LOCKDOWN. GET USED TO THAT, FIRESTAR. IT TENDS TO BE OUR MOST POPULAR CLASS AROUND HERE.
AND BY THE WAY, HI, ANGELICA. WELCOME ABOARD.
YEAH, THANKS, BOBBY. GOOD TO, YOU KNOW...THAT IS...YOU'RE LOOKING...
HOT.
...WELL.
UM, THANKS. YEAH, YOU TOO.
YOU CAN... LET GO OF MY HAND NOW. IT'S MELTING.
RIGHT, YEAH, IT CERTAINLY IS.
CONTROL YOUR HORMONES, LITTLE GIRL. THE MAN OF ICE ALREADY HAS A MATING PARTNER.
REALLY? I THOUGHT KITTY PRYDE WASN'T HERE ANYMORE?
I WASN'T REFERRING TO KITTY PRYDE.
HENRY, SINCE WE HAVE NO IDEA WHAT WILL HAPPEN IF THIS MACHINE IS TRIGGERED, I NEED TO KNOW THAT'S NOT ABOUT TO HAPPEN.
RELAX, MY ESTEEMED HEADMISTRESS. THE BAMFS HAD MANAGED TO SPLICE INTO OUR CENTRAL BATTERY, BUT I'VE SINCE SEVERED THOSE CIRCUITS.
THEIR MACHINE IS NOW COMPLETELY WITHOUT POWER.
YEAH?
THEN WHY'S IT GLOWING?
UH-OH.

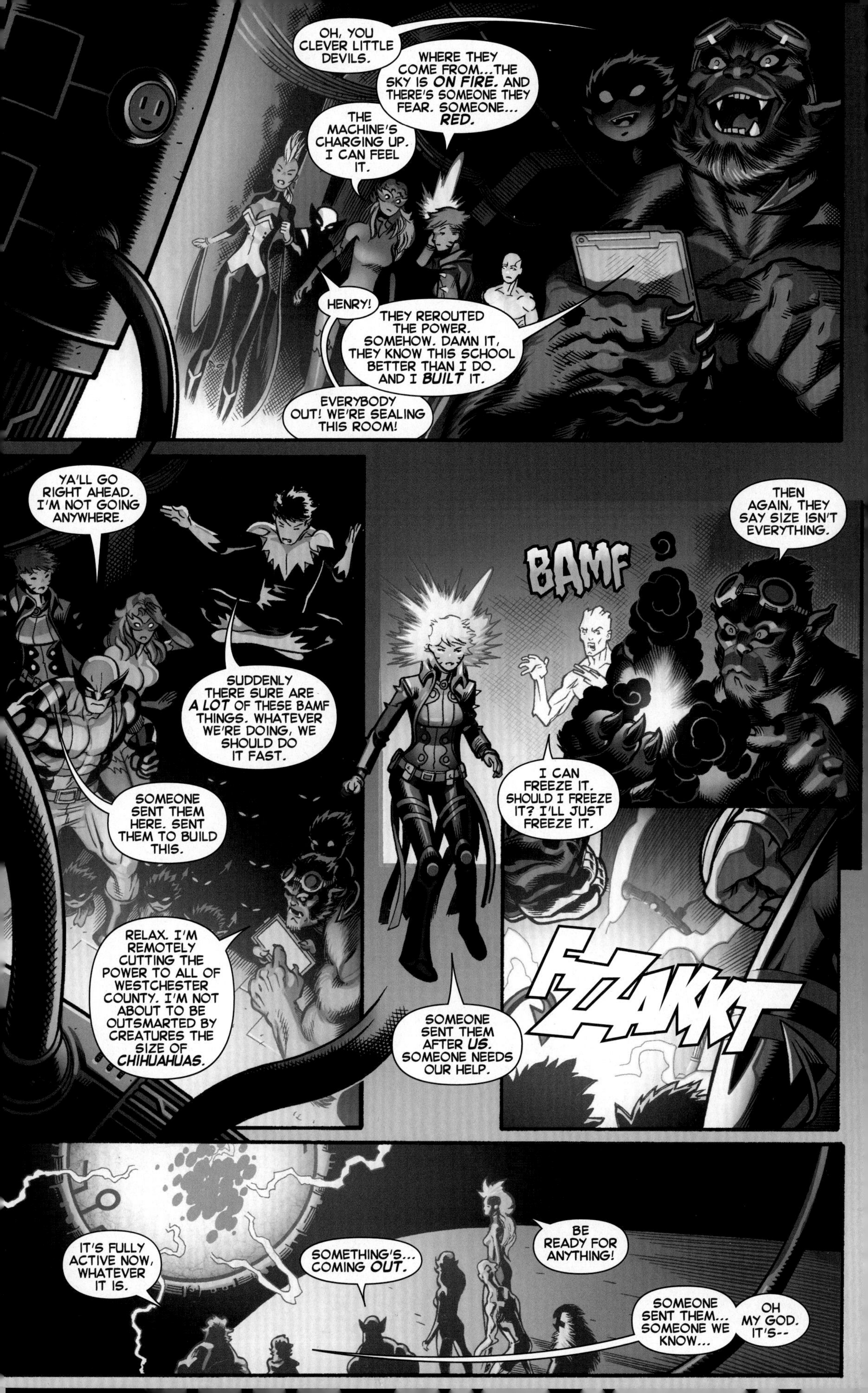
OH, YOU CLEVER LITTLE DEVILS.
WHERE THEY COME FROM...THE SKY IS ON FIRE. AND THERE'S SOMEONE THEY FEAR. SOMEONE... RED.
THE MACHINE'S CHARGING UP. I CAN FEEL IT.
HENRY!
THEY REROUTED THE POWER. SOMEHOW. DAMN IT, THEY KNOW THIS SCHOOL BETTER THAN I DO. AND I BUILT IT.
EVERYBODY OUT! WE'RE SEALING THIS ROOM!
YA'LL GO RIGHT AHEAD. I'M NOT GOING ANYWHERE.
SUDDENLY THERE SURE ARE A LOT OF THESE BAMF THINGS. WHATEVER WE'RE DOING, WE SHOULD DO IT FAST.
SOMEONE SENT THEM HERE. SENT THEM TO BUILD THIS.
RELAX. I'M REMOTELY CUTTING THE POWER TO ALL OF WESTCHESTER COUNTY. I'M NOT ABOUT TO BE OUTSMARTED BY CREATURES THE SIZE OF CHIHUAHUAS.
SOMEONE SENT THEM AFTER US. SOMEONE NEEDS OUR HELP.
BAMF
THEN AGAIN, THEY SAY SIZE ISN'T EVERYTHING.
I CAN FREEZE IT. SHOULD I FREEZE IT? I'LL JUST FREEZE IT.
FZZAKKT
IT'S FULLY ACTIVE NOW, WHATEVER IT IS.
SOMETHING'S... COMING OUT.
BE READY FOR ANYTHING!
SOMEONE SENT THEM... SOMEONE WE KNOW...
OH MY GOD. IT'S--

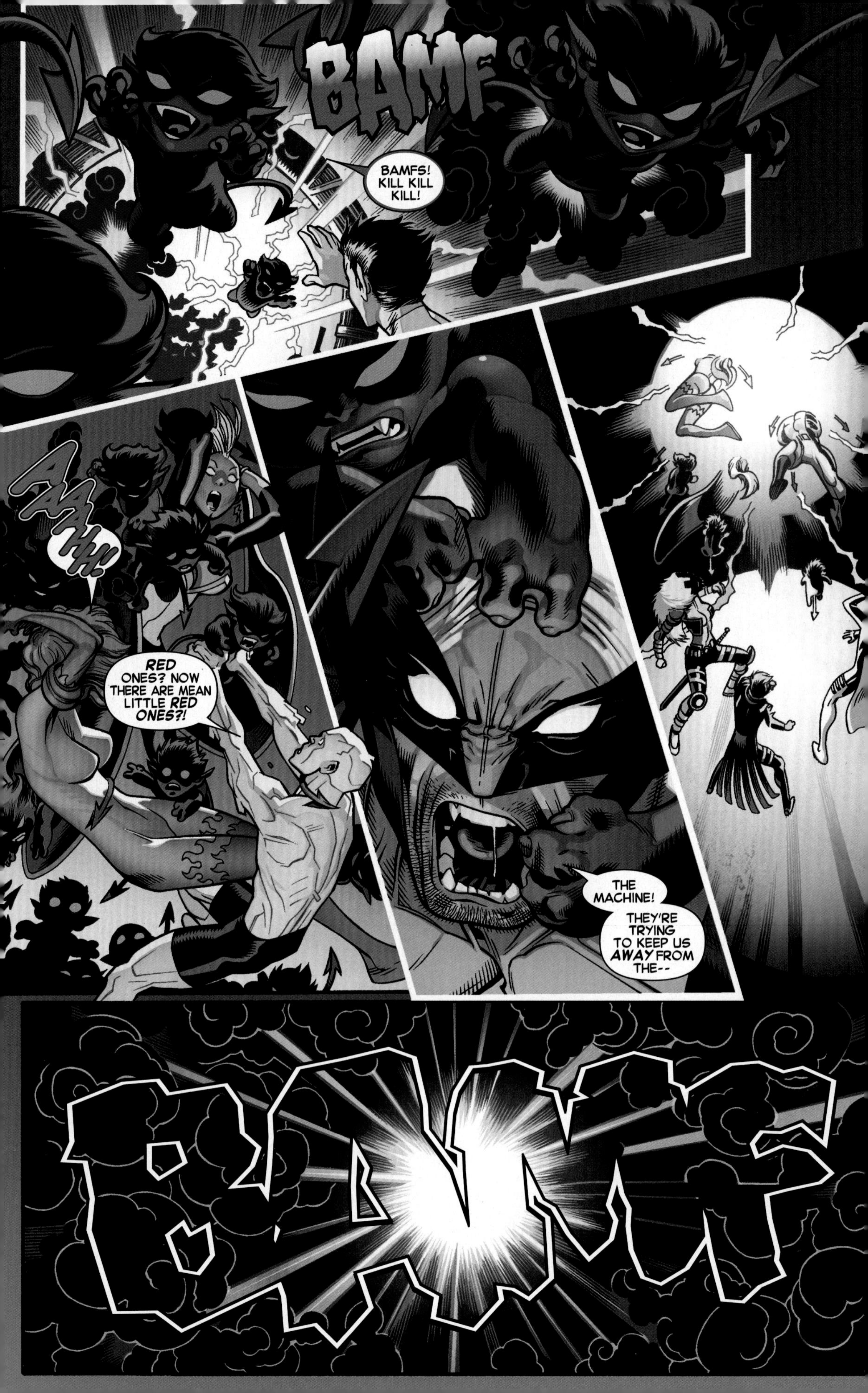
BAMF
BAMFS! KILL KILL KILL!
AAAHH!
RED ONES? NOW THERE ARE MEAN LITTLE RED ONES?!
THE MACHINE!
THEY'RE TRYING TO KEEP US AWAY FROM THE--
BAMF

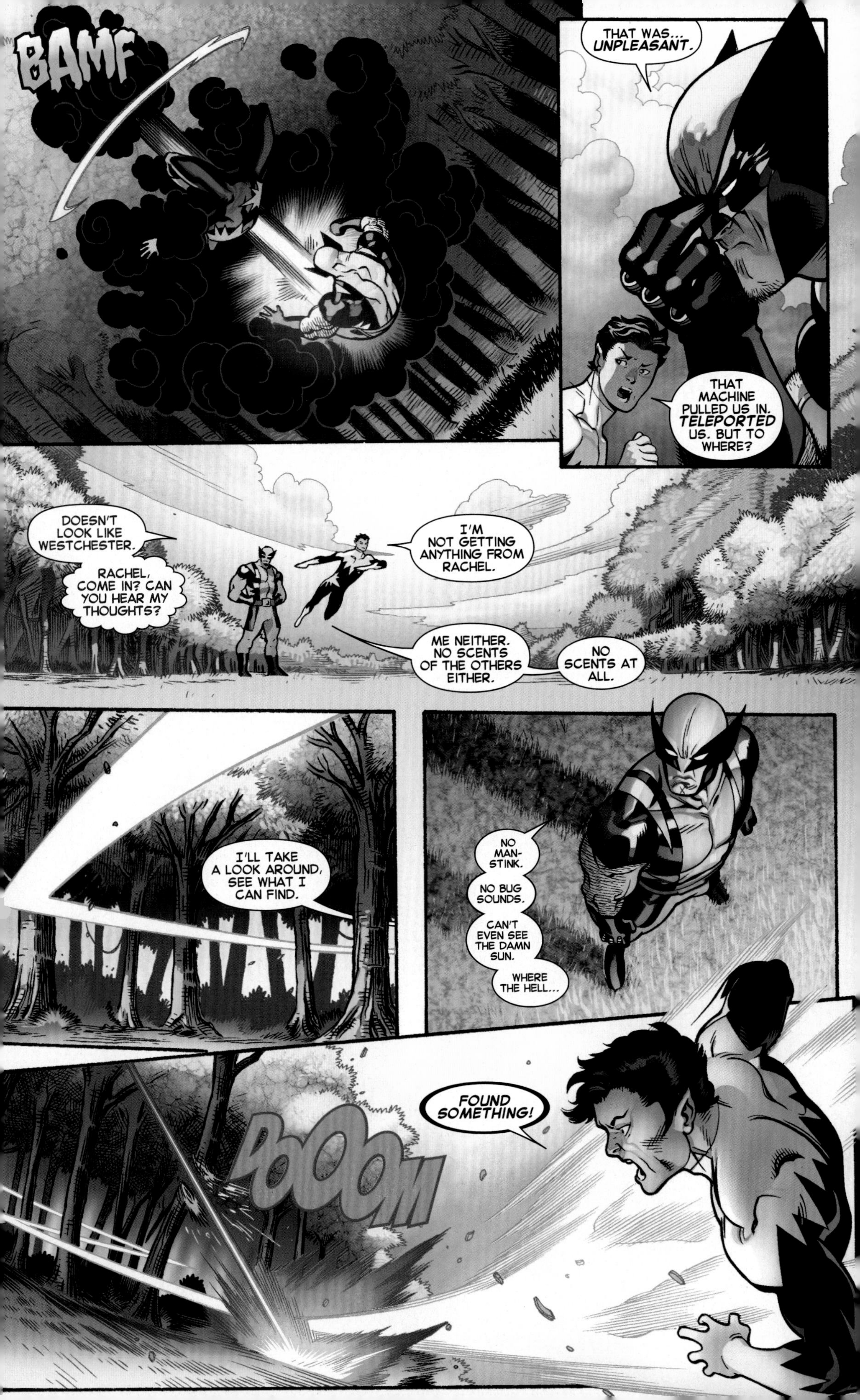
BAMF
THAT WAS... UNPLEASANT.
THAT MACHINE PULLED US IN. TELEPORTED US. BUT TO WHERE?
DOESN'T LOOK LIKE WESTCHESTER.
RACHEL, COME IN? CAN YOU HEAR MY THOUGHTS?
I'M NOT GETTING ANYTHING FROM RACHEL.
ME NEITHER. NO SCENTS OF THE OTHERS EITHER.
NO SCENTS AT ALL.
I'LL TAKE A LOOK AROUND, SEE WHAT I CAN FIND.
NO MAN-STINK.
NO BUG SOUNDS.
CAN'T EVEN SEE THE DAMN SUN.
WHERE THE HELL...
FOUND SOMETHING!
DOOOM

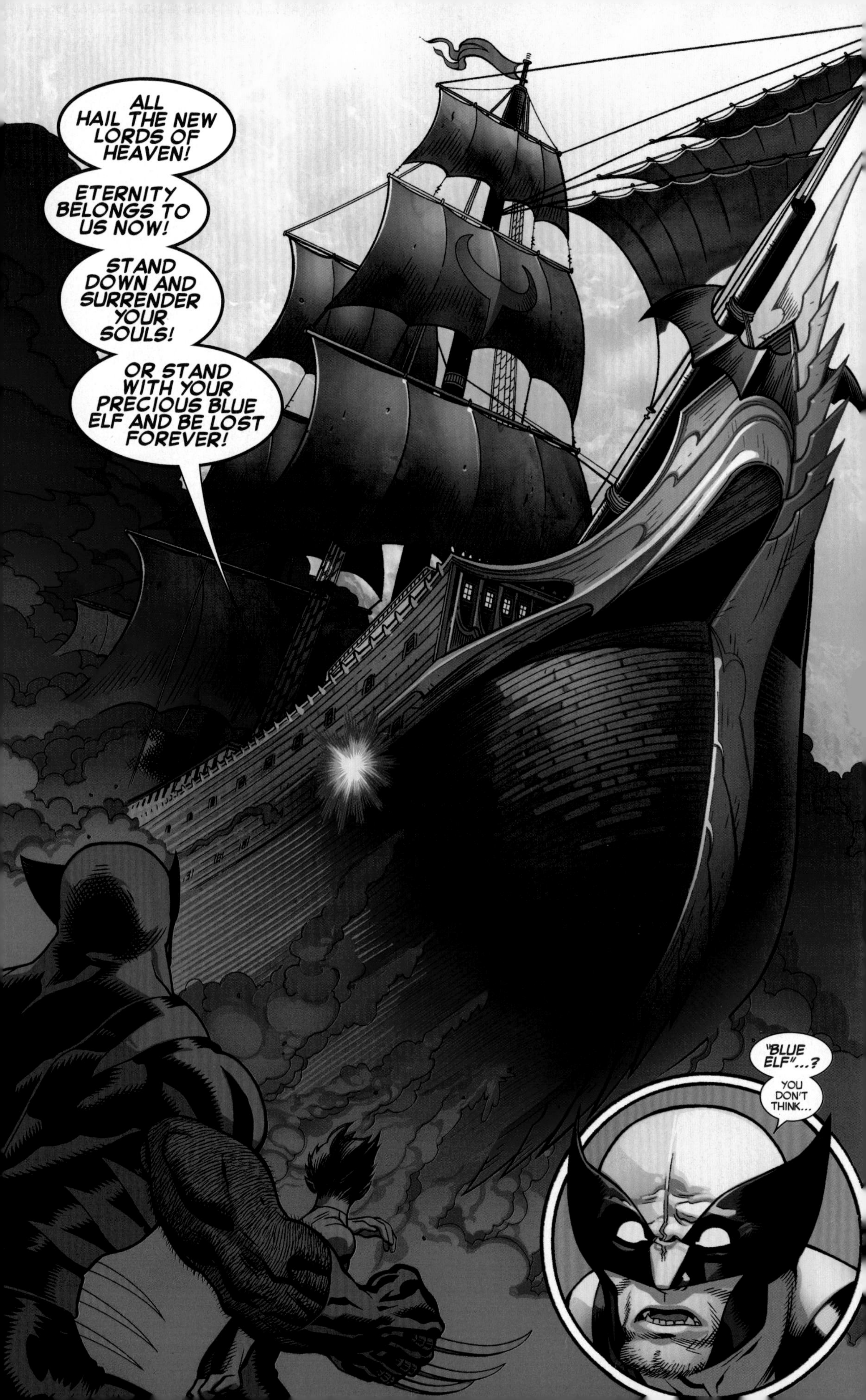
ALL HAIL THE NEW LORDS OF HEAVEN!
ETERNITY BELONGS TO US NOW!
STAND DOWN AND SURRENDER YOUR SOULS!
OR STAND WITH YOUR PRECIOUS BLUE ELF AND BE LOST FOREVER!
"BLUE ELF"...?
YOU DON'T THINK...

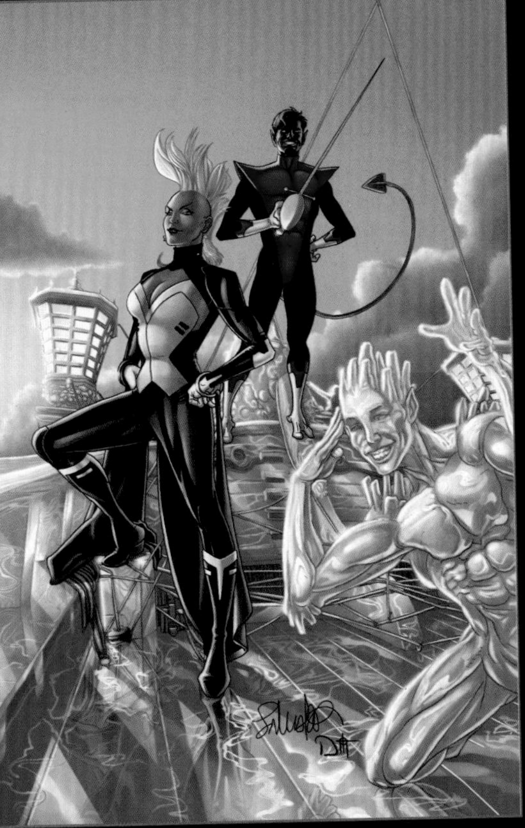

AMAZING X-MEN #1
LAUGHING OGRE VARIANT
BY SALVADOR LARROCA & DAVID OCAMPO

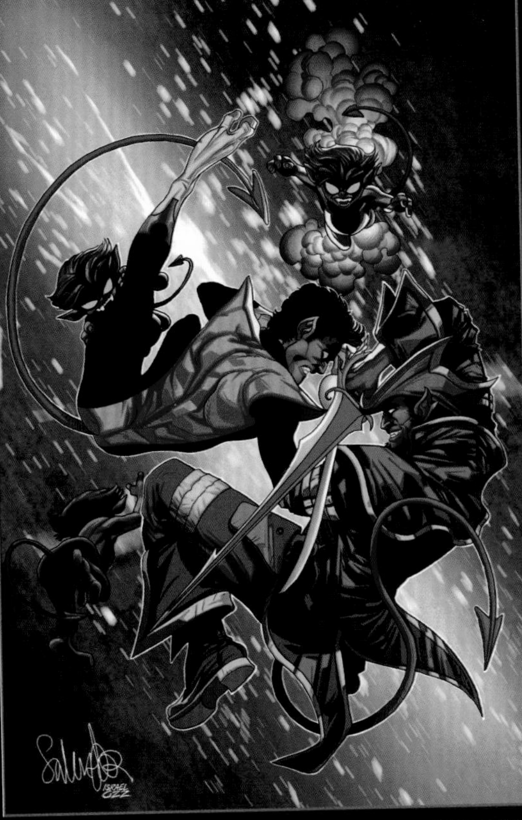

AMAZING X-MEN #1 HASTINGS VARIANT
BY SALVADOR LARROCA & ISRAEL SILVA

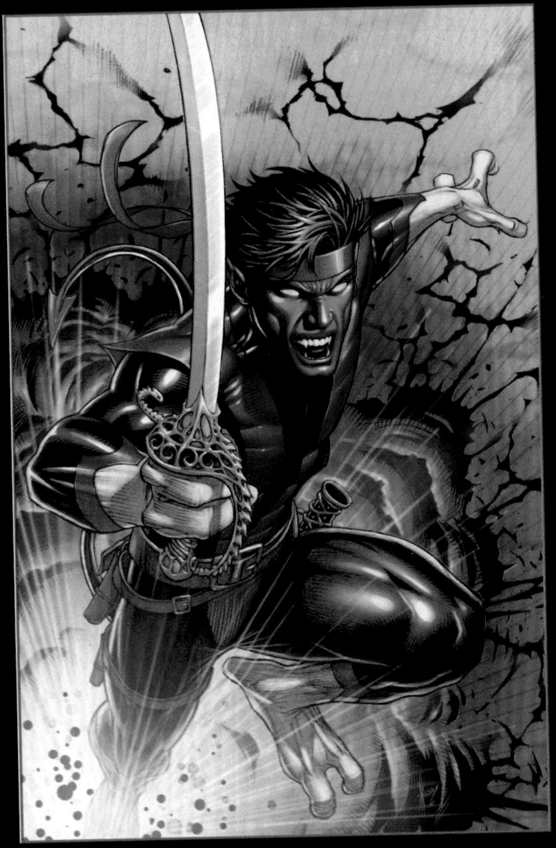

AMAZING X-MEN #2 VARIANT
BY DALE KEOWN & CHRIS SOTOMAYOR

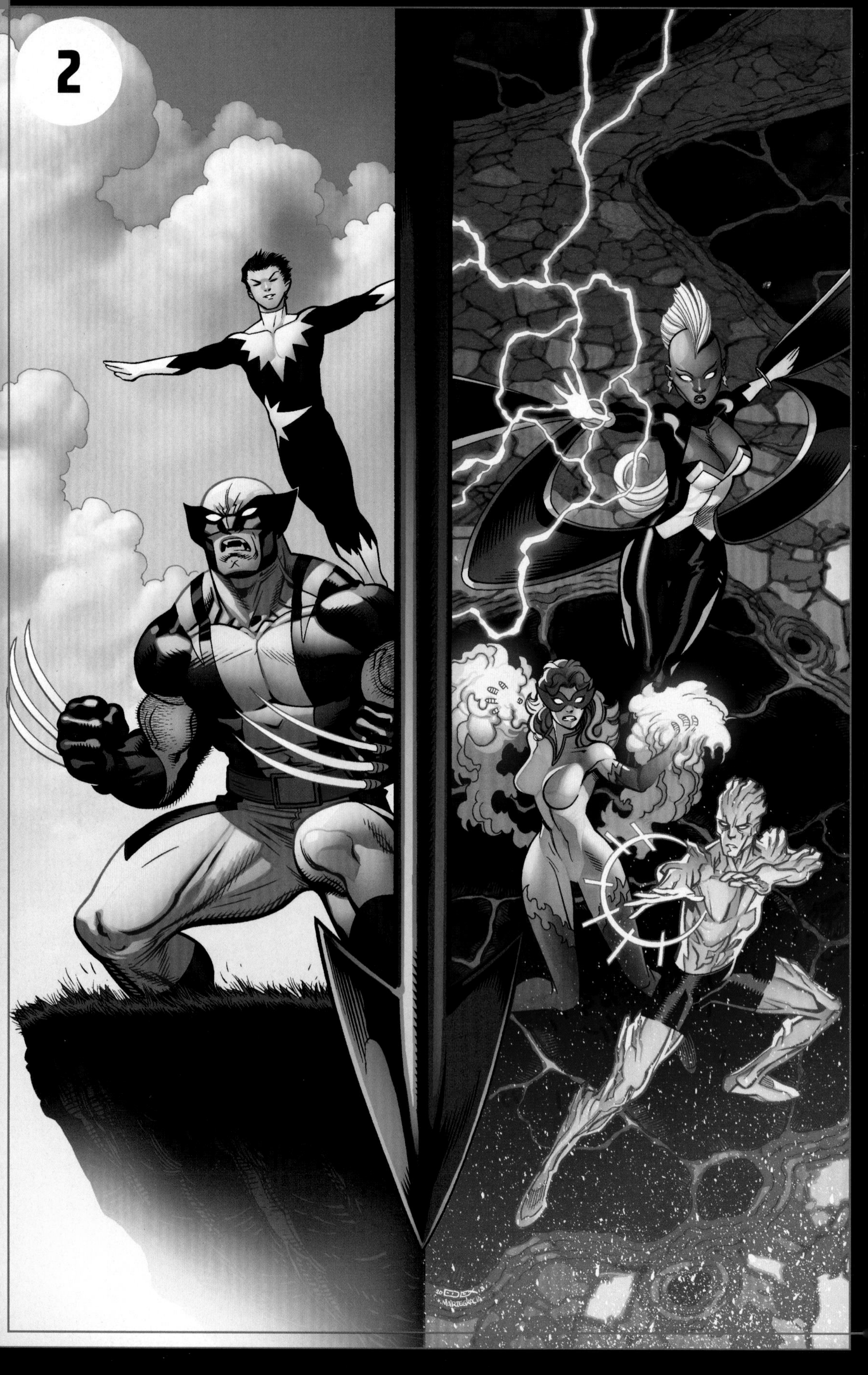
2

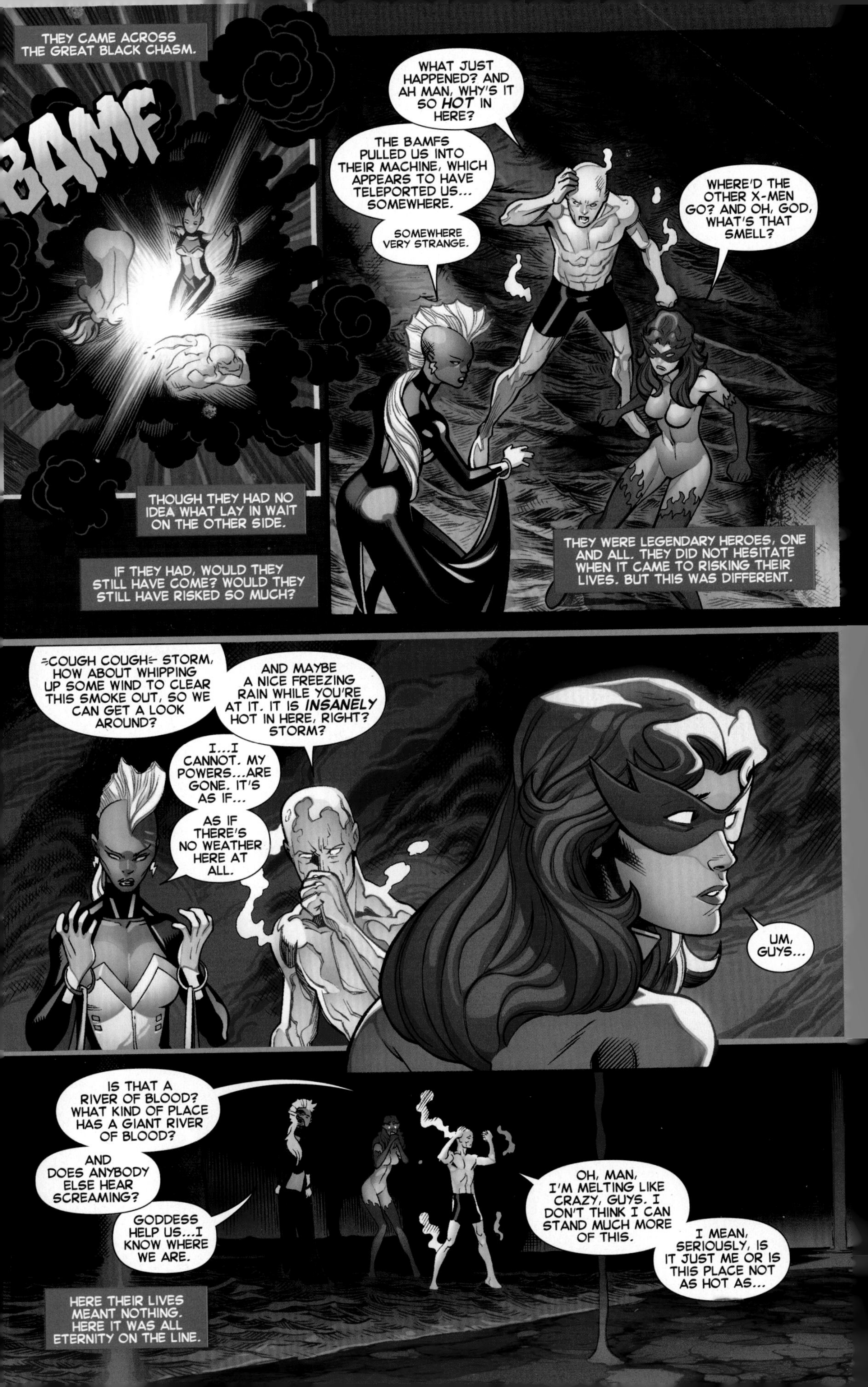
THEY CAME ACROSS THE GREAT BLACK CHASM.
BAMF
WHAT JUST HAPPENED? AND AH MAN, WHY'S IT SO HOT IN HERE?
THE BAMFS PULLED US INTO THEIR MACHINE, WHICH APPEARS TO HAVE TELEPORTED US... SOMEWHERE.
SOMEWHERE VERY STRANGE.
WHERE'D THE OTHER X-MEN GO? AND OH, GOD, WHAT'S THAT SMELL?
THOUGH THEY HAD NO IDEA WHAT LAY IN WAIT ON THE OTHER SIDE.
IF THEY HAD, WOULD THEY STILL HAVE COME? WOULD THEY STILL HAVE RISKED SO MUCH?
THEY WERE LEGENDARY HEROES, ONE AND ALL. THEY DID NOT HESITATE WHEN IT CAME TO RISKING THEIR LIVES. BUT THIS WAS DIFFERENT.
=COUGH COUGH= STORM, HOW ABOUT WHIPPING UP SOME WIND TO CLEAR THIS SMOKE OUT, SO WE CAN GET A LOOK AROUND?
AND MAYBE A NICE FREEZING RAIN WHILE YOU'RE AT IT. IT IS INSANELY HOT IN HERE, RIGHT? STORM?
I...I CANNOT. MY POWERS...ARE GONE. IT'S AS IF...
AS IF THERE'S NO WEATHER HERE AT ALL.
UM, GUYS...
IS THAT A RIVER OF BLOOD? WHAT KIND OF PLACE HAS A GIANT RIVER OF BLOOD?
AND DOES ANYBODY ELSE HEAR SCREAMING?
GODDESS HELP US...I KNOW WHERE WE ARE.
OH, MAN, I'M MELTING LIKE CRAZY, GUYS. I DON'T THINK I CAN STAND MUCH MORE OF THIS.
I MEAN, SERIOUSLY, IS IT JUST ME OR IS THIS PLACE NOT AS HOT AS...
HERE THEIR LIVES MEANT NOTHING. HERE IT WAS ALL ETERNITY ON THE LINE.

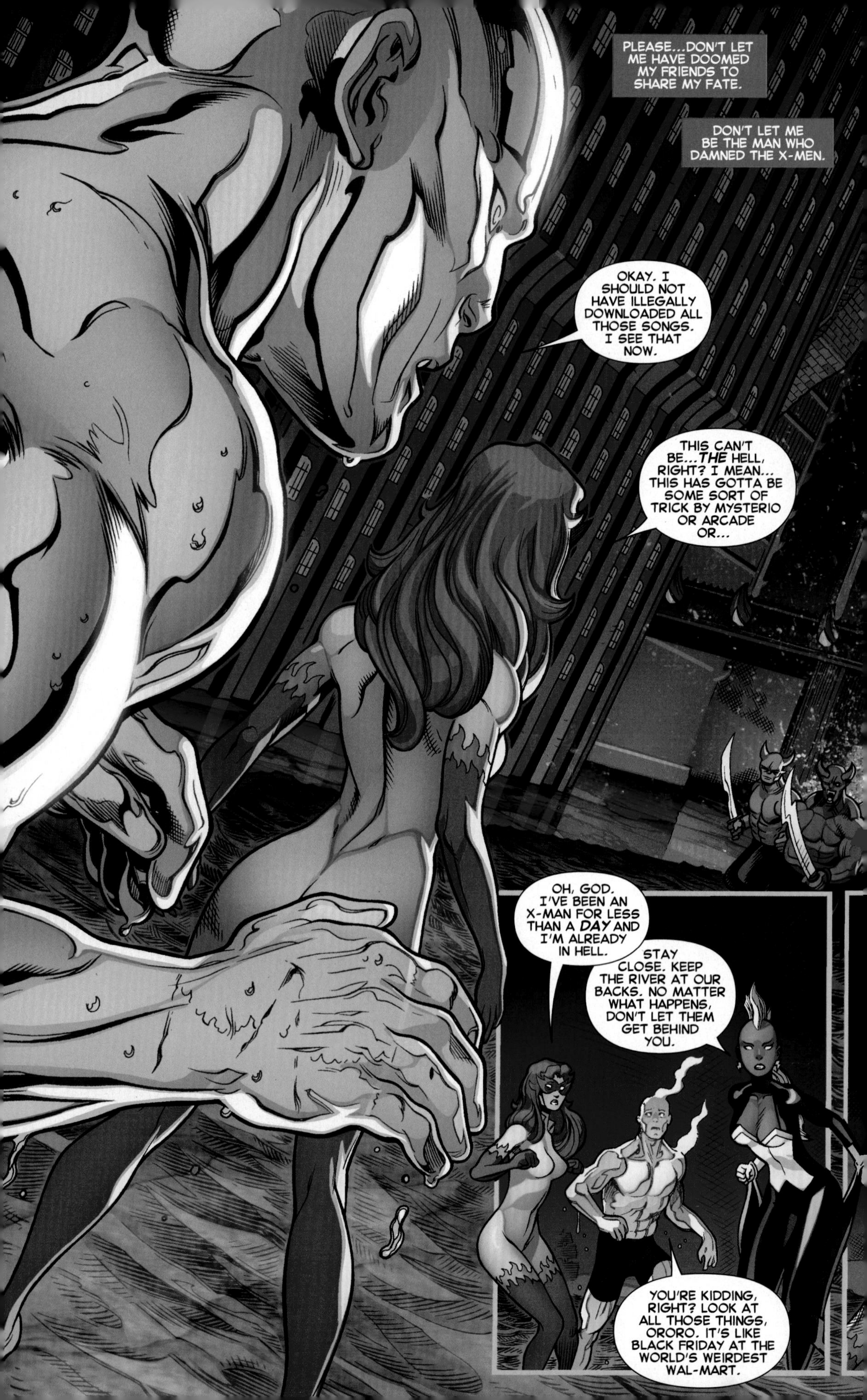
PLEASE...DON'T LET ME HAVE DOOMED MY FRIENDS TO SHARE MY FATE.
DON'T LET ME BE THE MAN WHO DAMNED THE X-MEN.
OKAY. I SHOULD NOT HAVE ILLEGALLY DOWNLOADED ALL THOSE SONGS. I SEE THAT NOW.
THIS CAN'T BE...*THE* HELL, RIGHT? I MEAN... THIS HAS GOTTA BE SOME SORT OF TRICK BY MYSTERIO OR ARCADE OR...
OH, GOD. I'VE BEEN AN X-MAN FOR LESS THAN A *DAY* AND I'M ALREADY IN HELL.
STAY CLOSE. KEEP THE RIVER AT OUR BACKS. NO MATTER WHAT HAPPENS, DON'T LET THEM GET BEHIND YOU.
YOU'RE KIDDING, RIGHT? LOOK AT ALL THOSE THINGS, ORORO. IT'S LIKE BLACK FRIDAY AT THE WORLD'S WEIRDEST WAL-MART.

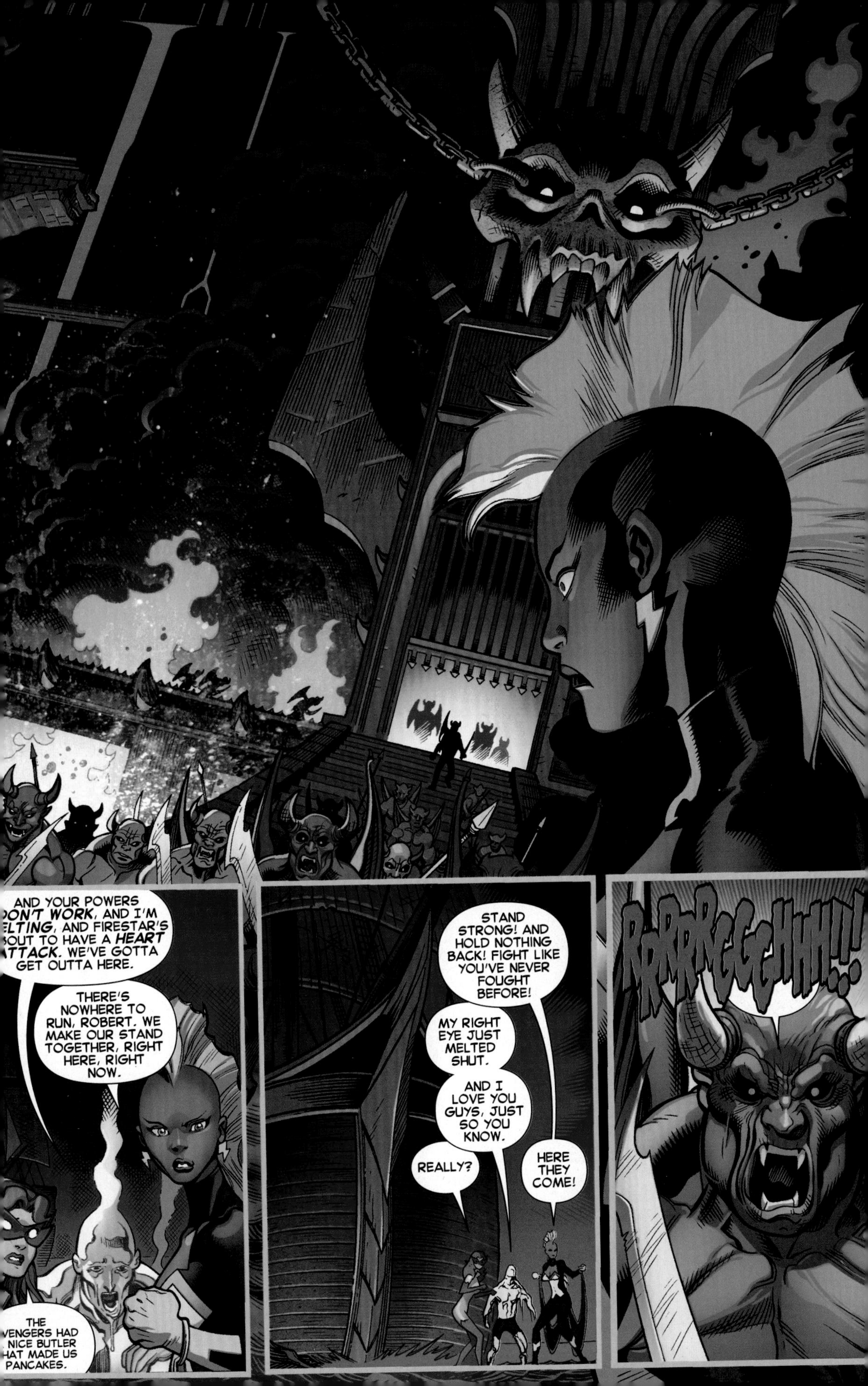
AND YOUR POWERS DON'T WORK, AND I'M ELTING, AND FIRESTAR'S BOUT TO HAVE A HEART TTACK. WE'VE GOTTA GET OUTTA HERE.
THERE'S NOWHERE TO RUN, ROBERT. WE MAKE OUR STAND TOGETHER, RIGHT HERE, RIGHT NOW.
THE VENGERS HAD NICE BUTLER HAT MADE US PANCAKES.
STAND STRONG! AND HOLD NOTHING BACK! FIGHT LIKE YOU'VE NEVER FOUGHT BEFORE!
MY RIGHT EYE JUST MELTED SHUT.
AND I LOVE YOU GUYS, JUST SO YOU KNOW.
REALLY?
HERE THEY COME!
RRRRRGGHHH!!!

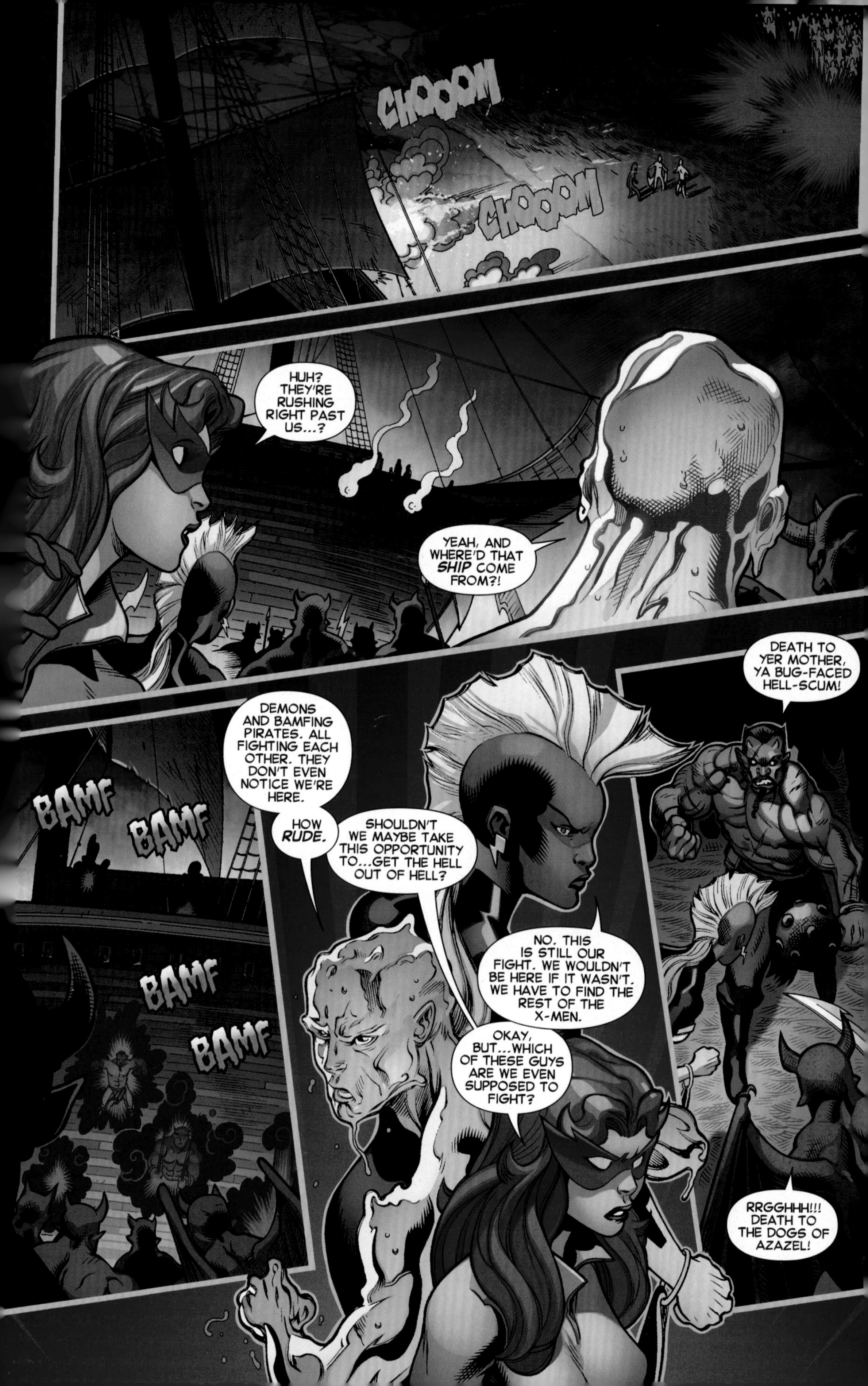
CHOOOM
CHOOOM
HUH? THEY'RE RUSHING RIGHT PAST US...?
YEAH, AND WHERE'D THAT SHIP COME FROM?!
DEMONS AND BAMFING PIRATES. ALL FIGHTING EACH OTHER. THEY DON'T EVEN NOTICE WE'RE HERE.
HOW RUDE.
SHOULDN'T WE MAYBE TAKE THIS OPPORTUNITY TO...GET THE HELL OUT OF HELL?
NO. THIS IS STILL OUR FIGHT. WE WOULDN'T BE HERE IF IT WASN'T. WE HAVE TO FIND THE REST OF THE X-MEN.
OKAY, BUT...WHICH OF THESE GUYS ARE WE EVEN SUPPOSED TO FIGHT?
BAMF
BAMF
BAMF
BAMF
DEATH TO YER MOTHER, YA BUG-FACED HELL-SCUM!
RRGGHHH!!! DEATH TO THE DOGS OF AZAZEL!

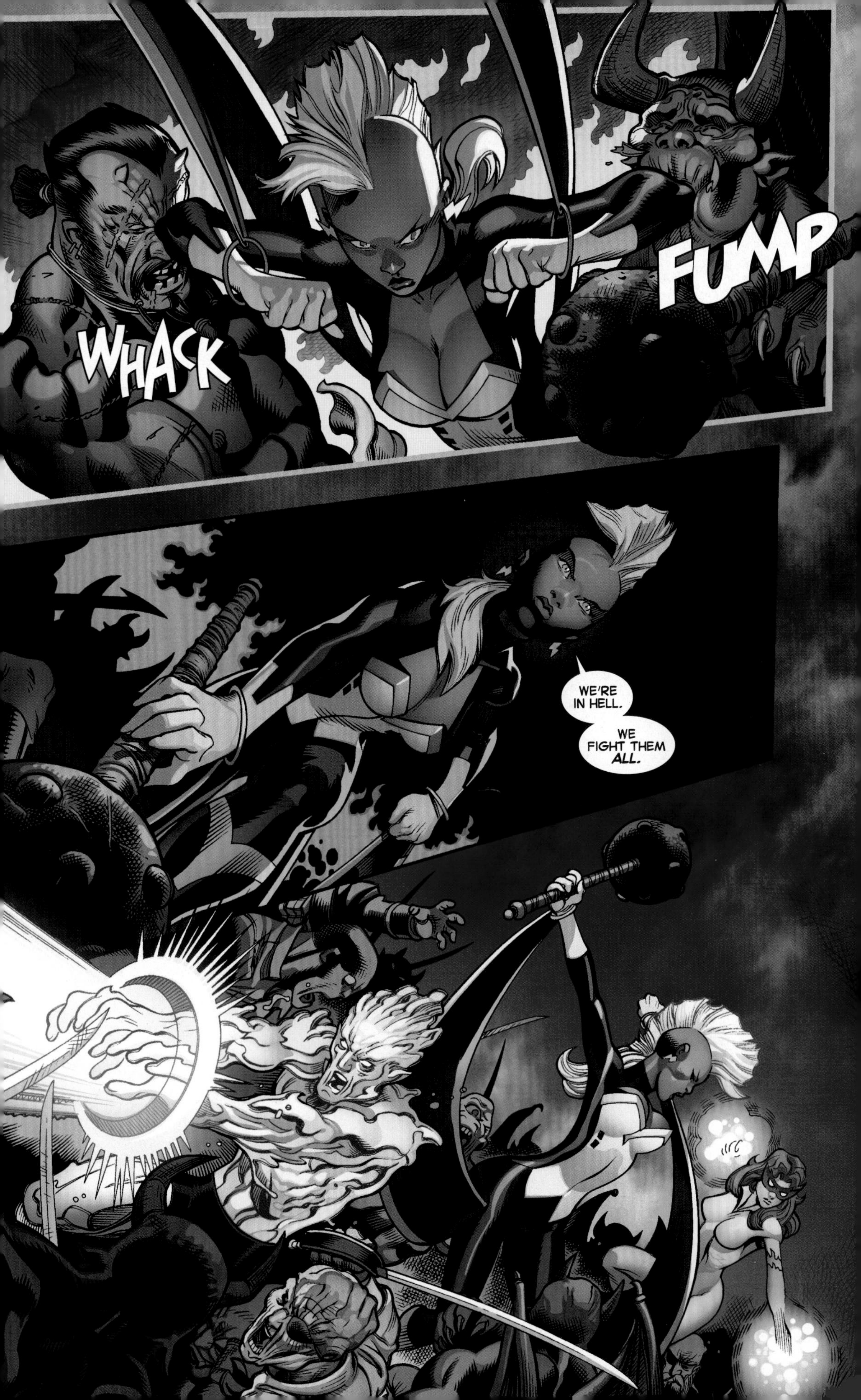
WHACK
FUMP
WE'RE IN HELL.
WE FIGHT THEM ALL.

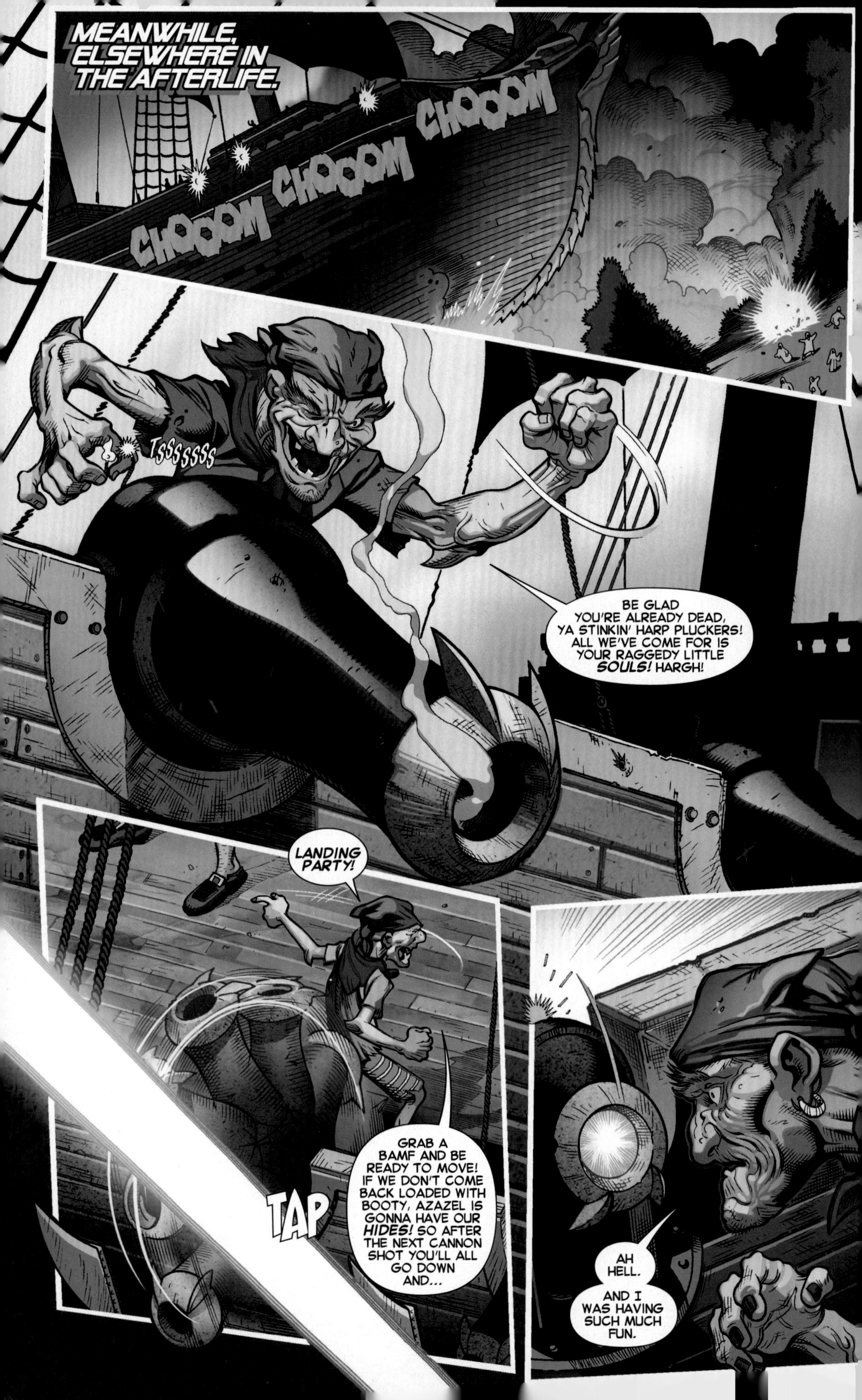
MEANWHILE, ELSEWHERE IN THE AFTERLIFE.
CHOOOM CHOOOM CHOOOM
TSSSSSSS
BE GLAD YOU'RE ALREADY DEAD, YA STINKIN' HARP PLUCKERS! ALL WE'VE COME FOR IS YOUR RAGGEDY LITTLE SOULS! HARGH!
LANDING PARTY!
GRAB A BAMF AND BE READY TO MOVE! IF WE DON'T COME BACK LOADED WITH BOOTY, AZAZEL IS GONNA HAVE OUR HIDES! SO AFTER THE NEXT CANNON SHOT YOU'LL ALL GO DOWN AND...
TAP
AH HELL.
AND I WAS HAVING SUCH MUCH FUN.

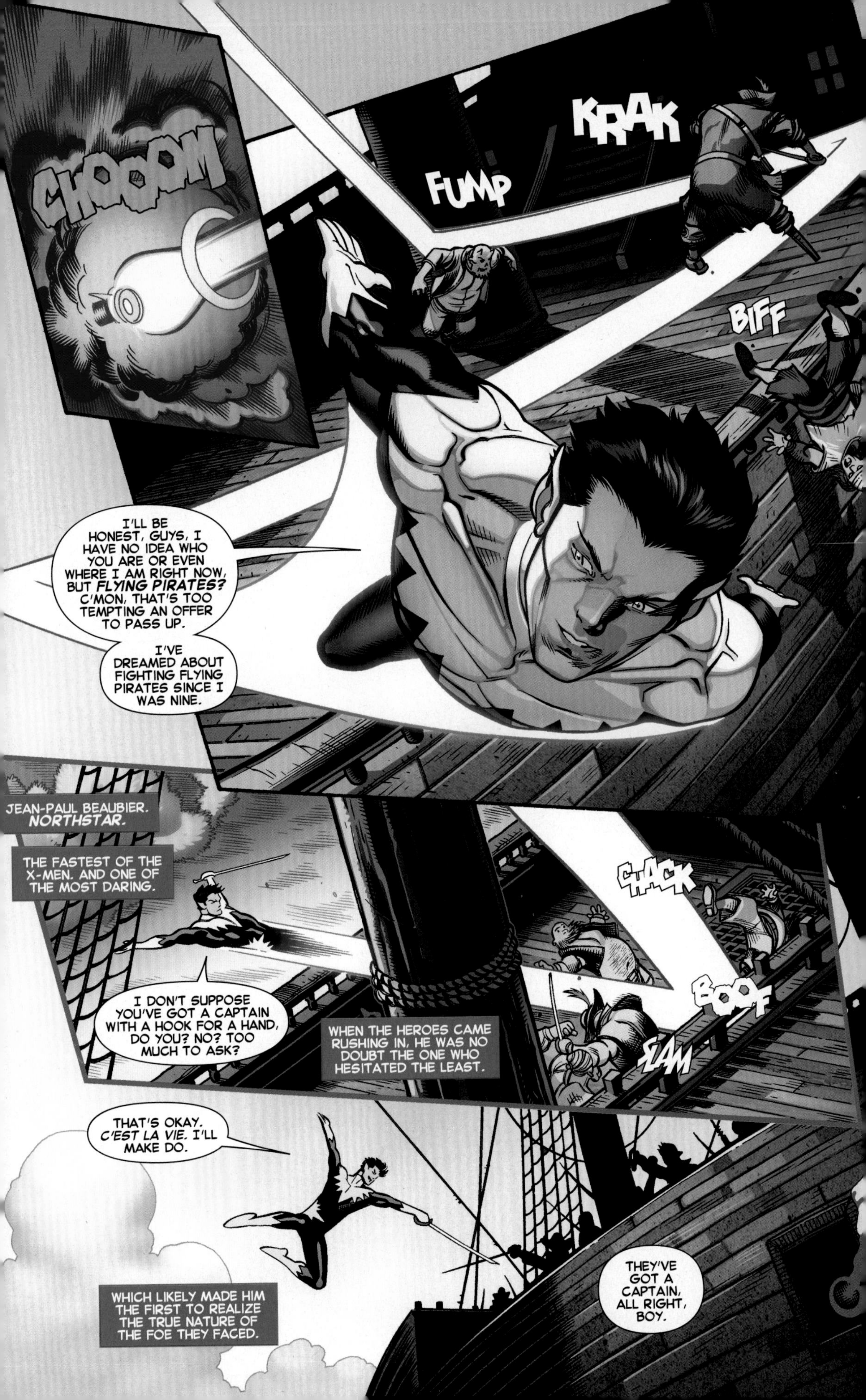
CHOOOM
KRAK
FUMP
BIFF
I'LL BE HONEST, GUYS, I HAVE NO IDEA WHO YOU ARE OR EVEN WHERE I AM RIGHT NOW, BUT FLYING PIRATES? C'MON, THAT'S TOO TEMPTING AN OFFER TO PASS UP.
I'VE DREAMED ABOUT FIGHTING FLYING PIRATES SINCE I WAS NINE.
JEAN-PAUL BEAUBIER. NORTHSTAR.
THE FASTEST OF THE X-MEN. AND ONE OF THE MOST DARING.
CHACK
I DON'T SUPPOSE YOU'VE GOT A CAPTAIN WITH A HOOK FOR A HAND, DO YOU? NO? TOO MUCH TO ASK?
WHEN THE HEROES CAME RUSHING IN, HE WAS NO DOUBT THE ONE WHO HESITATED THE LEAST.
BOOF
SLAM
THAT'S OKAY. C'EST LA VIE. I'LL MAKE DO.
WHICH LIKELY MADE HIM THE FIRST TO REALIZE THE TRUE NATURE OF THE FOE THEY FACED.
THEY'VE GOT A CAPTAIN, ALL RIGHT, BOY.

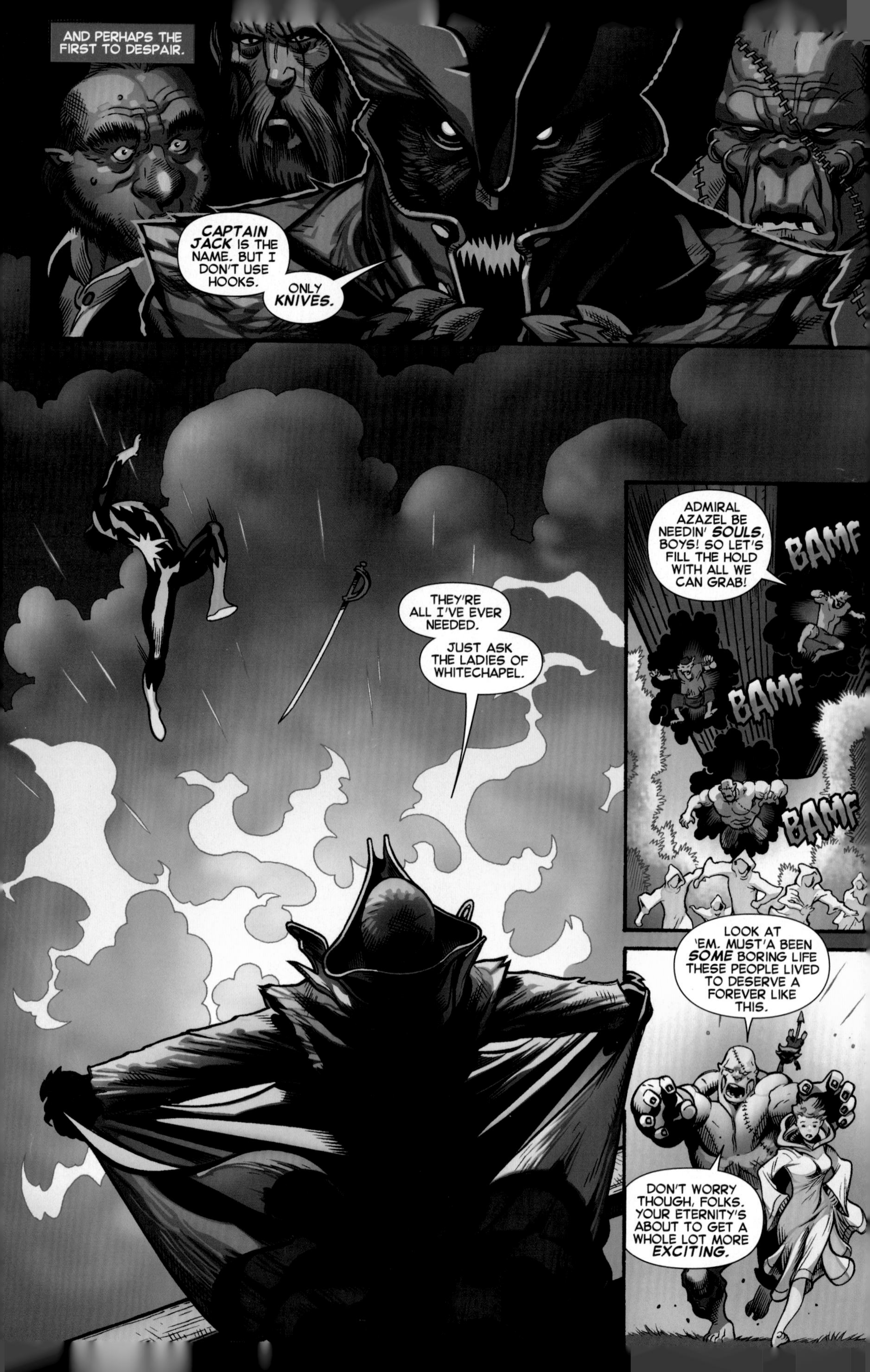
AND PERHAPS THE FIRST TO DESPAIR.
CAPTAIN JACK IS THE NAME. BUT I DON'T USE HOOKS.
ONLY KNIVES.
THEY'RE ALL I'VE EVER NEEDED.
JUST ASK THE LADIES OF WHITECHAPEL.
ADMIRAL AZAZEL BE NEEDIN' SOULS, BOYS! SO LET'S FILL THE HOLD WITH ALL WE CAN GRAB!
BAMF
BAMF
BAMF
LOOK AT 'EM. MUST'A BEEN SOME BORING LIFE THESE PEOPLE LIVED TO DESERVE A FOREVER LIKE THIS.
DON'T WORRY THOUGH, FOLKS. YOUR ETERNITY'S ABOUT TO GET A WHOLE LOT MORE EXCITING.

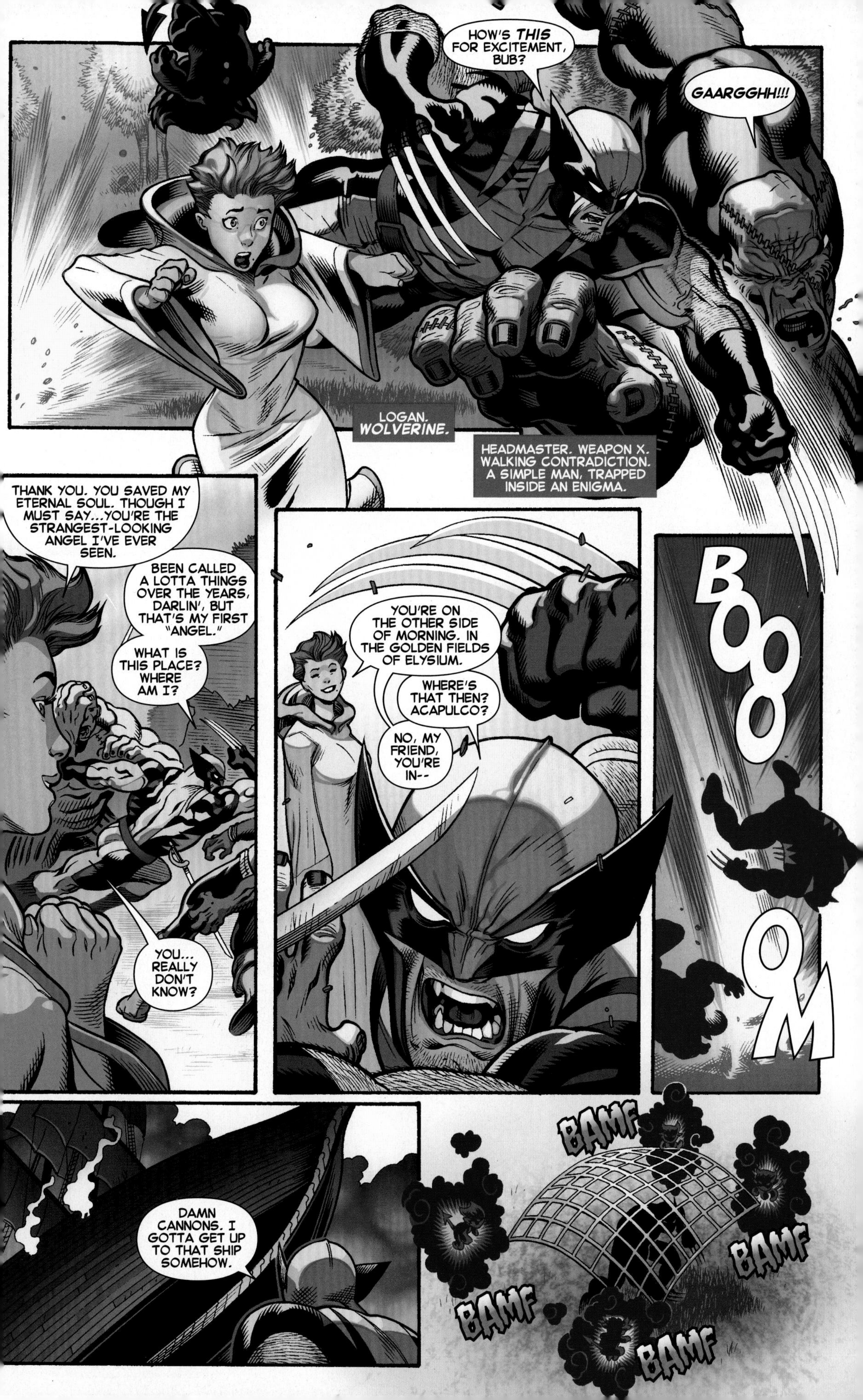
HOW'S *THIS* FOR EXCITEMENT, BUB?
GAARGGHH!!!
LOGAN. *WOLVERINE.*
HEADMASTER. WEAPON X. WALKING CONTRADICTION. A SIMPLE MAN, TRAPPED INSIDE AN ENIGMA.
THANK YOU. YOU SAVED MY ETERNAL SOUL. THOUGH I MUST SAY...YOU'RE THE STRANGEST-LOOKING ANGEL I'VE EVER SEEN.
BEEN CALLED A LOTTA THINGS OVER THE YEARS, DARLIN', BUT THAT'S MY FIRST "ANGEL."
WHAT IS THIS PLACE? WHERE AM I?
YOU... REALLY DON'T KNOW?
YOU'RE ON THE OTHER SIDE OF MORNING. IN THE GOLDEN FIELDS OF ELYSIUM.
WHERE'S THAT THEN? ACAPULCO?
NO, MY FRIEND, YOU'RE IN--
BOOOOM
DAMN CANNONS. I GOTTA GET UP TO THAT SHIP SOMEHOW.
BAMF
BAMF
BAMF
BAMF

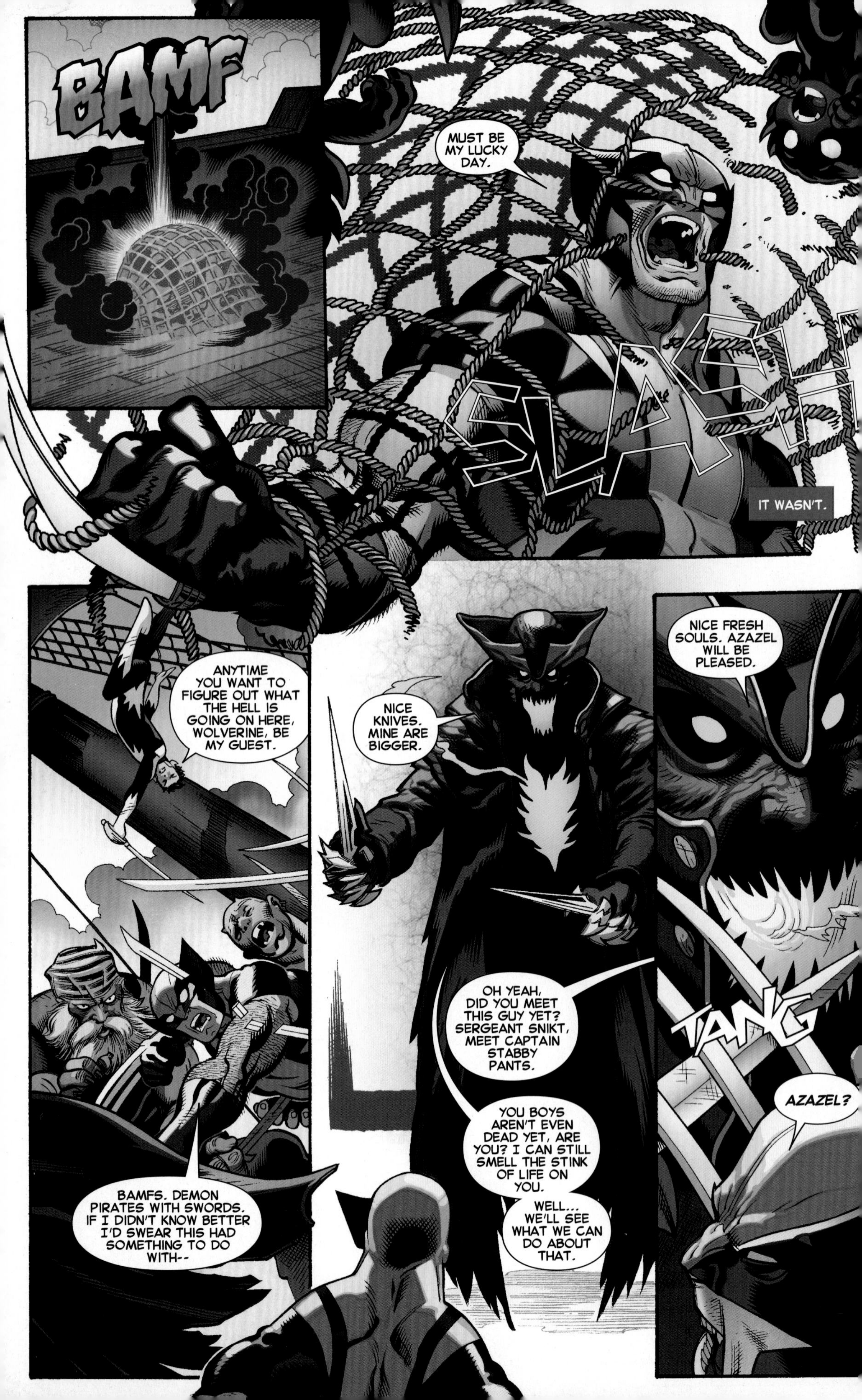
BAMF
MUST BE MY LUCKY DAY.
SLASH
IT WASN'T.
ANYTIME YOU WANT TO FIGURE OUT WHAT THE HELL IS GOING ON HERE, WOLVERINE, BE MY GUEST.
BAMFS. DEMON PIRATES WITH SWORDS. IF I DIDN'T KNOW BETTER I'D SWEAR THIS HAD SOMETHING TO DO WITH--
NICE KNIVES. MINE ARE BIGGER.
OH YEAH, DID YOU MEET THIS GUY YET? SERGEANT SNIKT, MEET CAPTAIN STABBY PANTS.
YOU BOYS AREN'T EVEN DEAD YET, ARE YOU? I CAN STILL SMELL THE STINK OF LIFE ON YOU.
WELL... WE'LL SEE WHAT WE CAN DO ABOUT THAT.
NICE FRESH SOULS. AZAZEL WILL BE PLEASED.
TANG
AZAZEL?

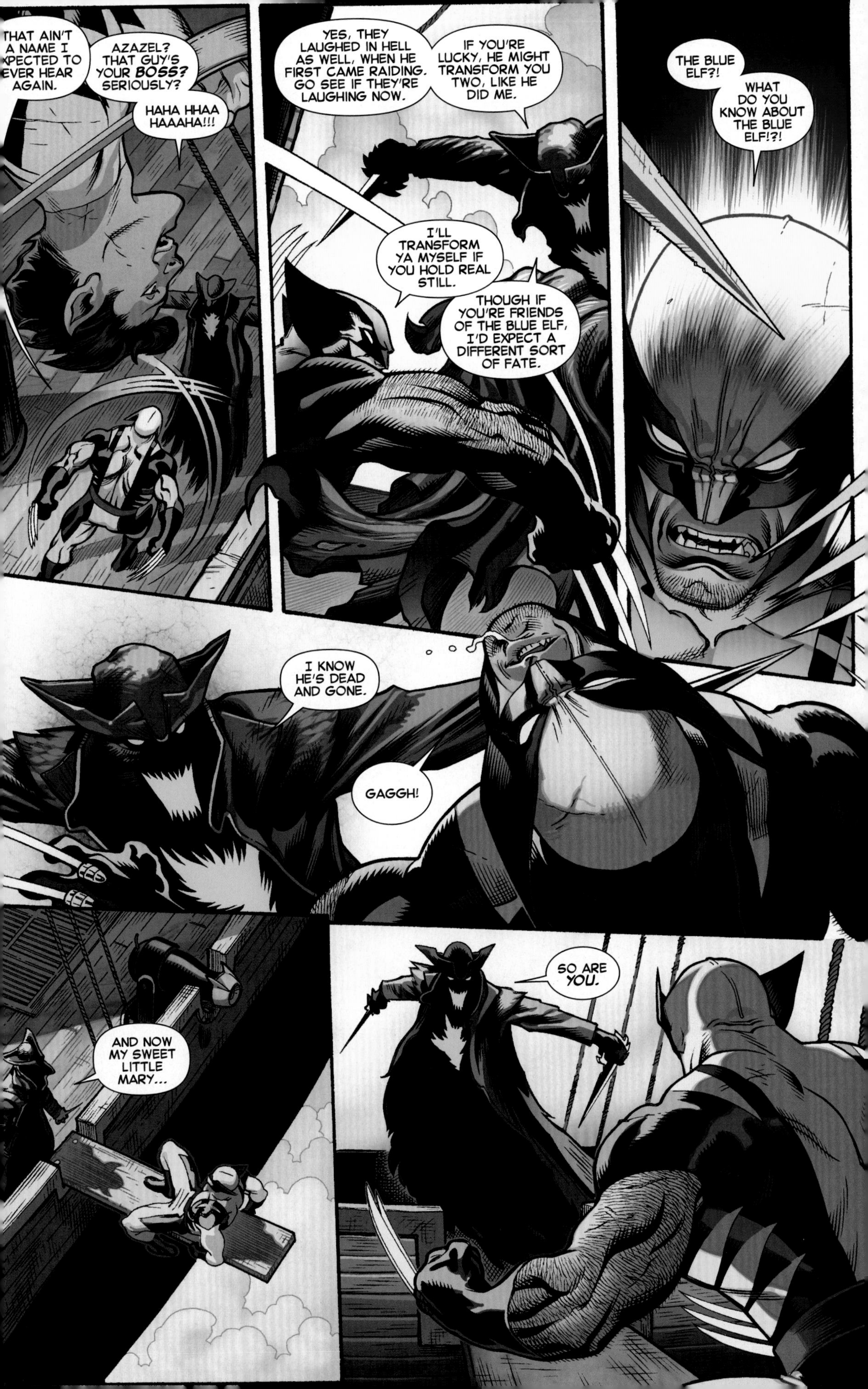

THAT AIN'T A NAME I EXPECTED TO EVER HEAR AGAIN.
AZAZEL? THAT GUY'S YOUR BOSS? SERIOUSLY?
HAHA HHAA HAAAHA!!!
YES, THEY LAUGHED IN HELL AS WELL, WHEN HE FIRST CAME RAIDING. GO SEE IF THEY'RE LAUGHING NOW.
IF YOU'RE LUCKY, HE MIGHT TRANSFORM YOU TWO, LIKE HE DID ME.
I'LL TRANSFORM YA MYSELF IF YOU HOLD REAL STILL.
THOUGH IF YOU'RE FRIENDS OF THE BLUE ELF, I'D EXPECT A DIFFERENT SORT OF FATE.
THE BLUE ELF?!
WHAT DO YOU KNOW ABOUT THE BLUE ELF!?!
I KNOW HE'S DEAD AND GONE.
GAGGH!
AND NOW MY SWEET LITTLE MARY...
SO ARE YOU.

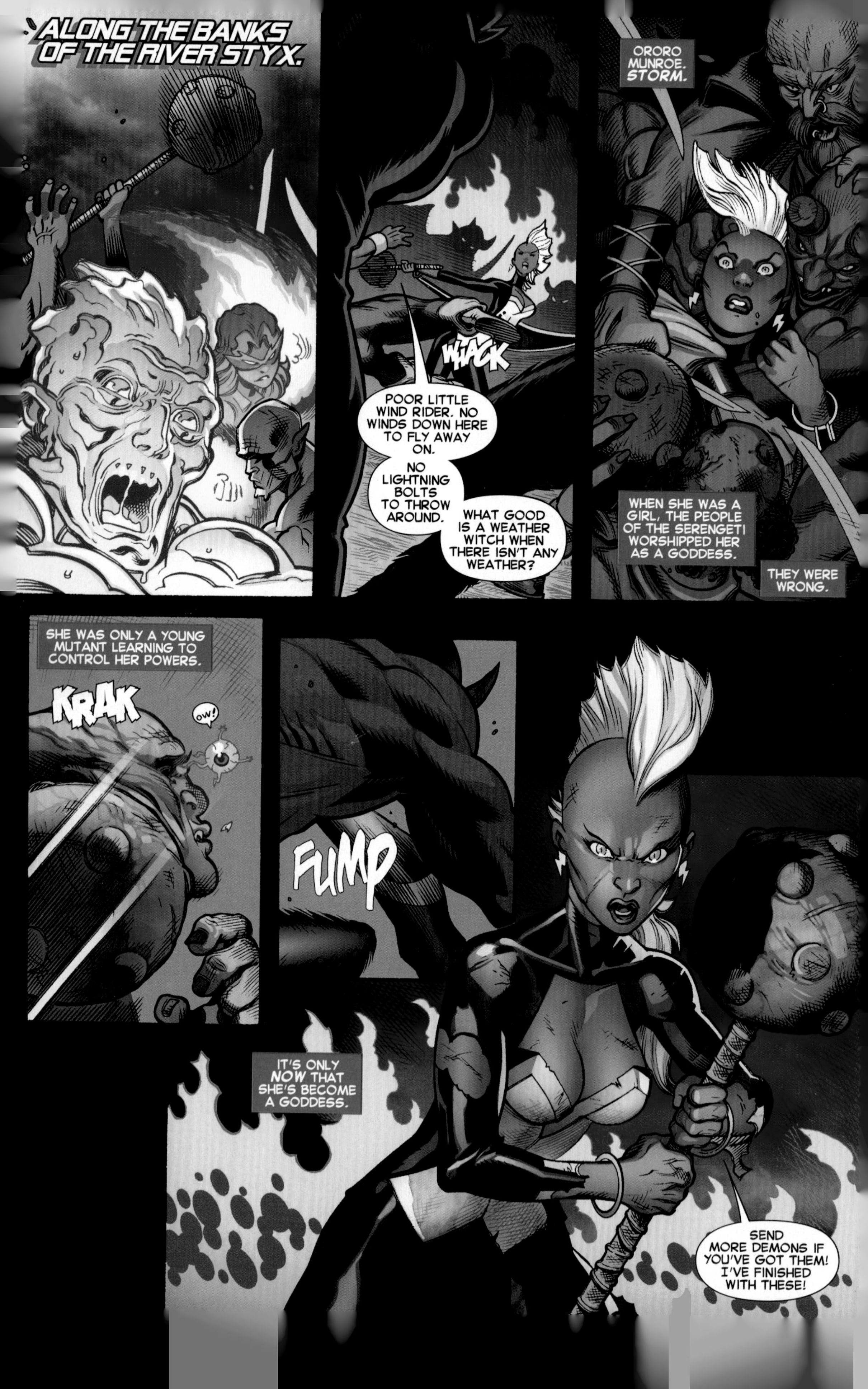

ALONG THE BANKS OF THE RIVER STYX.
WHACK
POOR LITTLE WIND RIDER. NO WINDS DOWN HERE TO FLY AWAY ON.
NO LIGHTNING BOLTS TO THROW AROUND.
WHAT GOOD IS A WEATHER WITCH WHEN THERE ISN'T ANY WEATHER?
ORORO MUNROE. STORM.
WHEN SHE WAS A GIRL, THE PEOPLE OF THE SERENGETI WORSHIPPED HER AS A GODDESS.
THEY WERE WRONG.
SHE WAS ONLY A YOUNG MUTANT LEARNING TO CONTROL HER POWERS.
KRAK
OW!
FUMP
IT'S ONLY NOW THAT SHE'S BECOME A GODDESS.
SEND MORE DEMONS IF YOU'VE GOT THEM! I'VE FINISHED WITH THESE!

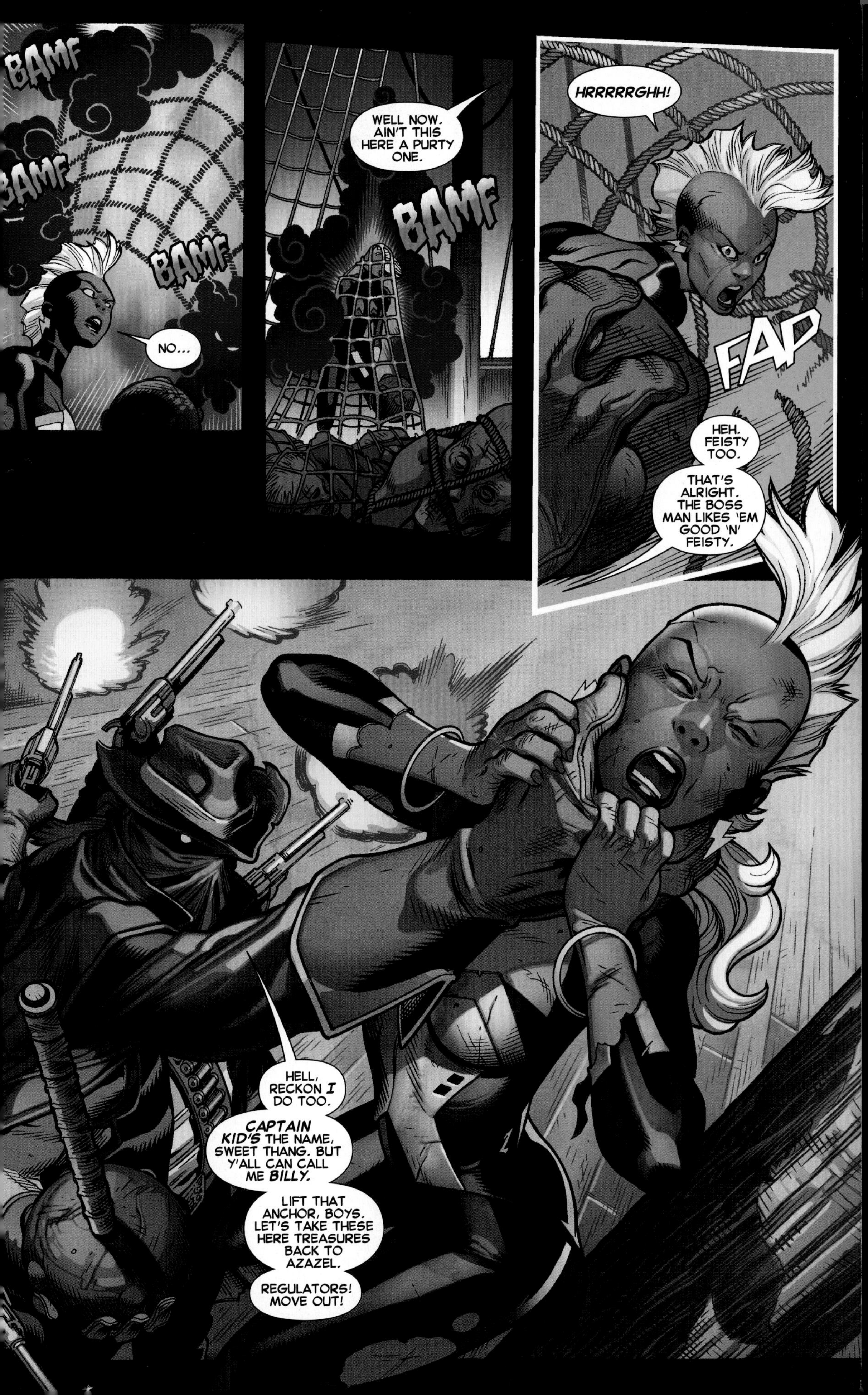
BAMF
BAMF
BAMF
NO...
WELL NOW. AIN'T THIS HERE A PURTY ONE.
BAMF
HRRRRRGHH!
FAP
HEH. FEISTY TOO.
THAT'S ALRIGHT. THE BOSS MAN LIKES 'EM GOOD 'N' FEISTY.
HELL, RECKON I DO TOO.
CAPTAIN KID'S THE NAME, SWEET THANG. BUT Y'ALL CAN CALL ME BILLY.
LIFT THAT ANCHOR, BOYS. LET'S TAKE THESE HERE TREASURES BACK TO AZAZEL.
REGULATORS! MOVE OUT!

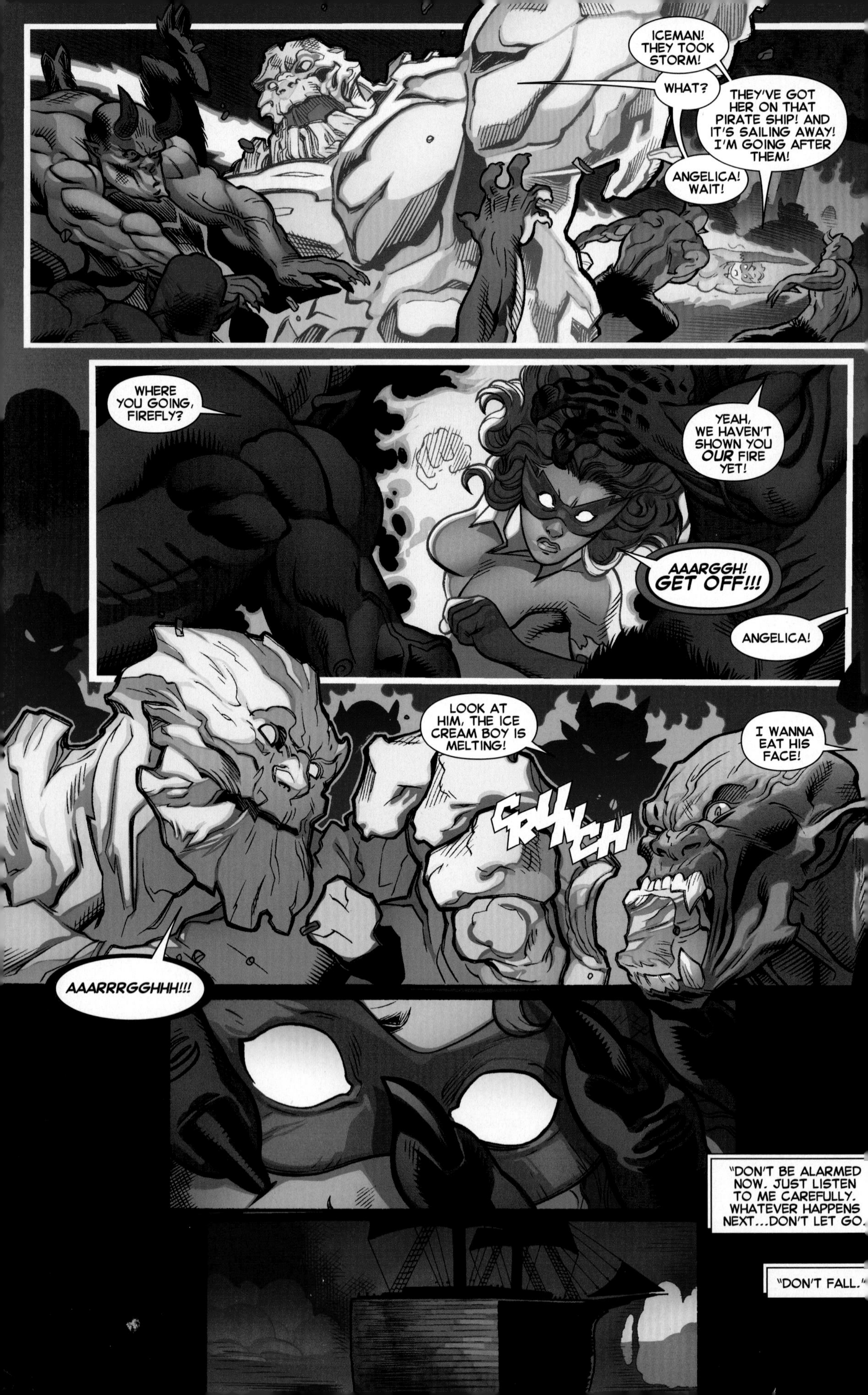
ICEMAN! THEY TOOK STORM!
WHAT?
THEY'VE GOT HER ON THAT PIRATE SHIP! AND IT'S SAILING AWAY! I'M GOING AFTER THEM!
ANGELICA! WAIT!
WHERE YOU GOING, FIREFLY?
YEAH, WE HAVEN'T SHOWN YOU OUR FIRE YET!
AAARGGH! GET OFF!!!
ANGELICA!
LOOK AT HIM, THE ICE CREAM BOY IS MELTING!
I WANNA EAT HIS FACE!
CRUNCH
AAARRRGGHHH!!!
"DON'T BE ALARMED NOW. JUST LISTEN TO ME CAREFULLY. WHATEVER HAPPENS NEXT...DON'T LET GO.
"DON'T FALL."

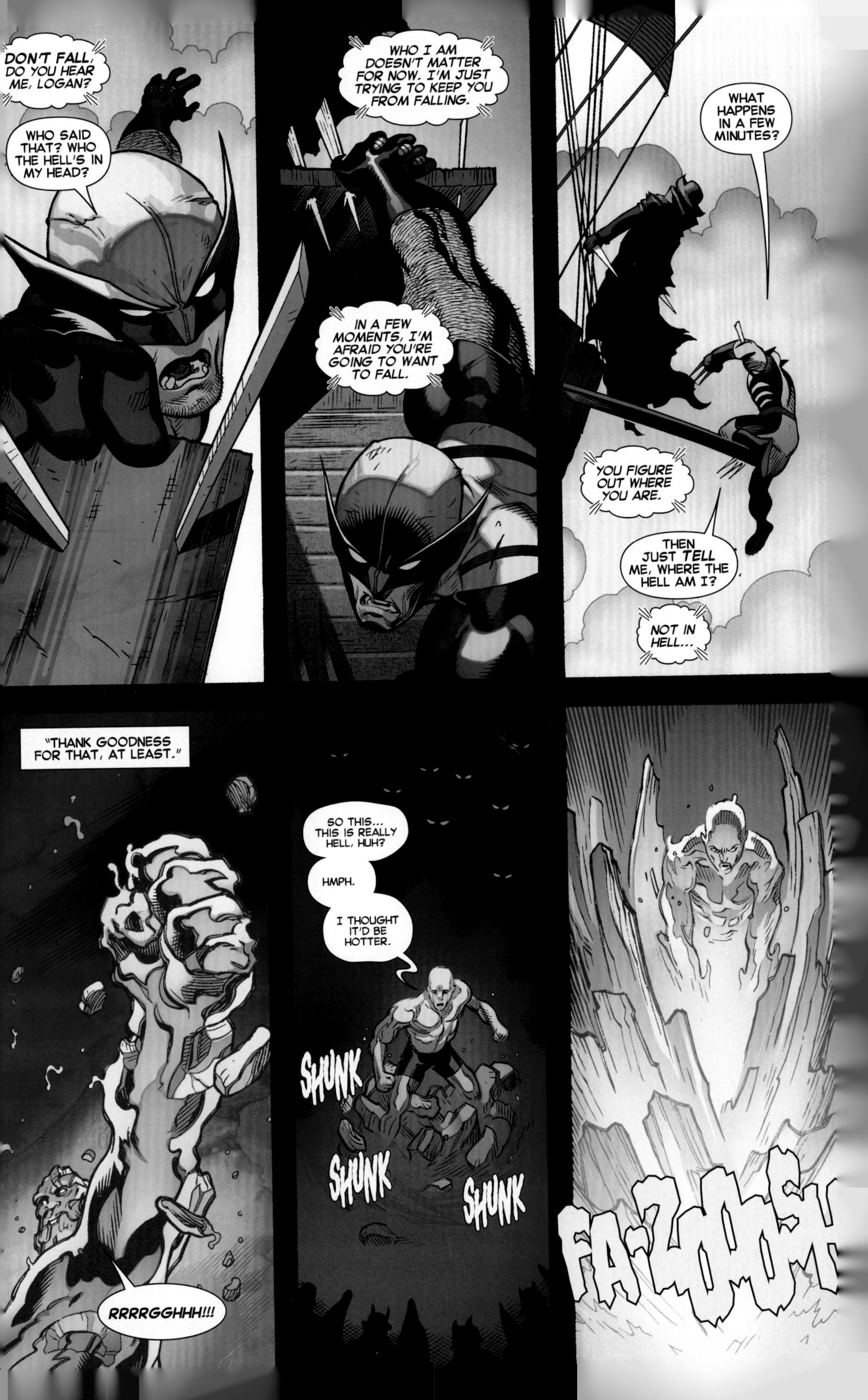
DON'T FALL, DO YOU HEAR ME, LOGAN?
WHO SAID THAT? WHO THE HELL'S IN MY HEAD?
WHO I AM DOESN'T MATTER FOR NOW. I'M JUST TRYING TO KEEP YOU FROM FALLING.
IN A FEW MOMENTS, I'M AFRAID YOU'RE GOING TO WANT TO FALL.
WHAT HAPPENS IN A FEW MINUTES?
YOU FIGURE OUT WHERE YOU ARE.
THEN JUST TELL ME, WHERE THE HELL AM I?
NOT IN HELL...
"THANK GOODNESS FOR THAT, AT LEAST."
RRRRGGHHH!!!
SO THIS... THIS IS REALLY HELL, HUH?
HMPH.
I THOUGHT IT'D BE HOTTER.
SHUNK
SHUNK
SHUNK
FA-ZOOSH

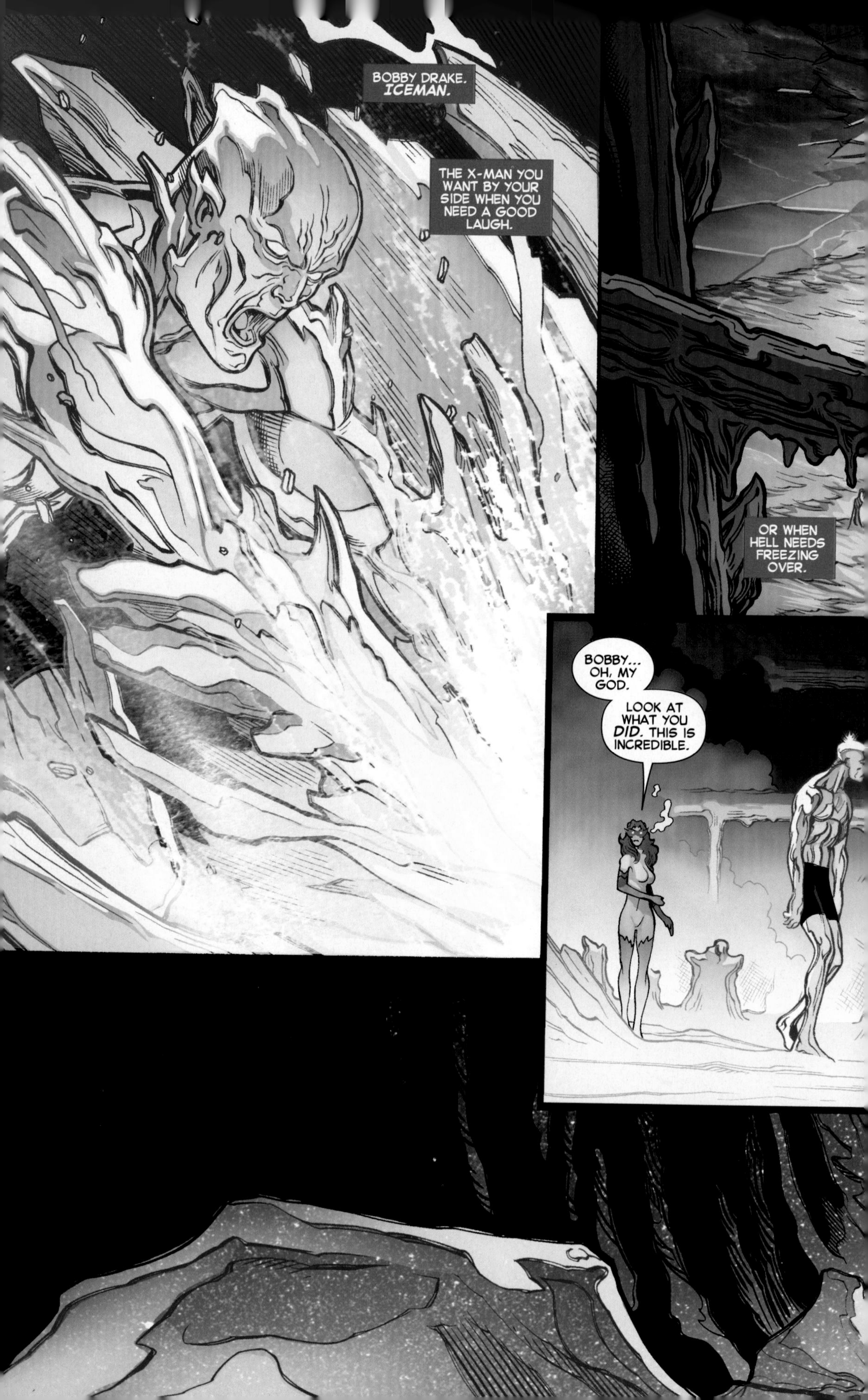
BOBBY DRAKE. *ICEMAN.*
THE X-MAN YOU WANT BY YOUR SIDE WHEN YOU NEED A GOOD LAUGH.
OR WHEN HELL NEEDS FREEZING OVER.
BOBBY... OH, MY GOD.
LOOK AT WHAT YOU *DID.* THIS IS INCREDIBLE.

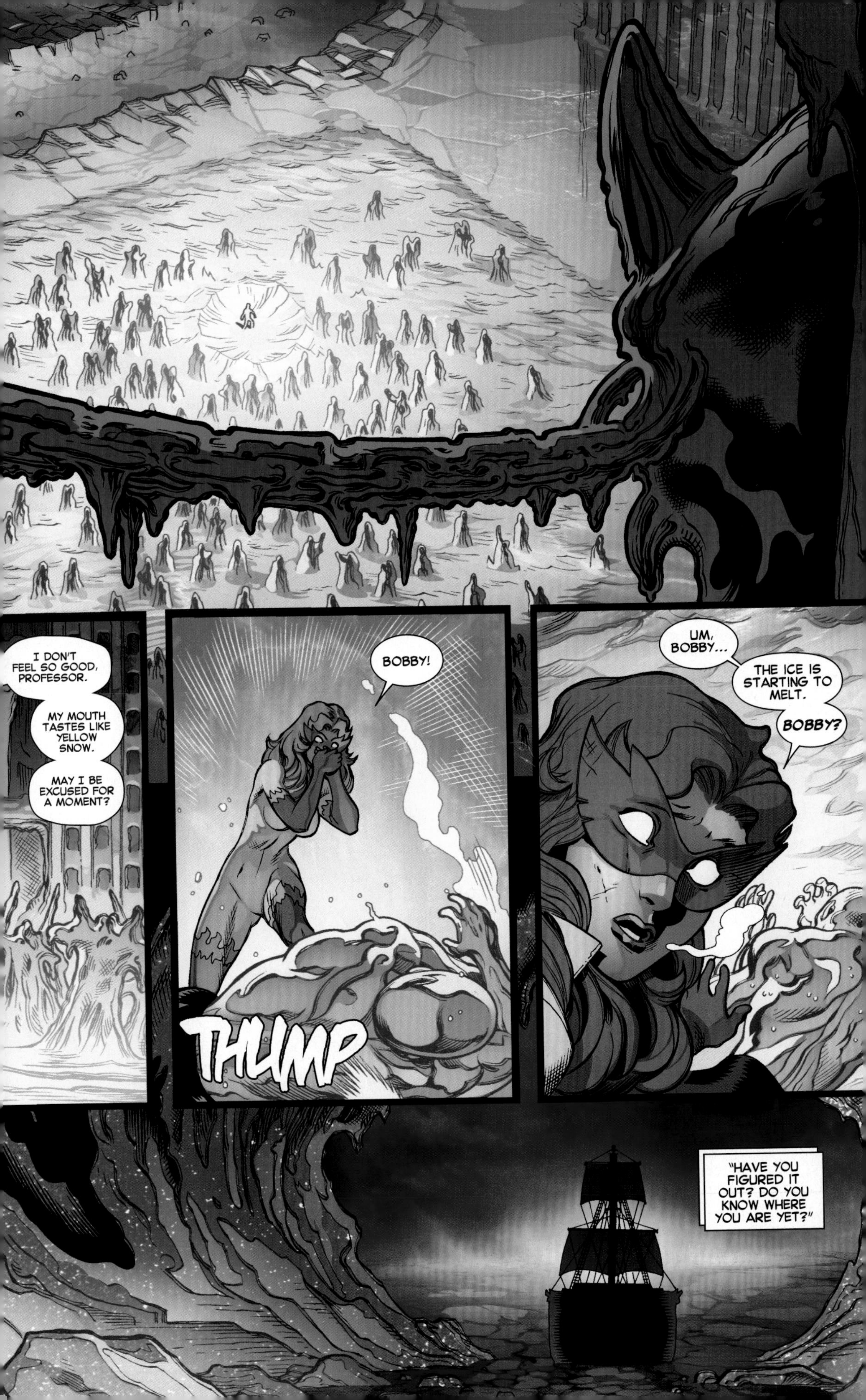
I DON'T FEEL SO GOOD, PROFESSOR.
MY MOUTH TASTES LIKE YELLOW SNOW.
MAY I BE EXCUSED FOR A MOMENT?
BOBBY!
THUMP
UM, BOBBY...
THE ICE IS STARTING TO MELT.
BOBBY?
"HAVE YOU FIGURED IT OUT? DO YOU KNOW WHERE YOU ARE YET?"

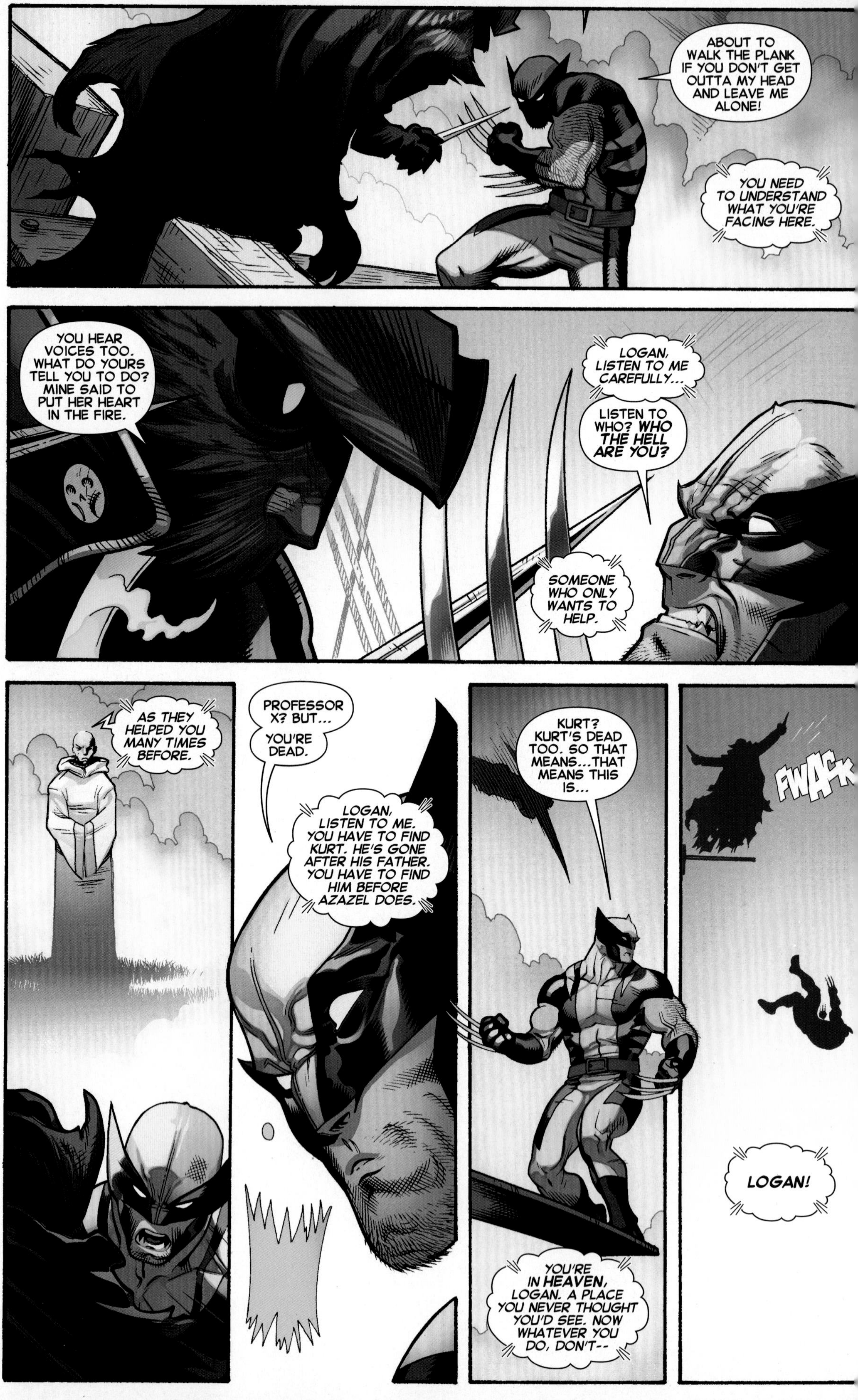
ABOUT TO WALK THE PLANK IF YOU DON'T GET OUTTA MY HEAD AND LEAVE ME ALONE!
YOU NEED TO UNDERSTAND WHAT YOU'RE FACING HERE.
YOU HEAR VOICES TOO. WHAT DO YOURS TELL YOU TO DO? MINE SAID TO PUT HER HEART IN THE FIRE.
LOGAN, LISTEN TO ME CAREFULLY...
LISTEN TO WHO? WHO THE HELL ARE YOU?
SOMEONE WHO ONLY WANTS TO HELP.
AS THEY HELPED YOU MANY TIMES BEFORE.
PROFESSOR X? BUT...
YOU'RE DEAD.
LOGAN, LISTEN TO ME. YOU HAVE TO FIND KURT. HE'S GONE AFTER HIS FATHER. YOU HAVE TO FIND HIM BEFORE AZAZEL DOES.
KURT? KURT'S DEAD TOO. SO THAT MEANS...THAT MEANS THIS IS...
YOU'RE IN HEAVEN, LOGAN. A PLACE YOU NEVER THOUGHT YOU'D SEE. NOW WHATEVER YOU DO, DON'T--
FWACK
LOGAN!

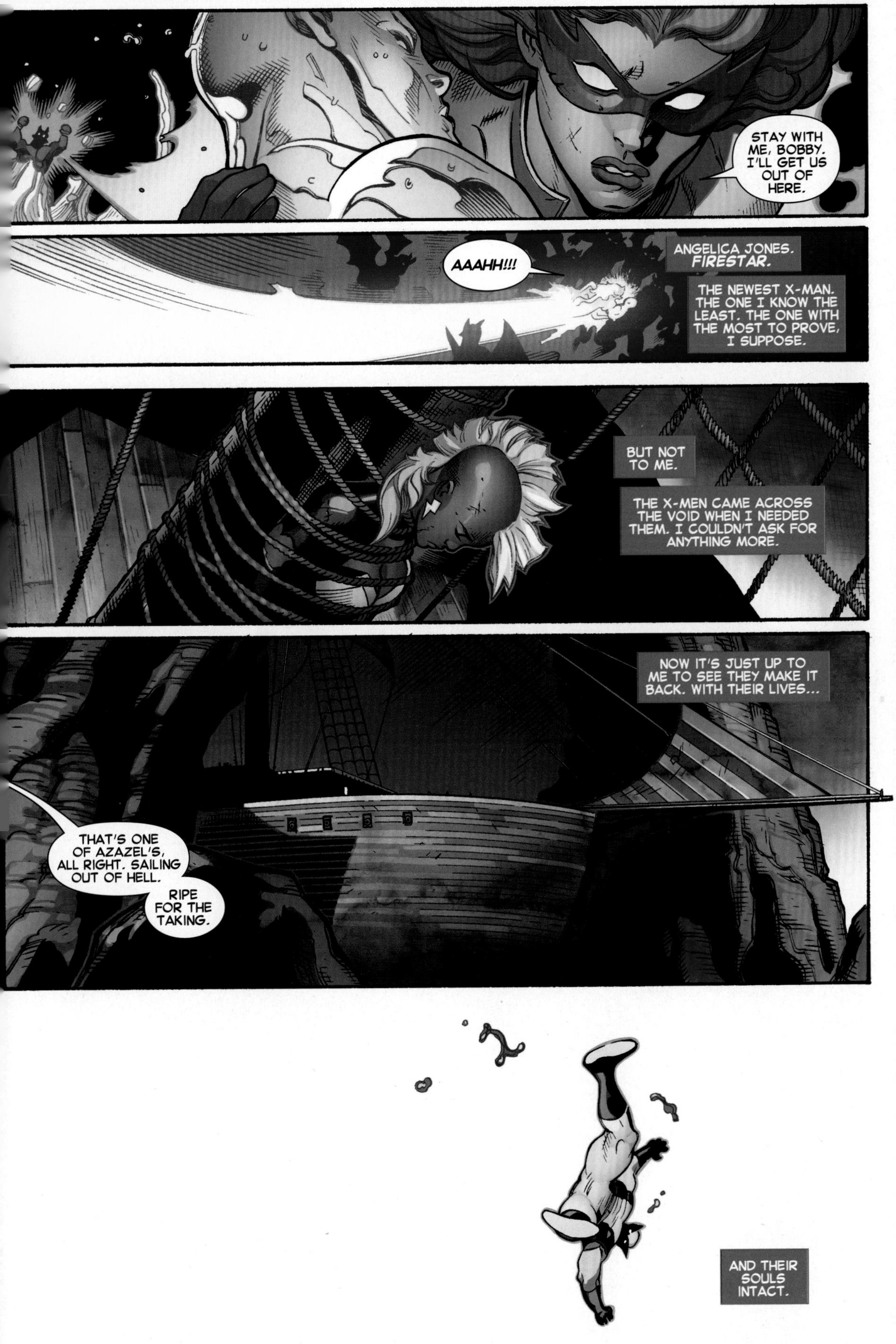
STAY WITH ME, BOBBY. I'LL GET US OUT OF HERE.
AAAHH!!!
ANGELICA JONES. FIRESTAR.
THE NEWEST X-MAN. THE ONE I KNOW THE LEAST. THE ONE WITH THE MOST TO PROVE, I SUPPOSE.
BUT NOT TO ME.
THE X-MEN CAME ACROSS THE VOID WHEN I NEEDED THEM. I COULDN'T ASK FOR ANYTHING MORE.
NOW IT'S JUST UP TO ME TO SEE THEY MAKE IT BACK. WITH THEIR LIVES...
THAT'S ONE OF AZAZEL'S, ALL RIGHT. SAILING OUT OF HELL.
RIPE FOR THE TAKING.
AND THEIR SOULS INTACT.

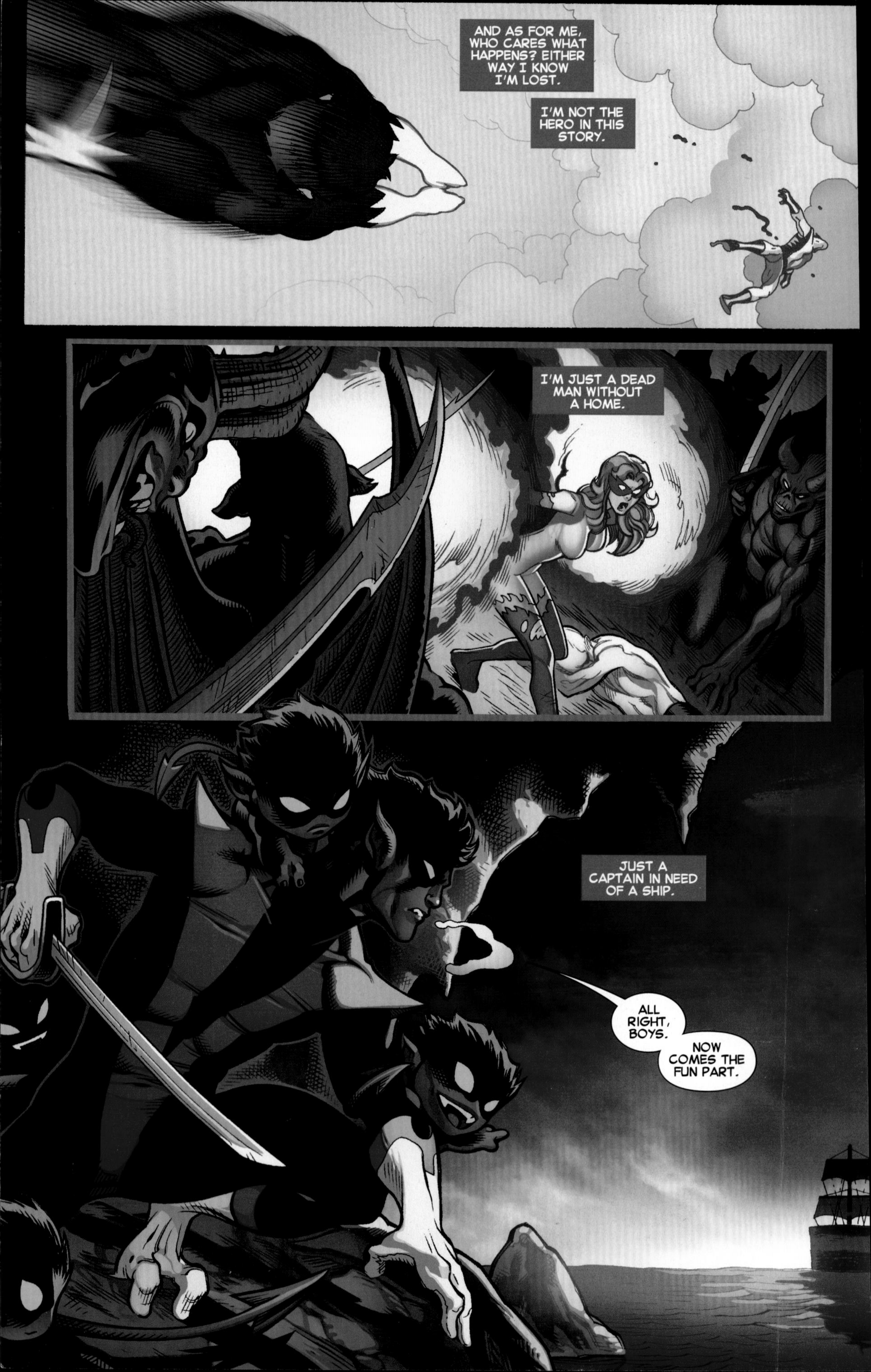
AND AS FOR ME, WHO CARES WHAT HAPPENS? EITHER WAY I KNOW I'M LOST.
I'M NOT THE HERO IN THIS STORY.
I'M JUST A DEAD MAN WITHOUT A HOME.
JUST A CAPTAIN IN NEED OF A SHIP.
ALL RIGHT, BOYS.
NOW COMES THE FUN PART.

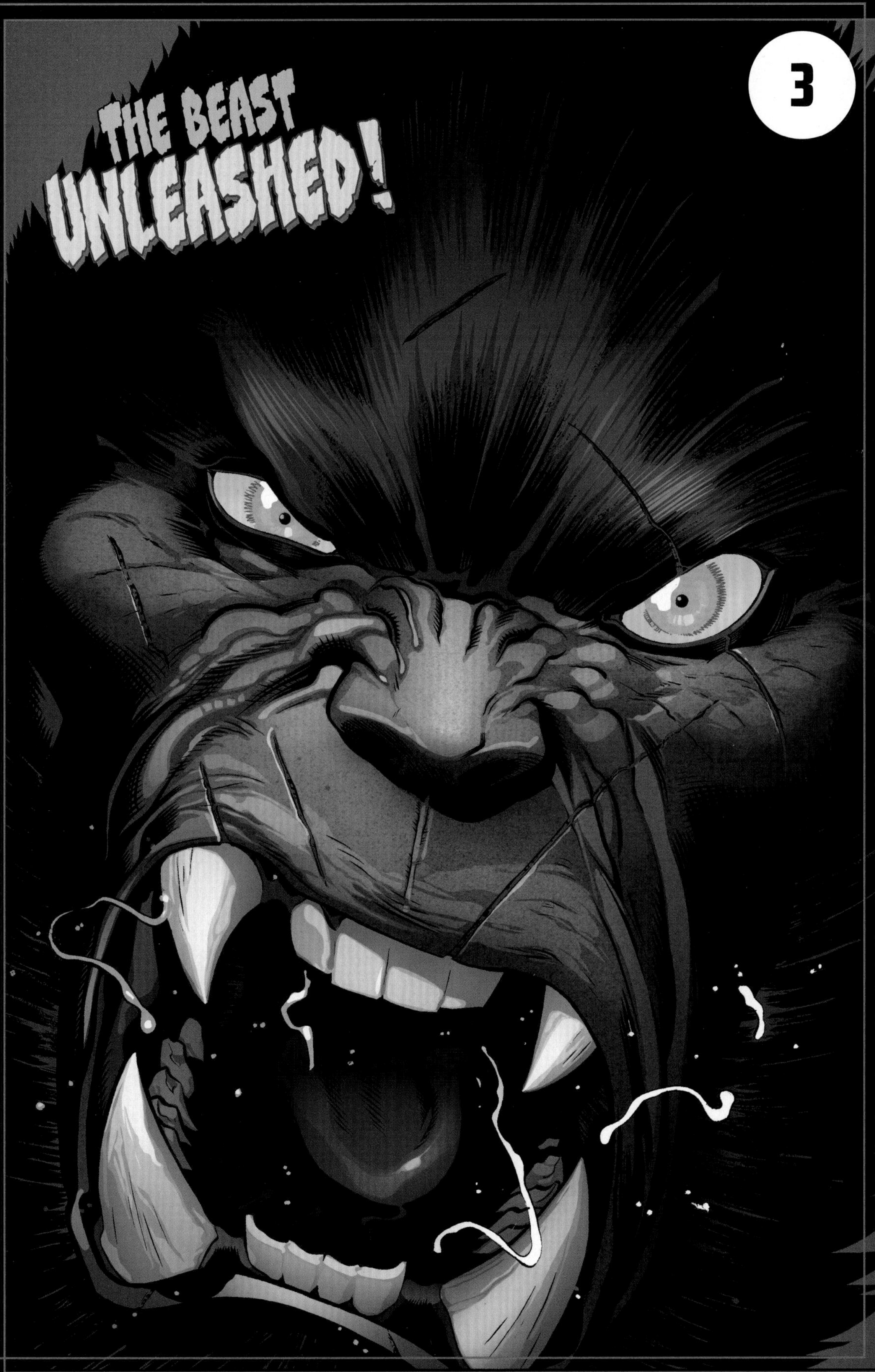
3
THE BEAST
UNLEASHED!

THE QUEST FOR NIGHTCRAWLER PART 3

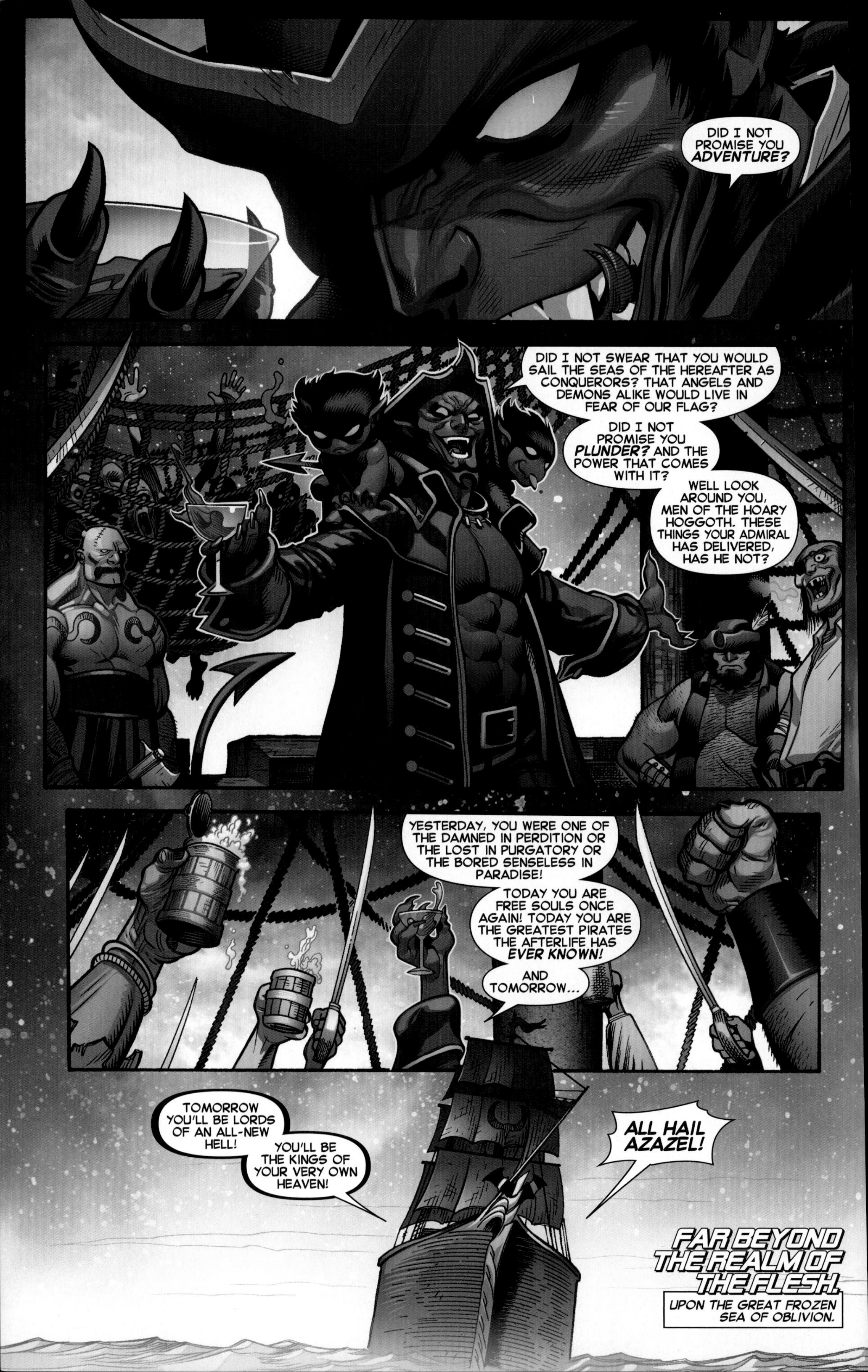
DID I NOT PROMISE YOU ADVENTURE?
DID I NOT SWEAR THAT YOU WOULD SAIL THE SEAS OF THE HEREAFTER AS CONQUERORS? THAT ANGELS AND DEMONS ALIKE WOULD LIVE IN FEAR OF OUR FLAG?
DID I NOT PROMISE YOU PLUNDER? AND THE POWER THAT COMES WITH IT?
WELL LOOK AROUND YOU, MEN OF THE HOARY HOGGOTH. THESE THINGS YOUR ADMIRAL HAS DELIVERED, HAS HE NOT?
YESTERDAY, YOU WERE ONE OF THE DAMNED IN PERDITION OR THE LOST IN PURGATORY OR THE BORED SENSELESS IN PARADISE!
TODAY YOU ARE FREE SOULS ONCE AGAIN! TODAY YOU ARE THE GREATEST PIRATES THE AFTERLIFE HAS EVER KNOWN!
AND TOMORROW...
TOMORROW YOU'LL BE LORDS OF AN ALL-NEW HELL!
YOU'LL BE THE KINGS OF YOUR VERY OWN HEAVEN!
ALL HAIL AZAZEL!
FAR BEYOND THE REALM OF THE FLESH.
UPON THE GREAT FROZEN SEA OF OBLIVION.

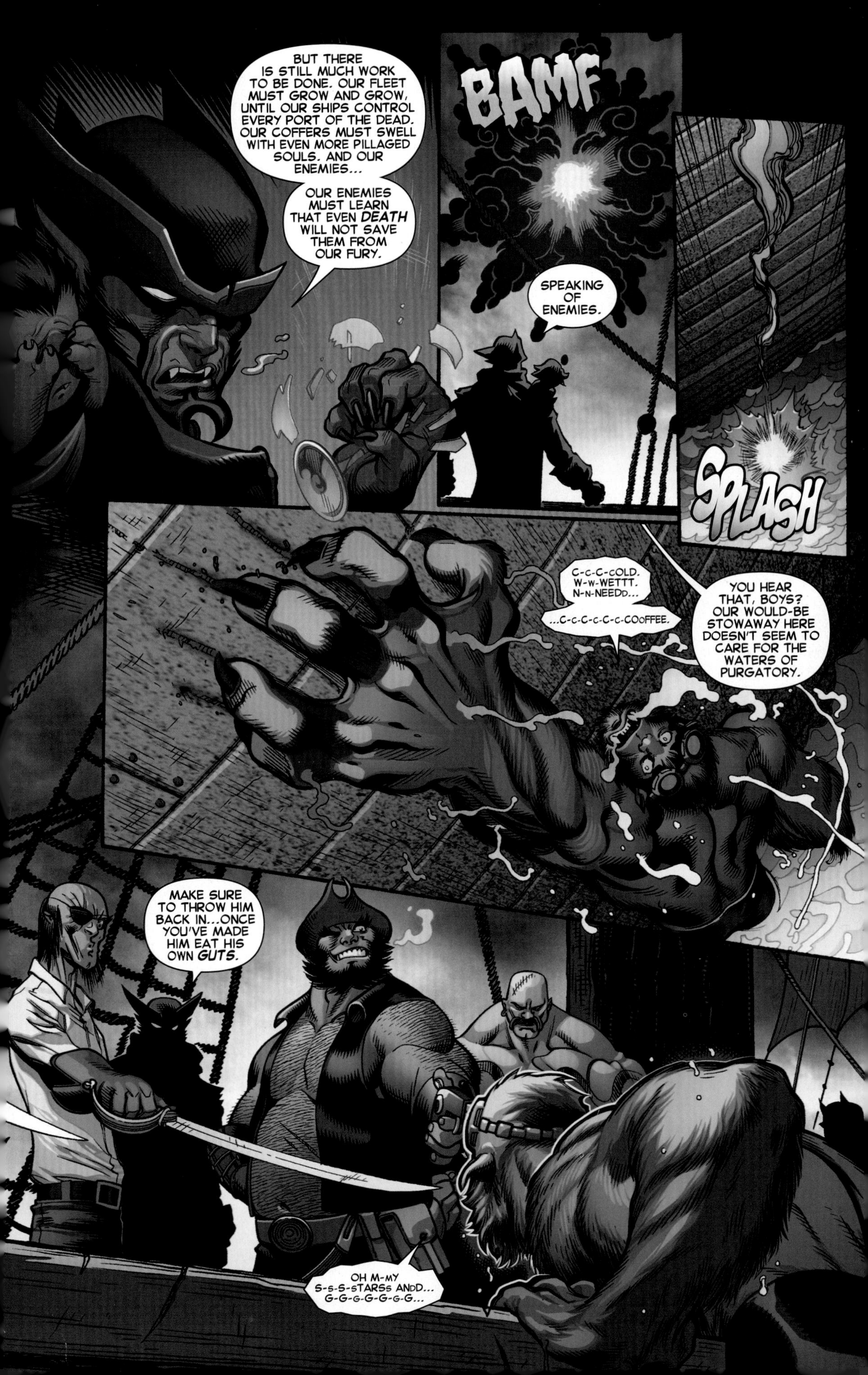
BUT THERE IS STILL MUCH WORK TO BE DONE. OUR FLEET MUST GROW AND GROW, UNTIL OUR SHIPS CONTROL EVERY PORT OF THE DEAD. OUR COFFERS MUST SWELL WITH EVEN MORE PILLAGED SOULS. AND OUR ENEMIES...
OUR ENEMIES MUST LEARN THAT EVEN DEATH WILL NOT SAVE THEM FROM OUR FURY.
BAMF
SPEAKING OF ENEMIES.
SPLASH
C-C-C-COLD. W-W-WETTT. N-N-NEEDD...
...C-C-C-C-C-C-COOFFEE.
YOU HEAR THAT, BOYS? OUR WOULD-BE STOWAWAY HERE DOESN'T SEEM TO CARE FOR THE WATERS OF PURGATORY.
MAKE SURE TO THROW HIM BACK IN...ONCE YOU'VE MADE HIM EAT HIS OWN GUTS.
OH M-MY S-S-S-STARSS ANDD... G-G-G-G-G-G-G...

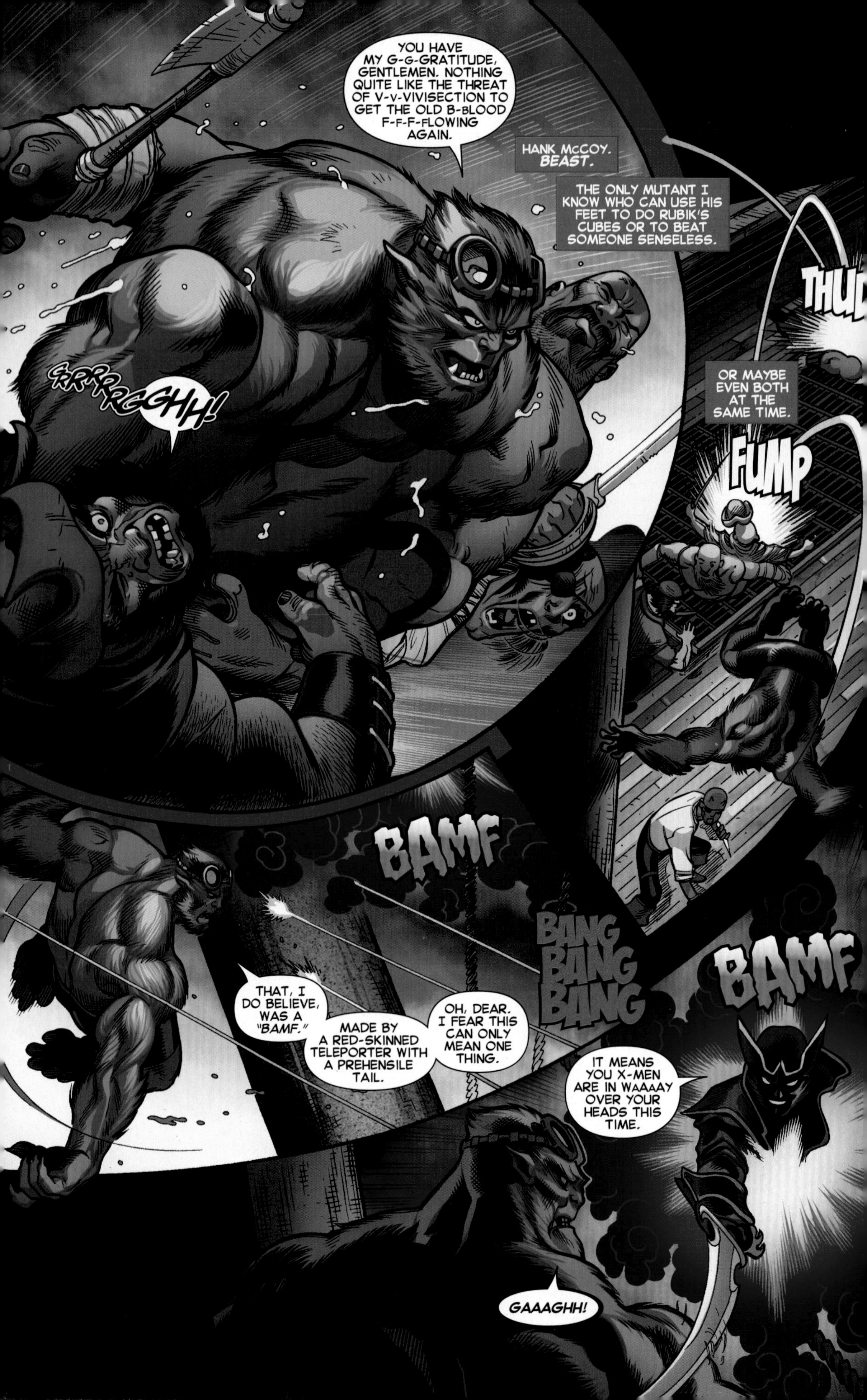
YOU HAVE MY G-G-GRATITUDE, GENTLEMEN. NOTHING QUITE LIKE THE THREAT OF V-V-VIVISECTION TO GET THE OLD B-BLOOD F-F-F-FLOWING AGAIN.
HANK McCOY. BEAST.
THE ONLY MUTANT I KNOW WHO CAN USE HIS FEET TO DO RUBIK'S CUBES OR TO BEAT SOMEONE SENSELESS.
THUD
GRRRRRGGHH!
OR MAYBE EVEN BOTH AT THE SAME TIME.
FUMP
BAMF
BANG BANG BANG
BAMF
THAT, I DO BELIEVE, WAS A "BAMF."
MADE BY A RED-SKINNED TELEPORTER WITH A PREHENSILE TAIL.
OH, DEAR. I FEAR THIS CAN ONLY MEAN ONE THING.
IT MEANS YOU X-MEN ARE IN WAAAAY OVER YOUR HEADS THIS TIME.
GAAAGHH!

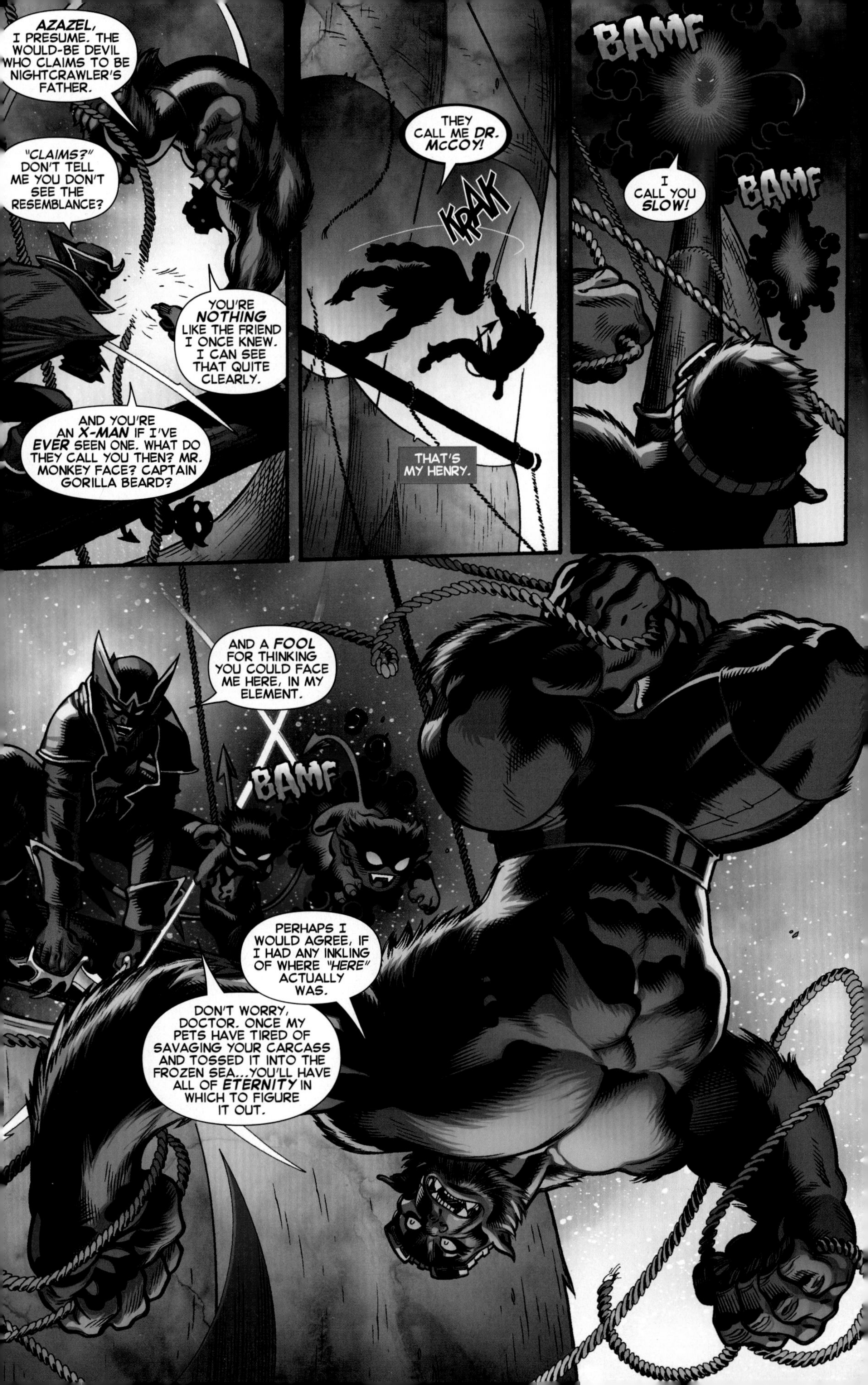
AZAZEL, I PRESUME. THE WOULD-BE DEVIL WHO CLAIMS TO BE NIGHTCRAWLER'S FATHER.
"CLAIMS?" DON'T TELL ME YOU DON'T SEE THE RESEMBLANCE?
YOU'RE NOTHING LIKE THE FRIEND I ONCE KNEW. I CAN SEE THAT QUITE CLEARLY.
AND YOU'RE AN X-MAN IF I'VE EVER SEEN ONE. WHAT DO THEY CALL YOU THEN? MR. MONKEY FACE? CAPTAIN GORILLA BEARD?
THEY CALL ME DR. McCOY!
KRAK
THAT'S MY HENRY.
BAMF
I CALL YOU SLOW!
BAMF
AND A FOOL FOR THINKING YOU COULD FACE ME HERE, IN MY ELEMENT.
BAMF
PERHAPS I WOULD AGREE, IF I HAD ANY INKLING OF WHERE "HERE" ACTUALLY WAS.
DON'T WORRY, DOCTOR. ONCE MY PETS HAVE TIRED OF SAVAGING YOUR CARCASS AND TOSSED IT INTO THE FROZEN SEA...YOU'LL HAVE ALL OF ETERNITY IN WHICH TO FIGURE IT OUT.

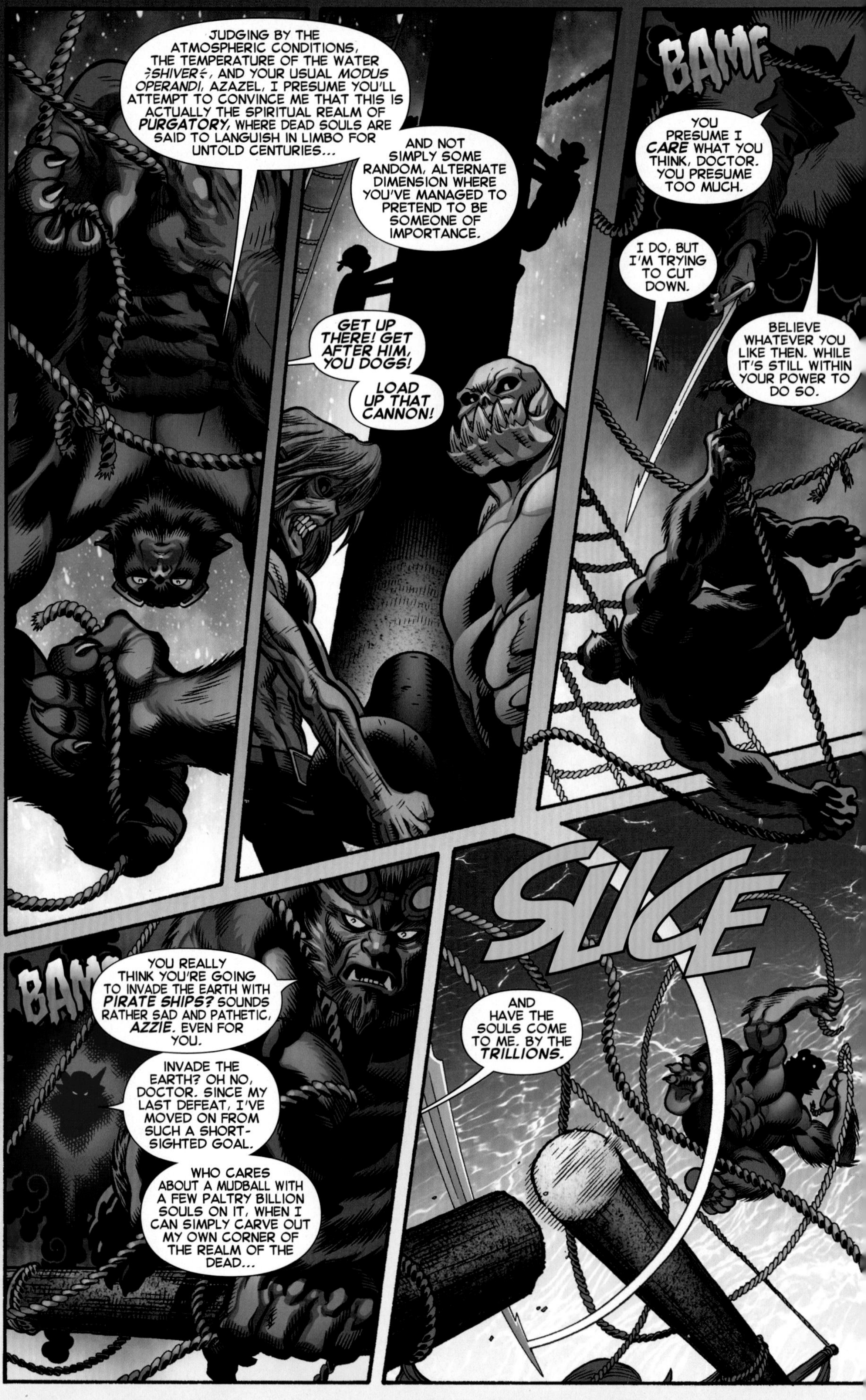
JUDGING BY THE ATMOSPHERIC CONDITIONS, THE TEMPERATURE OF THE WATER *SHIVER*, AND YOUR USUAL MODUS OPERANDI, AZAZEL, I PRESUME YOU'LL ATTEMPT TO CONVINCE ME THAT THIS IS ACTUALLY THE SPIRITUAL REALM OF PURGATORY, WHERE DEAD SOULS ARE SAID TO LANGUISH IN LIMBO FOR UNTOLD CENTURIES...
AND NOT SIMPLY SOME RANDOM, ALTERNATE DIMENSION WHERE YOU'VE MANAGED TO PRETEND TO BE SOMEONE OF IMPORTANCE.
GET UP THERE! GET AFTER HIM, YOU DOGS!
LOAD UP THAT CANNON!
BAMF
YOU PRESUME I CARE WHAT YOU THINK, DOCTOR. YOU PRESUME TOO MUCH.
I DO, BUT I'M TRYING TO CUT DOWN.
BELIEVE WHATEVER YOU LIKE THEN. WHILE IT'S STILL WITHIN YOUR POWER TO DO SO.
YOU REALLY THINK YOU'RE GOING TO INVADE THE EARTH WITH PIRATE SHIPS? SOUNDS RATHER SAD AND PATHETIC, AZZIE. EVEN FOR YOU.
INVADE THE EARTH? OH NO, DOCTOR. SINCE MY LAST DEFEAT, I'VE MOVED ON FROM SUCH A SHORT-SIGHTED GOAL.
WHO CARES ABOUT A MUDBALL WITH A FEW PALTRY BILLION SOULS ON IT, WHEN I CAN SIMPLY CARVE OUT MY OWN CORNER OF THE REALM OF THE DEAD...
SLICE
AND HAVE THE SOULS COME TO ME. BY THE TRILLIONS.

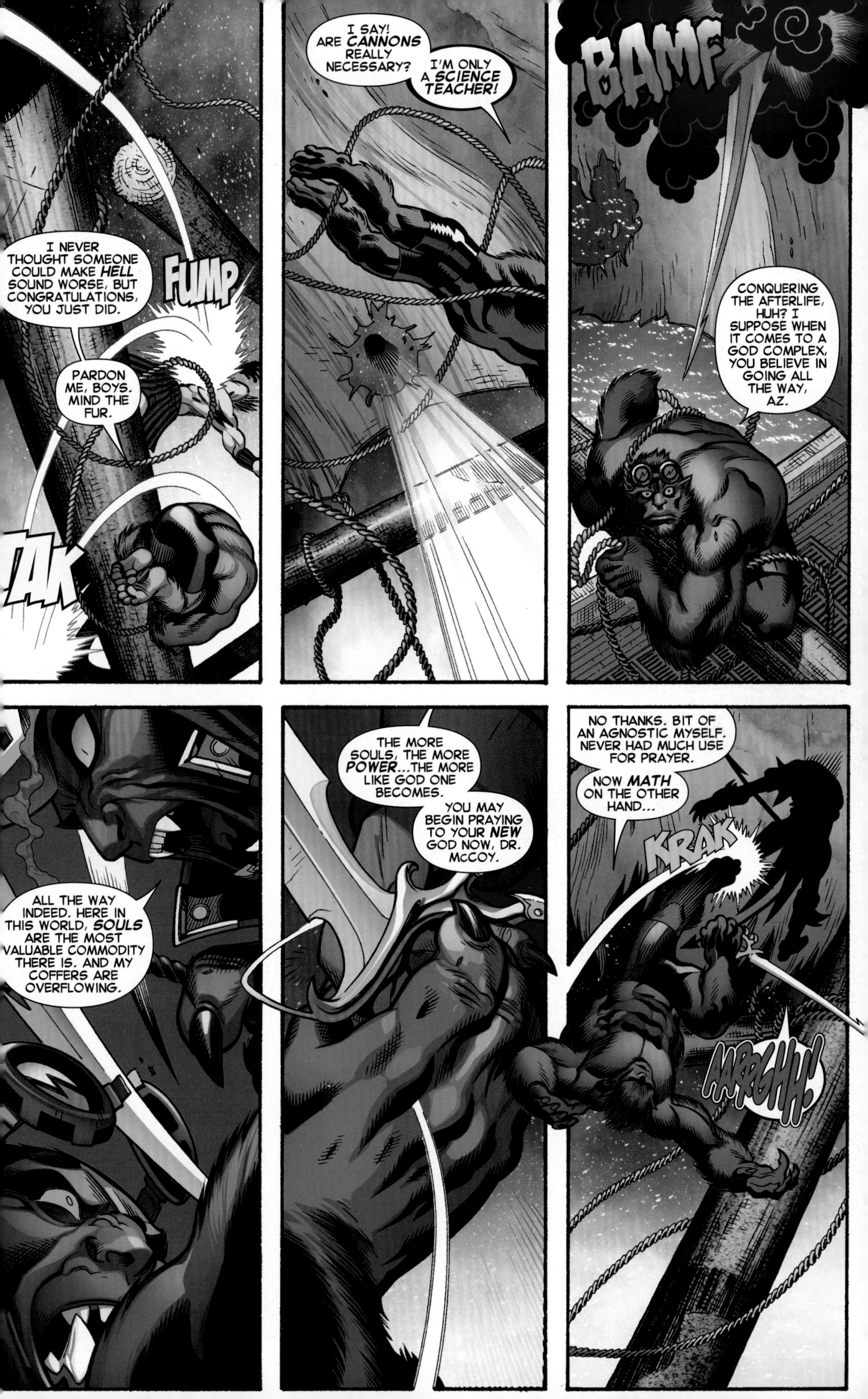
I NEVER THOUGHT SOMEONE COULD MAKE *HELL* SOUND WORSE, BUT CONGRATULATIONS, YOU JUST DID.
FUMP
PARDON ME, BOYS. MIND THE FUR.
TAK
I SAY! ARE *CANNONS* REALLY NECESSARY?
I'M ONLY A *SCIENCE TEACHER!*
BAMF
CONQUERING THE AFTERLIFE, HUH? I SUPPOSE WHEN IT COMES TO A GOD COMPLEX, YOU BELIEVE IN GOING ALL THE WAY, AZ.
ALL THE WAY INDEED. HERE IN THIS WORLD, *SOULS* ARE THE MOST VALUABLE COMMODITY THERE IS. AND MY COFFERS ARE OVERFLOWING.
THE MORE SOULS, THE MORE *POWER*...THE MORE LIKE GOD ONE BECOMES.
YOU MAY BEGIN PRAYING TO YOUR *NEW* GOD NOW, DR. McCOY.
NO THANKS. BIT OF AN AGNOSTIC MYSELF. NEVER HAD MUCH USE FOR PRAYER.
NOW *MATH* ON THE OTHER HAND...
KRAK
AARRGHH!

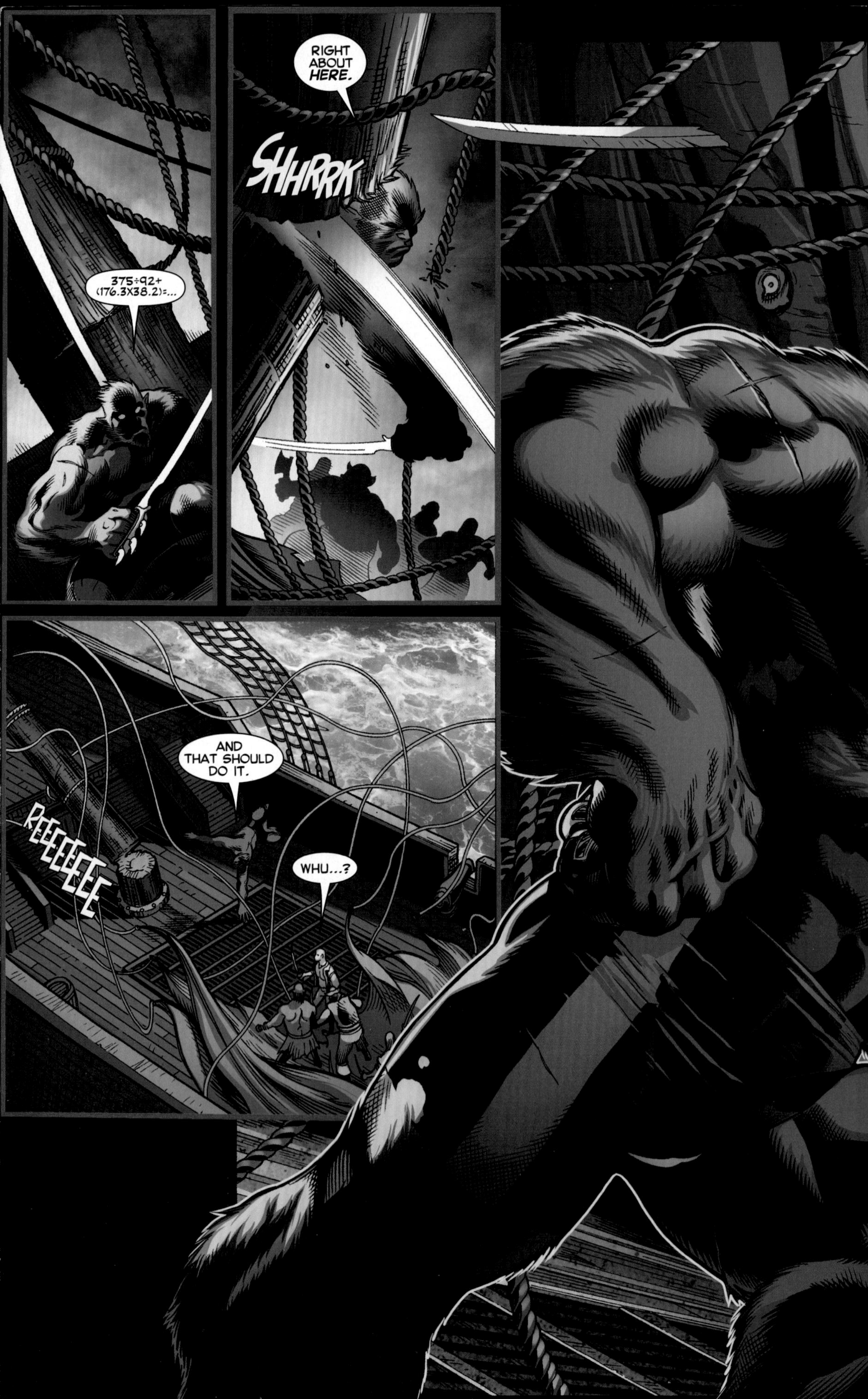
375÷92+
(176.3X38.2)=...
RIGHT ABOUT HERE.
SHHRRK
AND THAT SHOULD DO IT.
REEEEEEEE
WHU...?

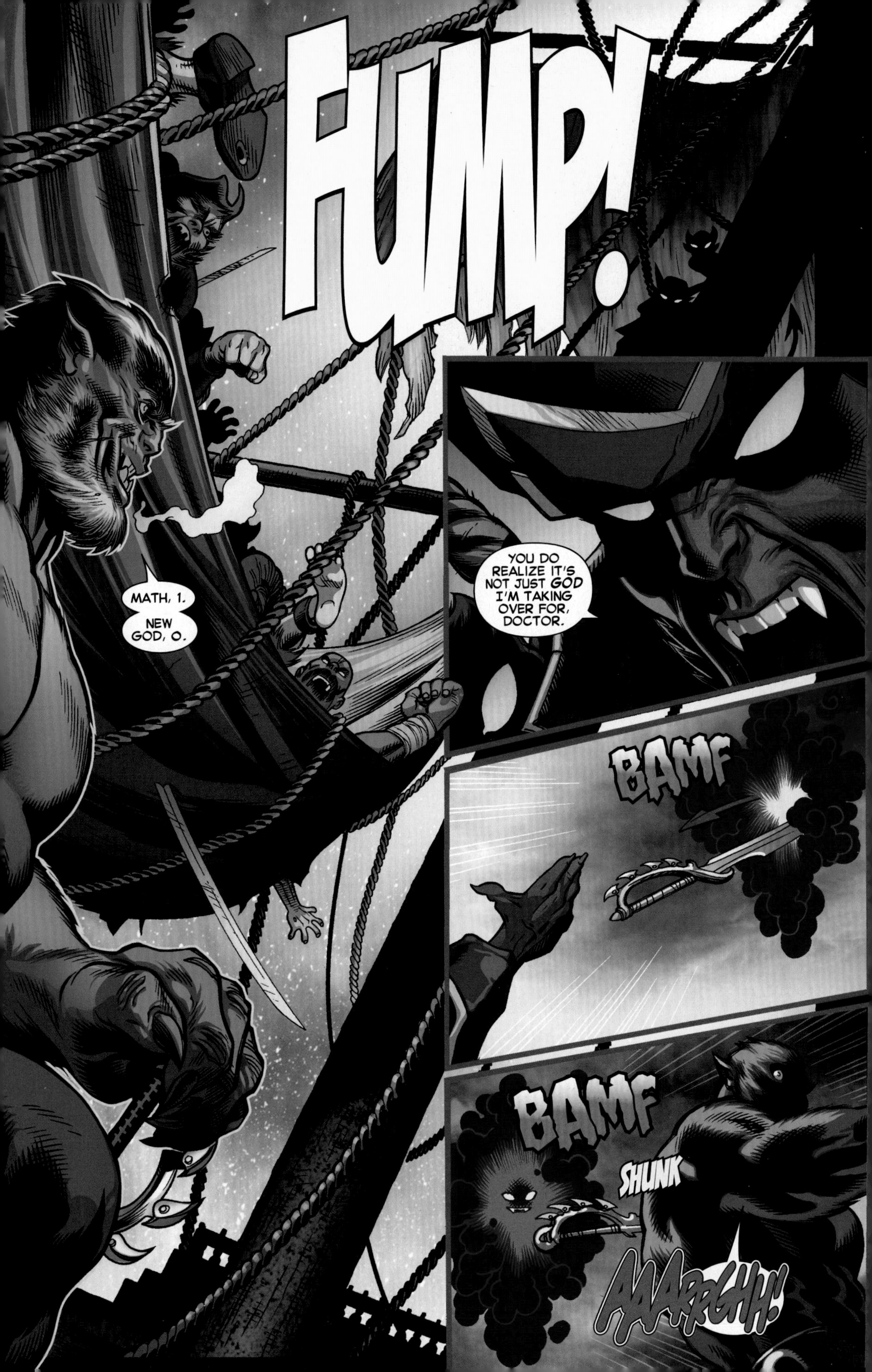
FUMP!
MATH, 1.
NEW GOD, 0.
YOU DO REALIZE IT'S NOT JUST GOD I'M TAKING OVER FOR, DOCTOR.
BAMF
BAMF
SHUNK
AAARRGHH!

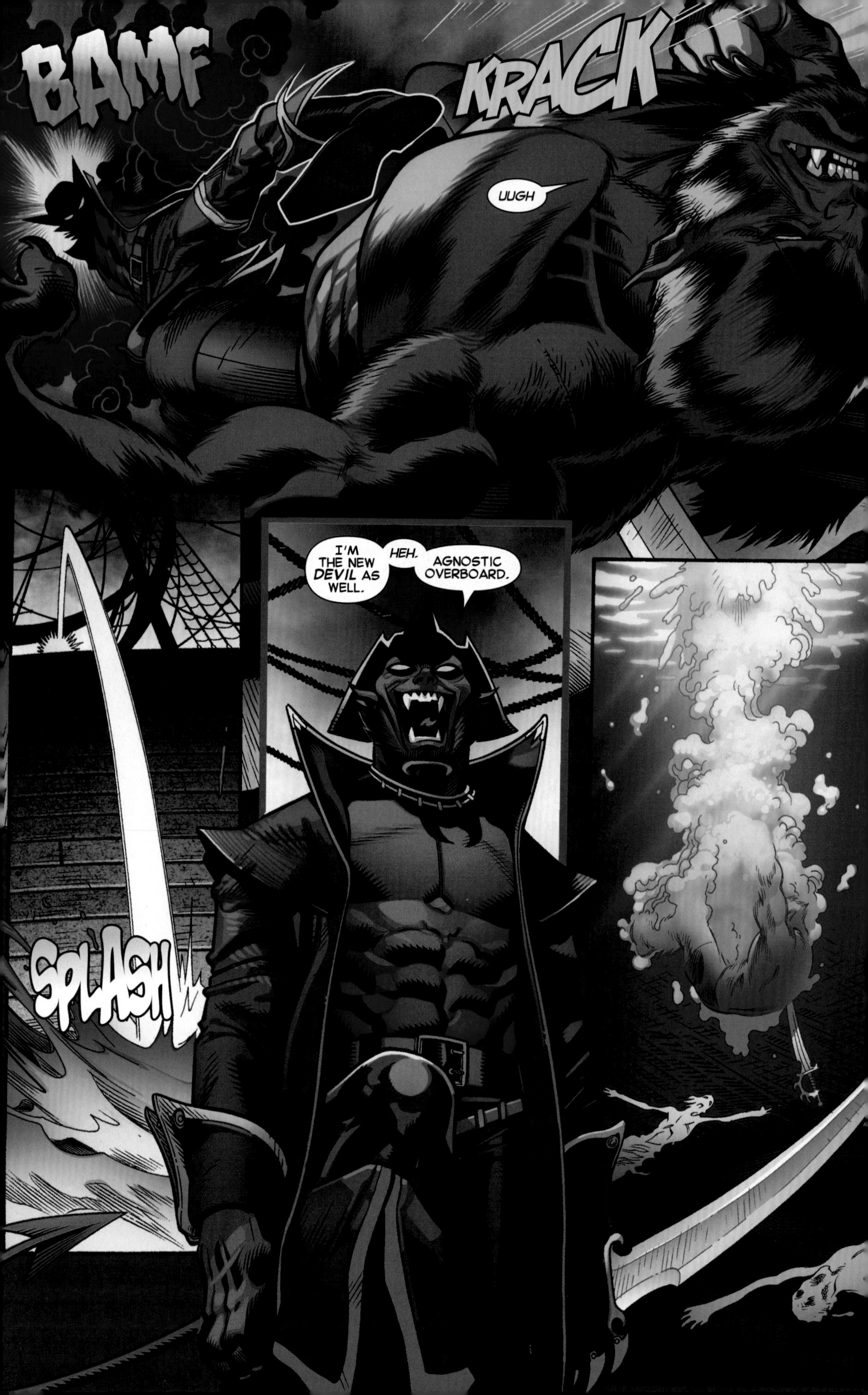
BAMF
KRACK
UUGH
SPLASH
I'M THE NEW DEVIL AS WELL.
HEH.
AGNOSTIC OVERBOARD.

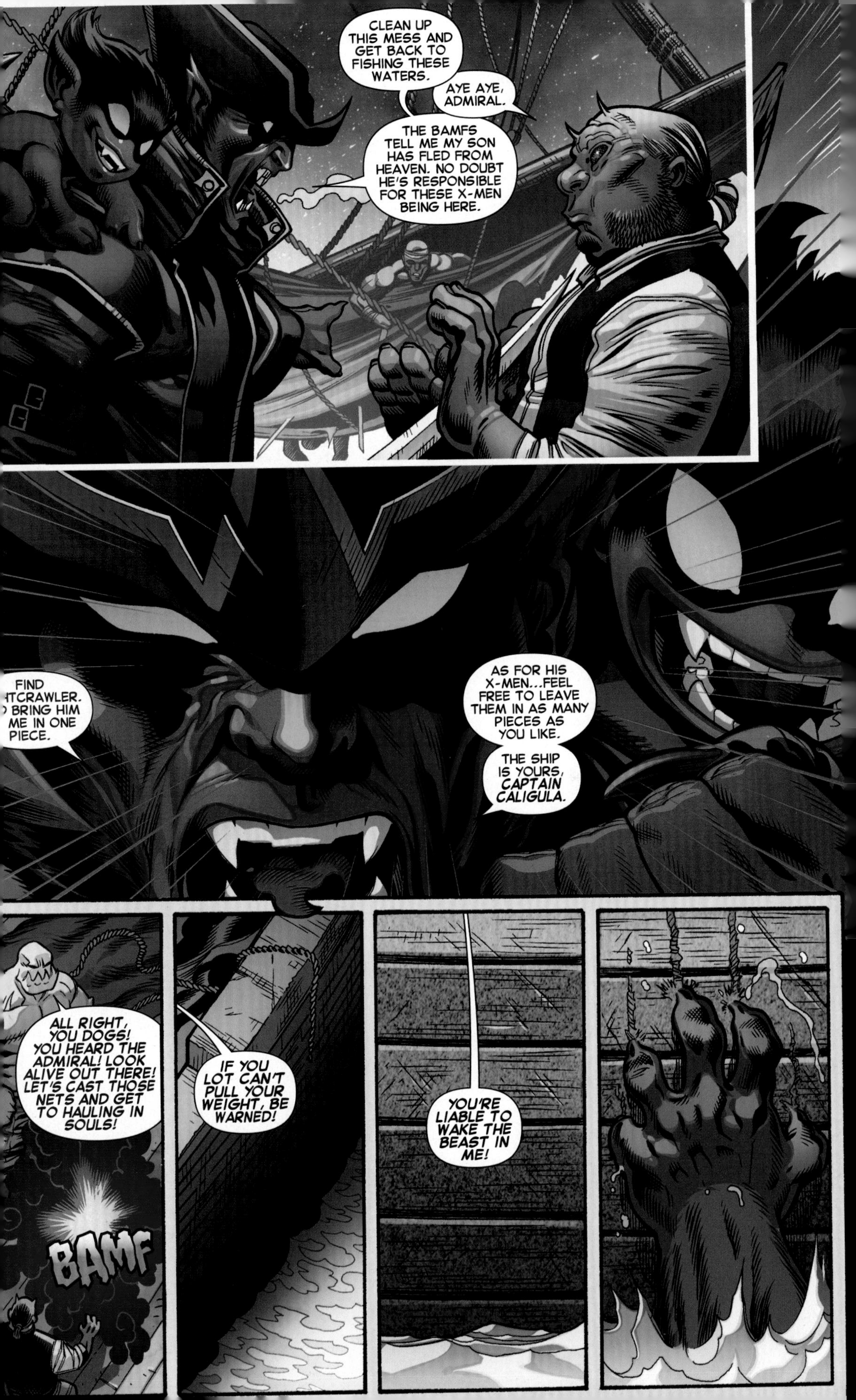
CLEAN UP THIS MESS AND GET BACK TO FISHING THESE WATERS.
AYE AYE, ADMIRAL.
THE BAMFS TELL ME MY SON HAS FLED FROM HEAVEN. NO DOUBT HE'S RESPONSIBLE FOR THESE X-MEN BEING HERE.
FIND
TCRAWLER.
BRING HIM
ME IN ONE
PIECE.
AS FOR HIS X-MEN...FEEL FREE TO LEAVE THEM IN AS MANY PIECES AS YOU LIKE.
THE SHIP IS YOURS, CAPTAIN CALIGULA.
ALL RIGHT, YOU DOGS! YOU HEARD THE ADMIRAL! LOOK ALIVE OUT THERE! LET'S CAST THOSE NETS AND GET TO HAULING IN SOULS!
BAMF
IF YOU LOT CAN'T PULL YOUR WEIGHT, BE WARNED!
YOU'RE LIABLE TO WAKE THE BEAST IN ME!

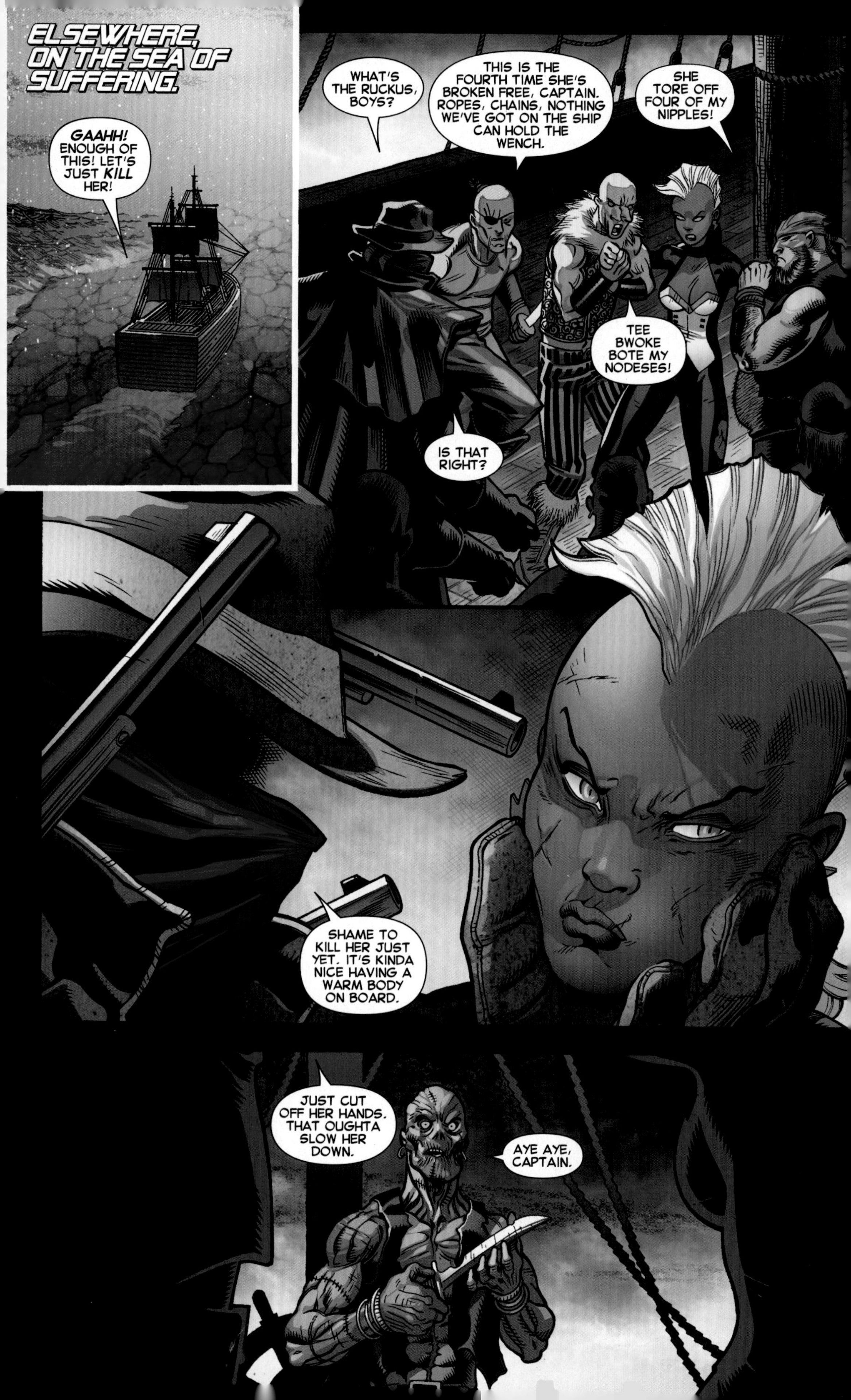
ELSEWHERE, ON THE SEA OF SUFFERING.
GAAHH! ENOUGH OF THIS! LET'S JUST KILL HER!
WHAT'S THE RUCKUS, BOYS?
THIS IS THE FOURTH TIME SHE'S BROKEN FREE, CAPTAIN. ROPES, CHAINS, NOTHING WE'VE GOT ON THE SHIP CAN HOLD THE WENCH.
SHE TORE OFF FOUR OF MY NIPPLES!
TEE BWOKE BOTE MY NODESES!
IS THAT RIGHT?
SHAME TO KILL HER JUST YET. IT'S KINDA NICE HAVING A WARM BODY ON BOARD.
JUST CUT OFF HER HANDS. THAT OUGHTA SLOW HER DOWN.
AYE AYE, CAPTAIN.

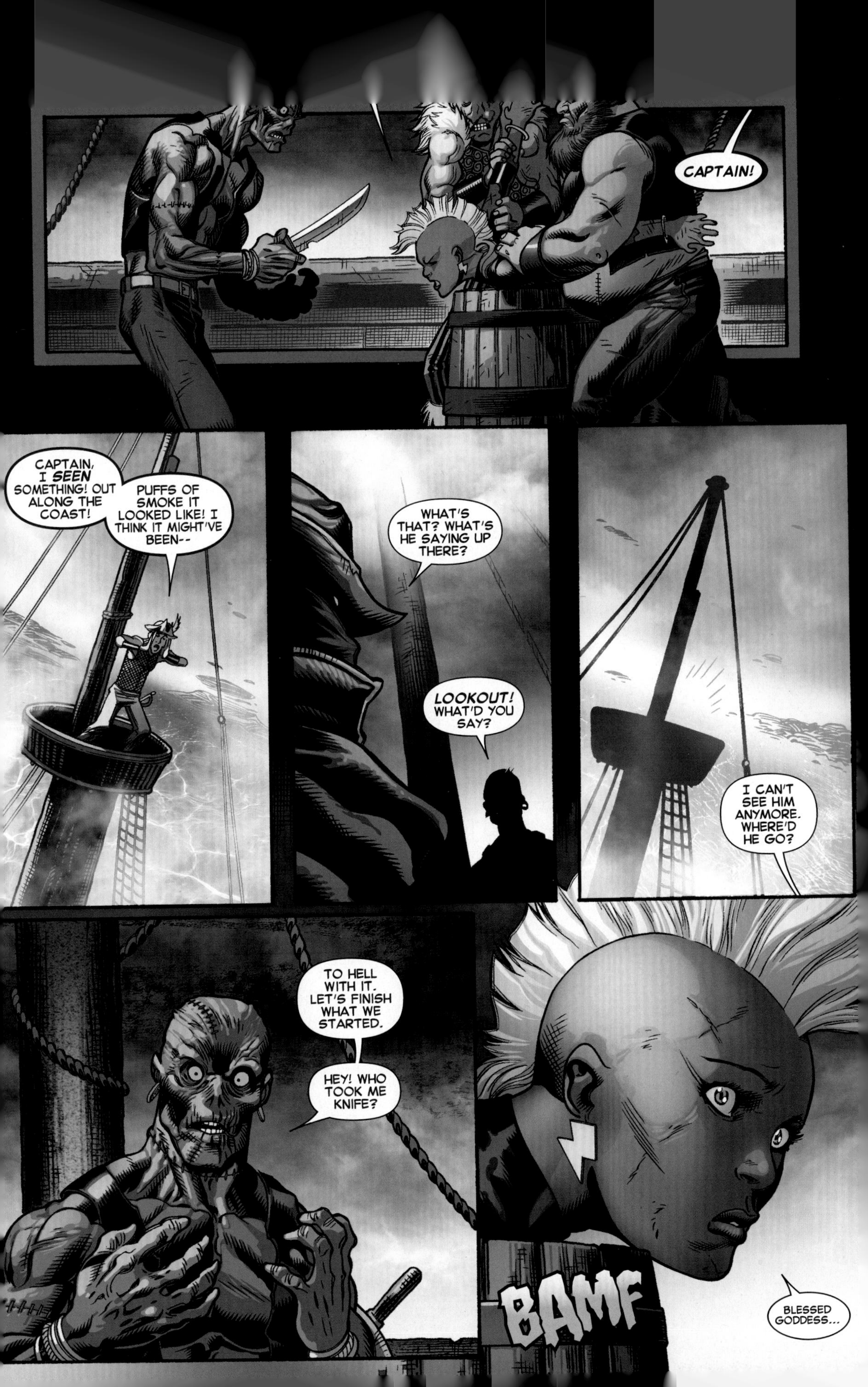
CAPTAIN!
CAPTAIN, I **SEEN** SOMETHING! OUT ALONG THE COAST!
PUFFS OF SMOKE IT LOOKED LIKE! I THINK IT MIGHT'VE BEEN--
WHAT'S THAT? WHAT'S HE SAYING UP THERE?
LOOKOUT! WHAT'D YOU SAY?
I CAN'T SEE HIM ANYMORE. WHERE'D HE GO?
TO HELL WITH IT. LET'S FINISH WHAT WE STARTED.
HEY! WHO TOOK ME KNIFE?
BAMF
BLESSED GODDESS...

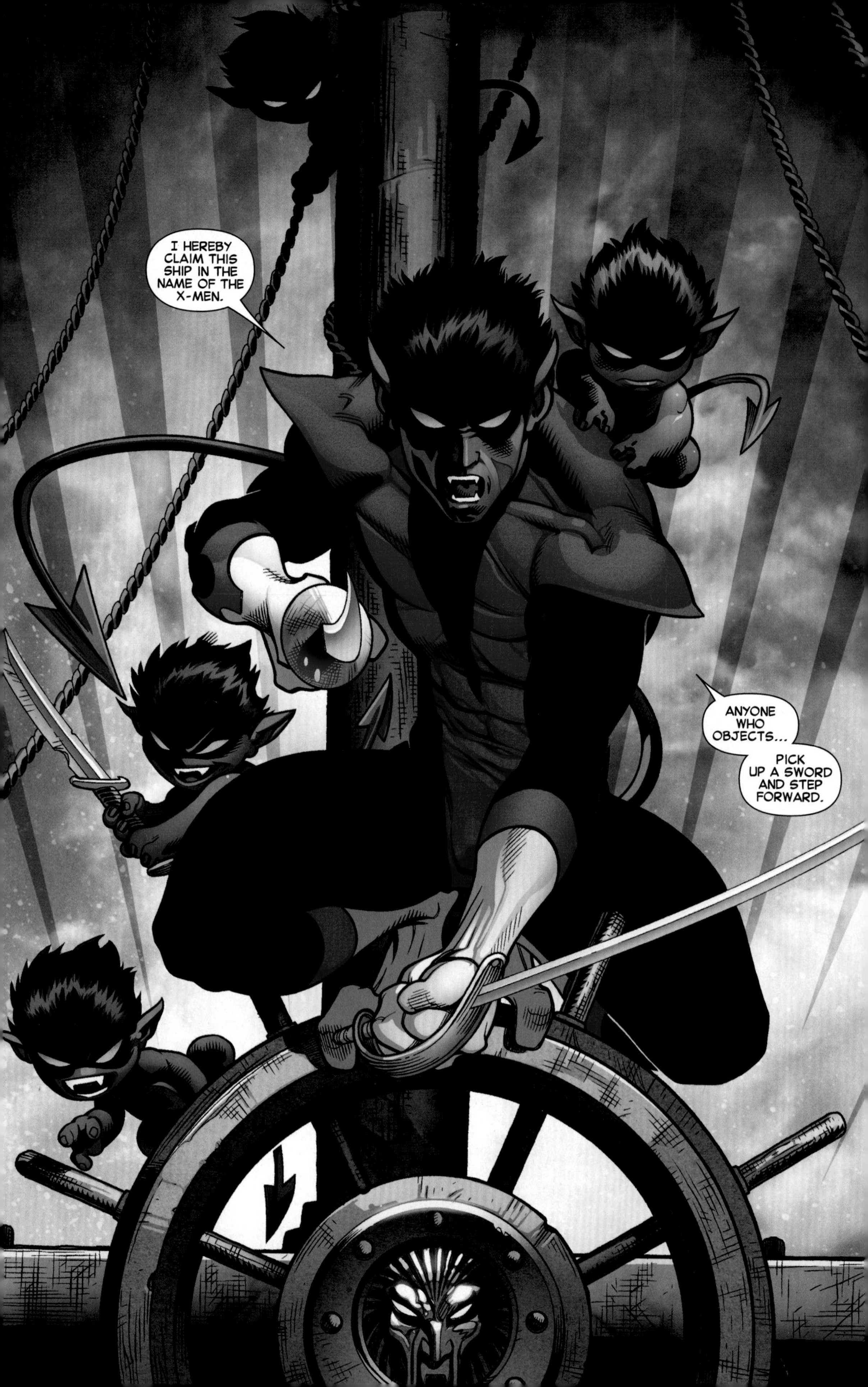
I HEREBY CLAIM THIS SHIP IN THE NAME OF THE X-MEN.
ANYONE WHO OBJECTS...
PICK UP A SWORD AND STEP FORWARD.

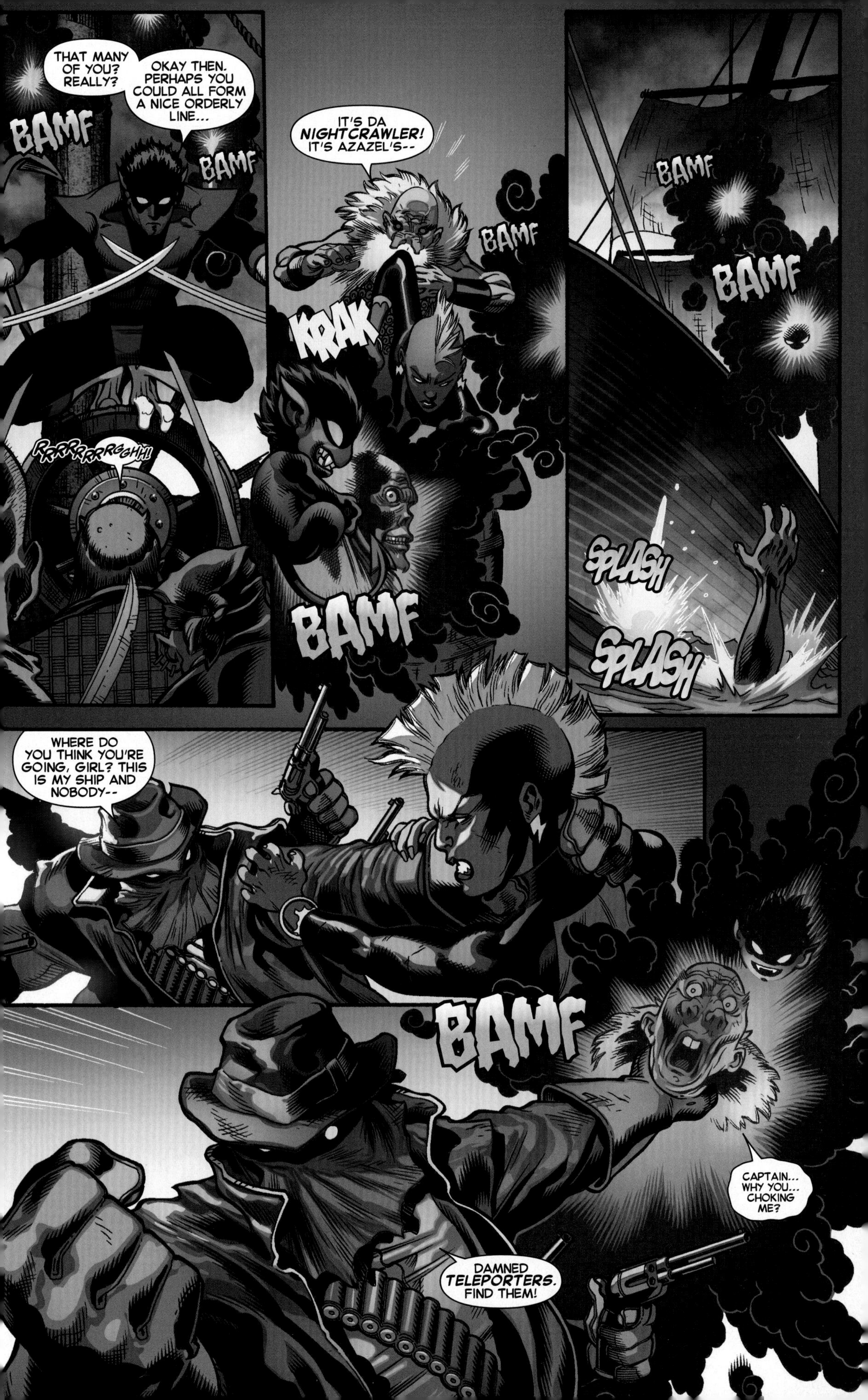
THAT MANY OF YOU? REALLY?
OKAY THEN. PERHAPS YOU COULD ALL FORM A NICE ORDERLY LINE...
BAMF
BAMF
RRRRRRRRGHH!
IT'S DA NIGHTCRAWLER! IT'S AZAZEL'S--
BAMF
KRAK
BAMF
BAMF
BAMF
SPLASH
SPLASH
WHERE DO YOU THINK YOU'RE GOING, GIRL? THIS IS MY SHIP AND NOBODY--
BAMF
CAPTAIN... WHY YOU... CHOKING ME?
DAMNED TELEPORTERS. FIND THEM!

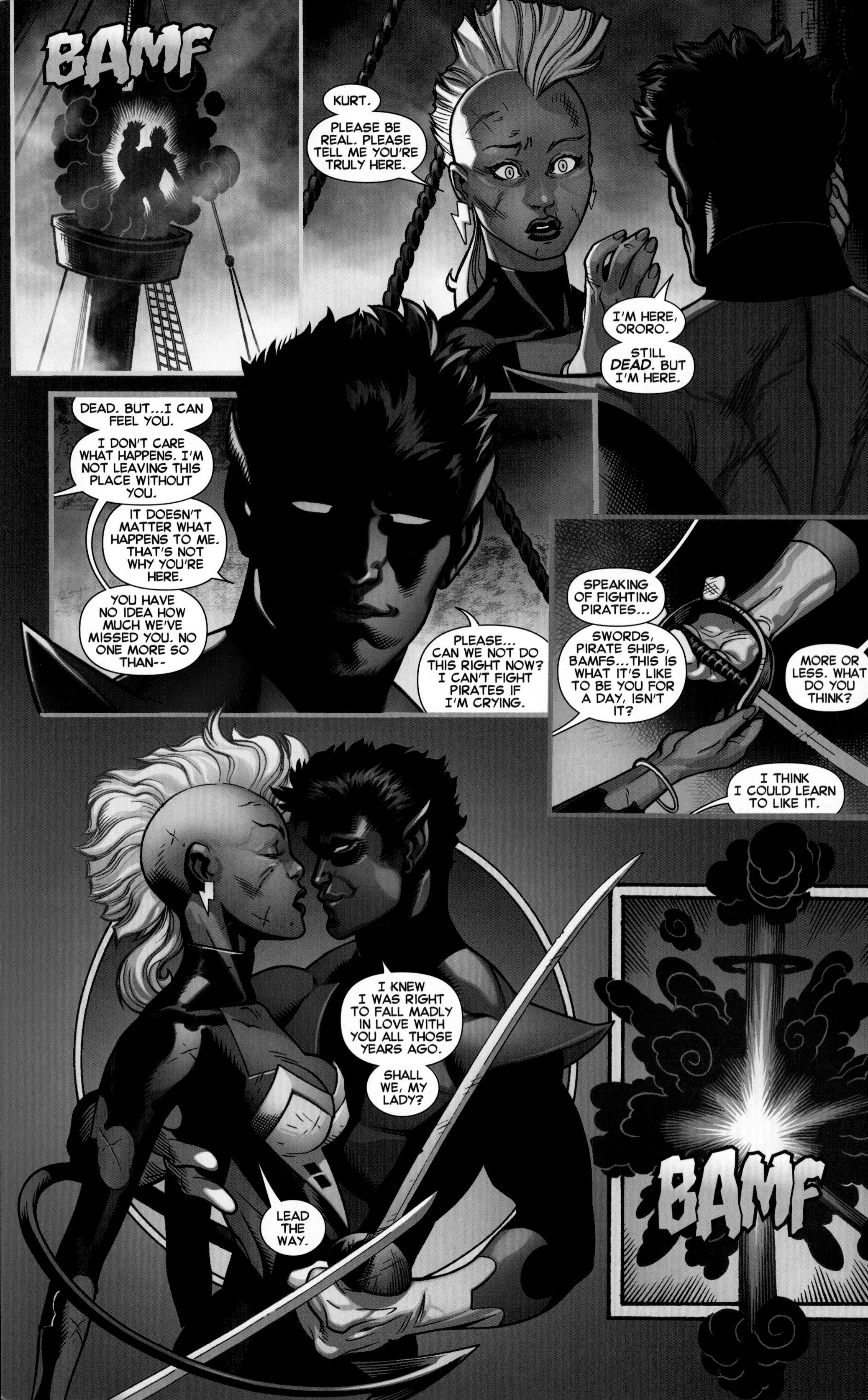
BAMF
KURT.
PLEASE BE REAL. PLEASE TELL ME YOU'RE TRULY HERE.
I'M HERE, ORORO.
STILL DEAD. BUT I'M HERE.
DEAD. BUT...I CAN FEEL YOU.
I DON'T CARE WHAT HAPPENS. I'M NOT LEAVING THIS PLACE WITHOUT YOU.
IT DOESN'T MATTER WHAT HAPPENS TO ME. THAT'S NOT WHY YOU'RE HERE.
YOU HAVE NO IDEA HOW MUCH WE'VE MISSED YOU. NO ONE MORE SO THAN--
PLEASE... CAN WE NOT DO THIS RIGHT NOW? I CAN'T FIGHT PIRATES IF I'M CRYING.
SPEAKING OF FIGHTING PIRATES...
SWORDS, PIRATE SHIPS, BAMFS...THIS IS WHAT IT'S LIKE TO BE YOU FOR A DAY, ISN'T IT?
MORE OR LESS. WHAT DO YOU THINK?
I THINK I COULD LEARN TO LIKE IT.
I KNEW I WAS RIGHT TO FALL MADLY IN LOVE WITH YOU ALL THOSE YEARS AGO.
SHALL WE, MY LADY?
LEAD THE WAY.
BAMF

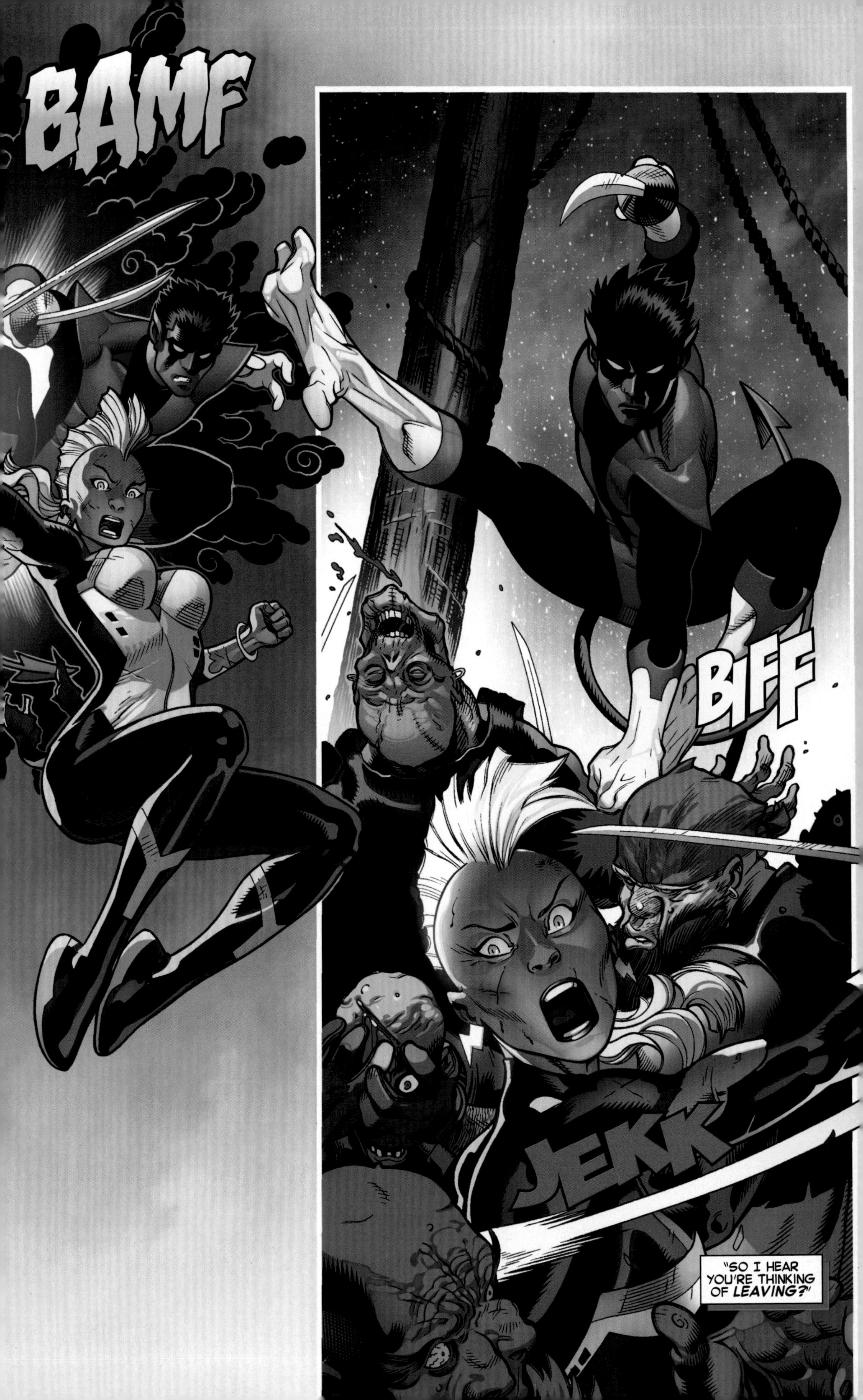
BAMF
BIFF
JEKK
"SO I HEAR YOU'RE THINKING OF *LEAVING?*"

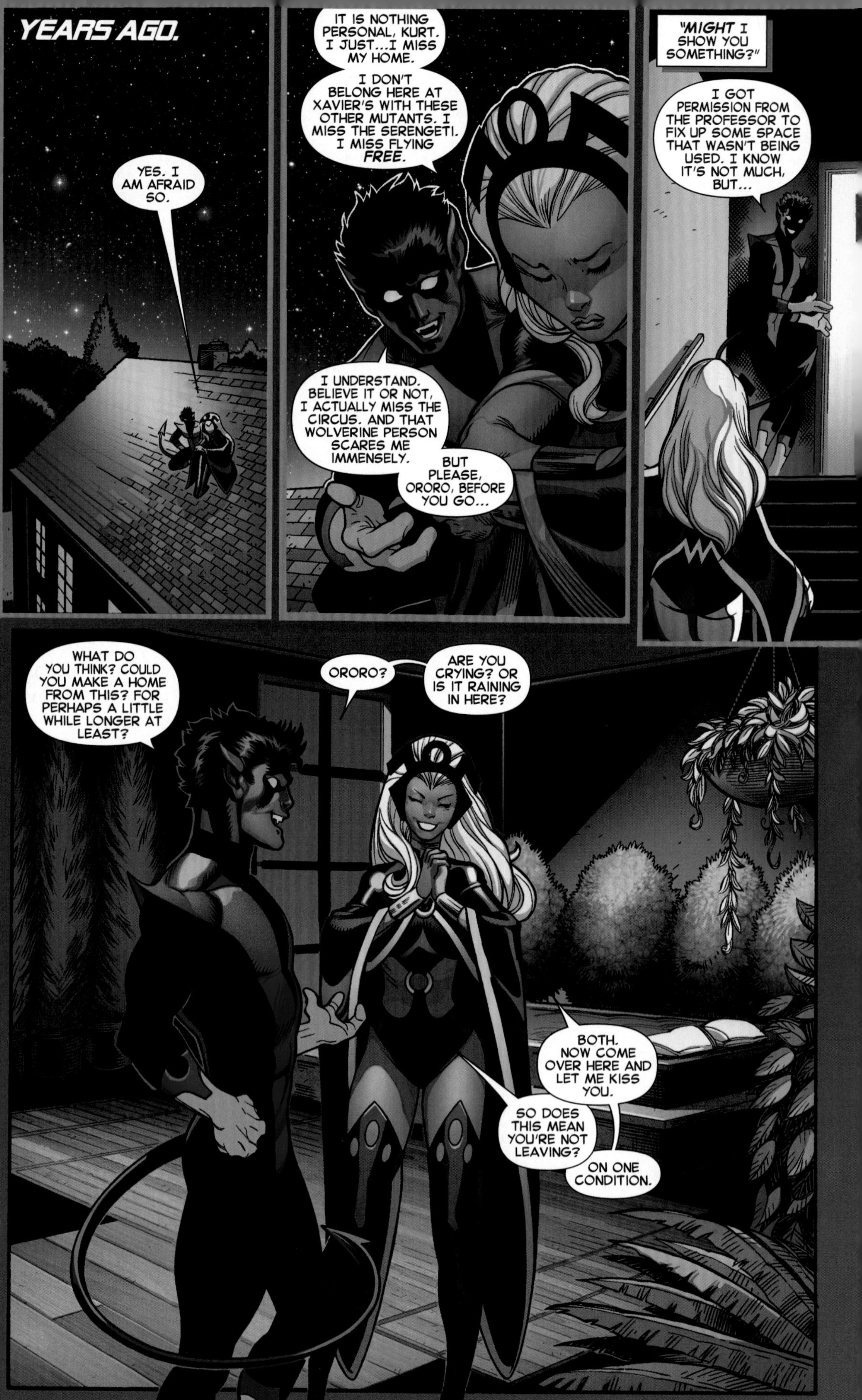
YEARS AGO.
YES. I AM AFRAID SO.
IT IS NOTHING PERSONAL, KURT. I JUST...I MISS MY HOME.
I DON'T BELONG HERE AT XAVIER'S WITH THESE OTHER MUTANTS. I MISS THE SERENGETI. I MISS FLYING FREE.
I UNDERSTAND. BELIEVE IT OR NOT, I ACTUALLY MISS THE CIRCUS. AND THAT WOLVERINE PERSON SCARES ME IMMENSELY.
BUT PLEASE, ORORO, BEFORE YOU GO...
"MIGHT I SHOW YOU SOMETHING?"
I GOT PERMISSION FROM THE PROFESSOR TO FIX UP SOME SPACE THAT WASN'T BEING USED. I KNOW IT'S NOT MUCH, BUT...
WHAT DO YOU THINK? COULD YOU MAKE A HOME FROM THIS? FOR PERHAPS A LITTLE WHILE LONGER AT LEAST?
ORORO?
ARE YOU CRYING? OR IS IT RAINING IN HERE?
BOTH. NOW COME OVER HERE AND LET ME KISS YOU.
SO DOES THIS MEAN YOU'RE NOT LEAVING?
ON ONE CONDITION.

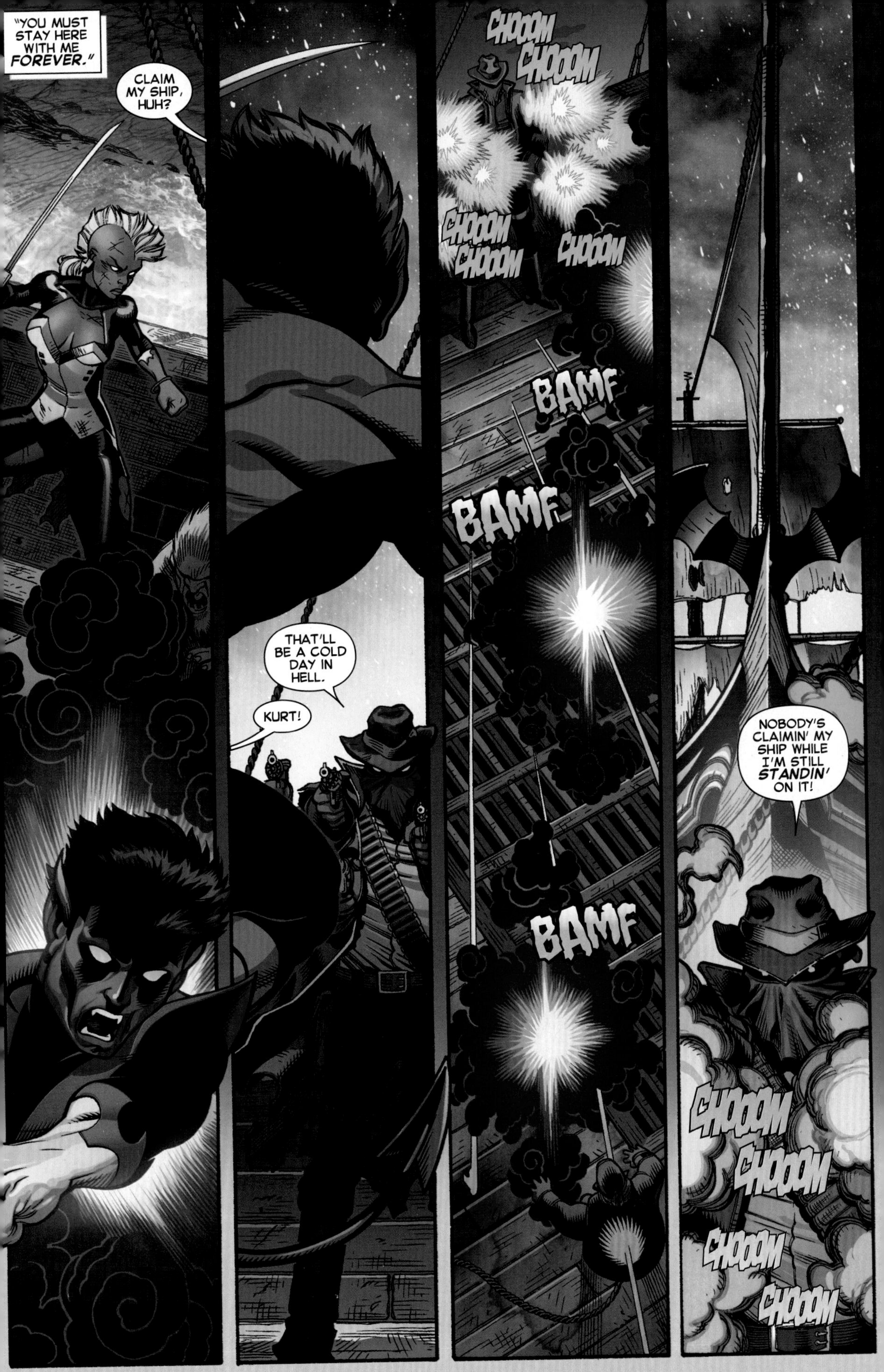
"YOU MUST STAY HERE WITH ME FOREVER."
CLAIM MY SHIP, HUH?
THAT'LL BE A COLD DAY IN HELL.
KURT!
CHOOOM CHOOOM
CHOOOM CHOOOM
CHOOOM
BAMF
BAMF
BAMF
NOBODY'S CLAIMIN' MY SHIP WHILE I'M STILL STANDIN' ON IT!
CHOOOM CHOOOM
CHOOOM
CHOOOM

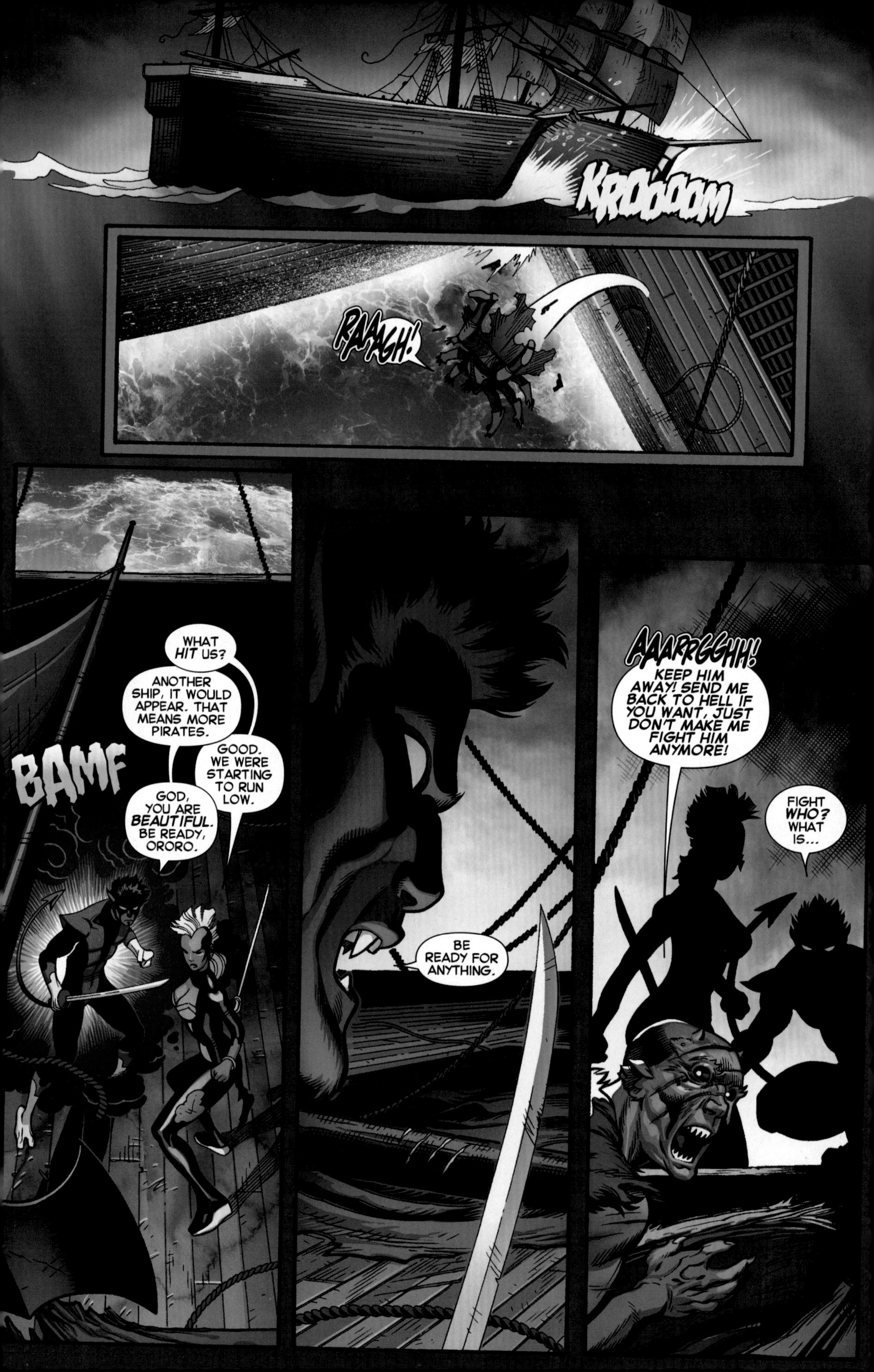
KROOOOM
RAAAGH!
WHAT HIT US?
ANOTHER SHIP, IT WOULD APPEAR. THAT MEANS MORE PIRATES.
GOOD. WE WERE STARTING TO RUN LOW.
BAMF
GOD, YOU ARE BEAUTIFUL. BE READY, ORORO.
BE READY FOR ANYTHING.
AAARRGGHH!
KEEP HIM AWAY! SEND ME BACK TO HELL IF YOU WANT, JUST DON'T MAKE ME FIGHT HIM ANYMORE!
FIGHT WHO? WHAT IS...

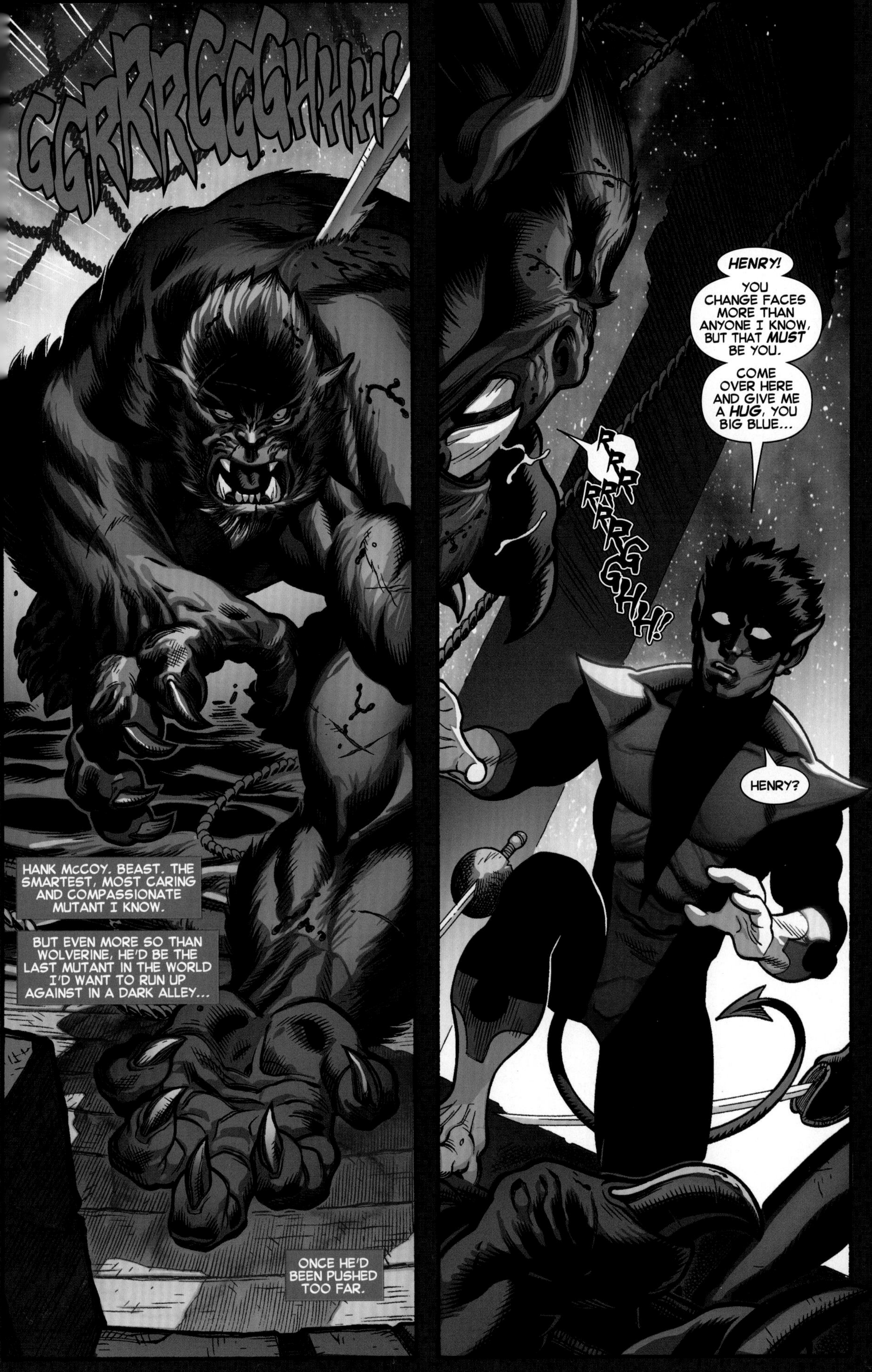
GGRRRGGGHHH!
HANK McCOY. BEAST. THE SMARTEST, MOST CARING AND COMPASSIONATE MUTANT I KNOW.
BUT EVEN MORE SO THAN WOLVERINE, HE'D BE THE LAST MUTANT IN THE WORLD I'D WANT TO RUN UP AGAINST IN A DARK ALLEY...
ONCE HE'D BEEN PUSHED TOO FAR.
HENRY! YOU CHANGE FACES MORE THAN ANYONE I KNOW, BUT THAT MUST BE YOU.
COME OVER HERE AND GIVE ME A HUG, YOU BIG BLUE...
RRRRRRRGGHHH!
HENRY?

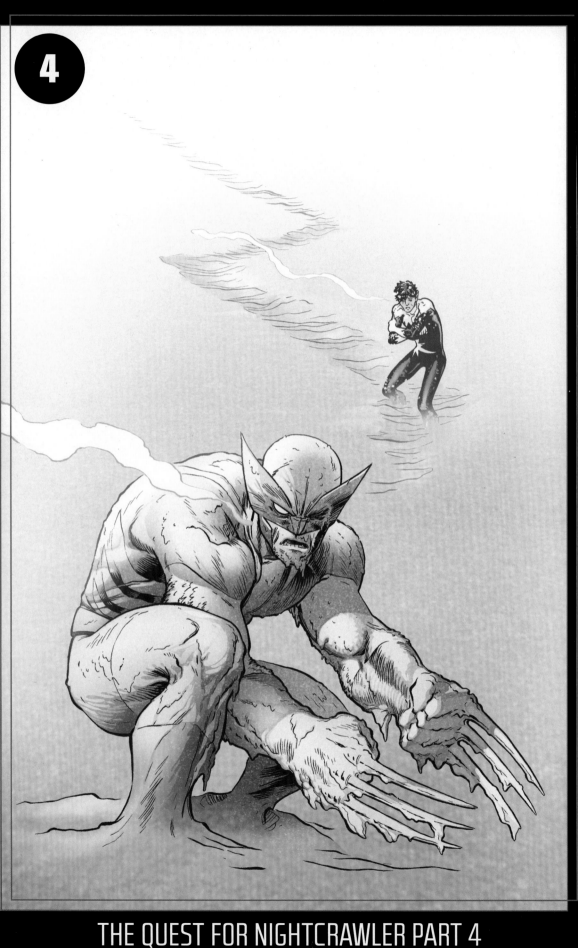

4

THE QUEST FOR NIGHTCRAWLER PART 4

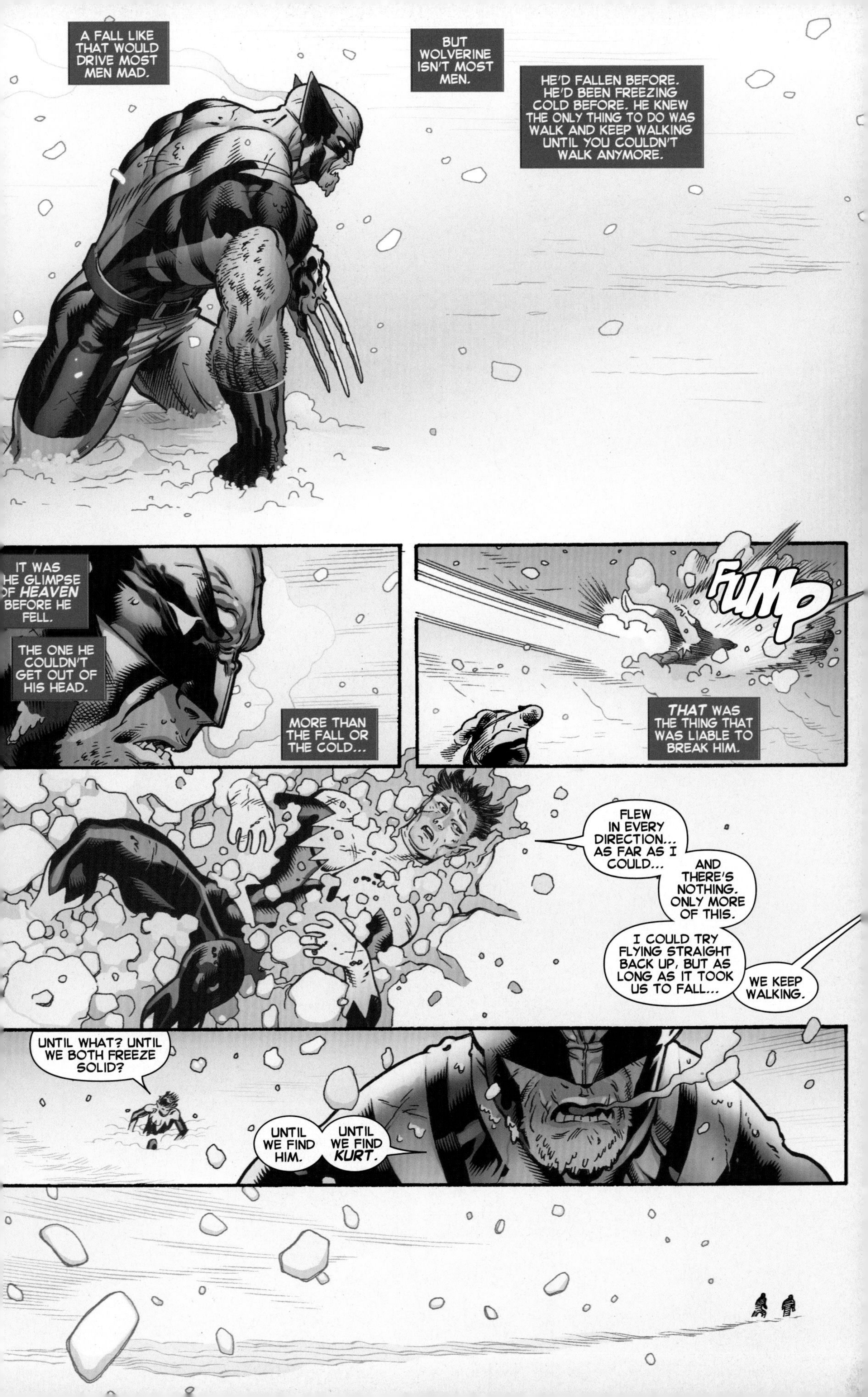
A FALL LIKE THAT WOULD DRIVE MOST MEN MAD.
BUT WOLVERINE ISN'T MOST MEN.
HE'D FALLEN BEFORE. HE'D BEEN FREEZING COLD BEFORE. HE KNEW THE ONLY THING TO DO WAS WALK AND KEEP WALKING UNTIL YOU COULDN'T WALK ANYMORE.
IT WAS HE GLIMPSE OF HEAVEN BEFORE HE FELL.
THE ONE HE COULDN'T GET OUT OF HIS HEAD.
MORE THAN THE FALL OR THE COLD...
FUMP
THAT WAS THE THING THAT WAS LIABLE TO BREAK HIM.
FLEW IN EVERY DIRECTION... AS FAR AS I COULD...
AND THERE'S NOTHING. ONLY MORE OF THIS.
I COULD TRY FLYING STRAIGHT BACK UP, BUT AS LONG AS IT TOOK US TO FALL...
WE KEEP WALKING.
UNTIL WHAT? UNTIL WE BOTH FREEZE SOLID?
UNTIL WE FIND HIM.
UNTIL WE FIND KURT.

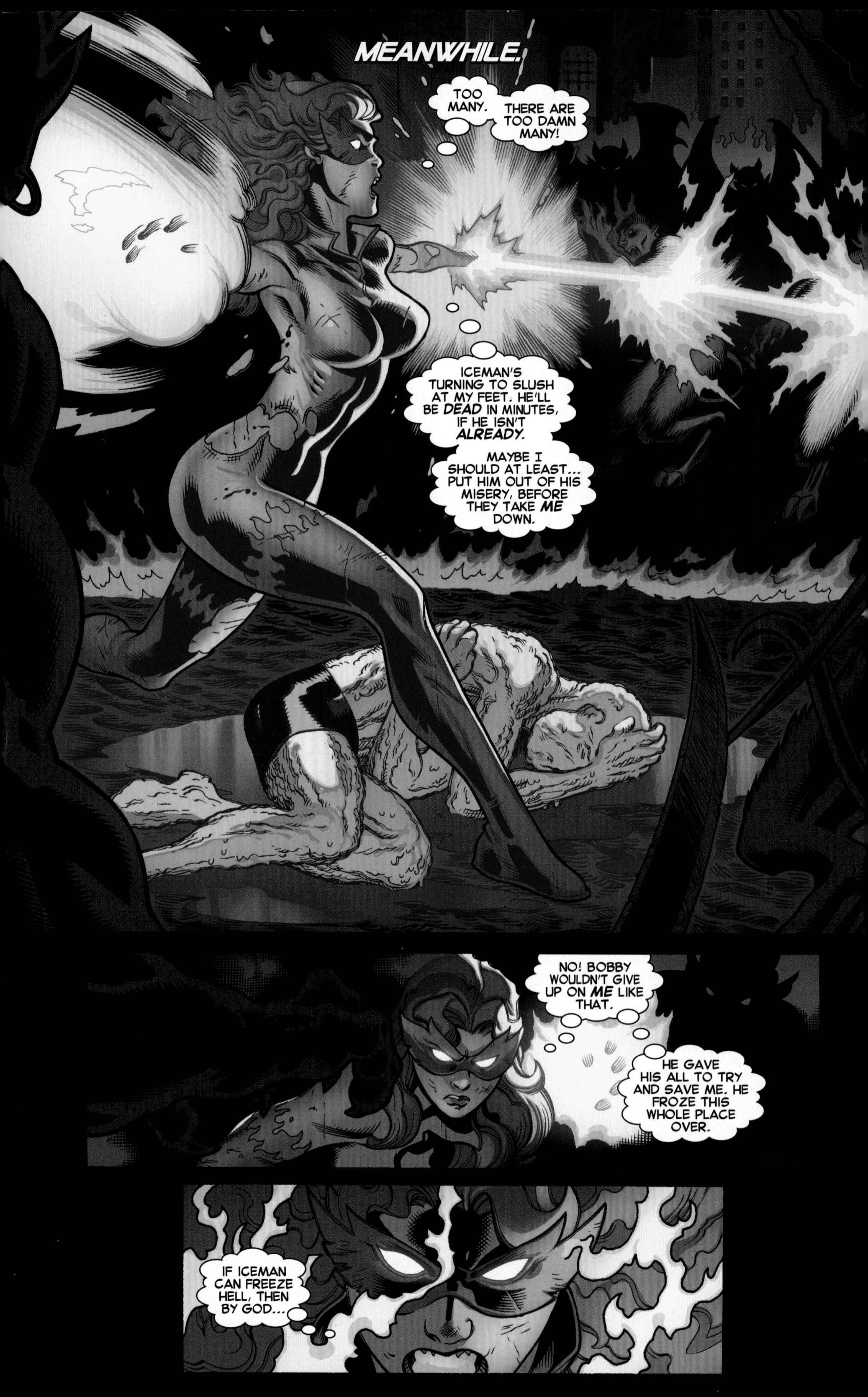
MEANWHILE.
TOO MANY.
THERE ARE TOO DAMN MANY!
ICEMAN'S TURNING TO SLUSH AT MY FEET. HE'LL BE DEAD IN MINUTES, IF HE ISN'T ALREADY.
MAYBE I SHOULD AT LEAST... PUT HIM OUT OF HIS MISERY, BEFORE THEY TAKE ME DOWN.
NO! BOBBY WOULDN'T GIVE UP ON ME LIKE THAT.
HE GAVE HIS ALL TO TRY AND SAVE ME. HE FROZE THIS WHOLE PLACE OVER.
IF ICEMAN CAN FREEZE HELL, THEN BY GOD...

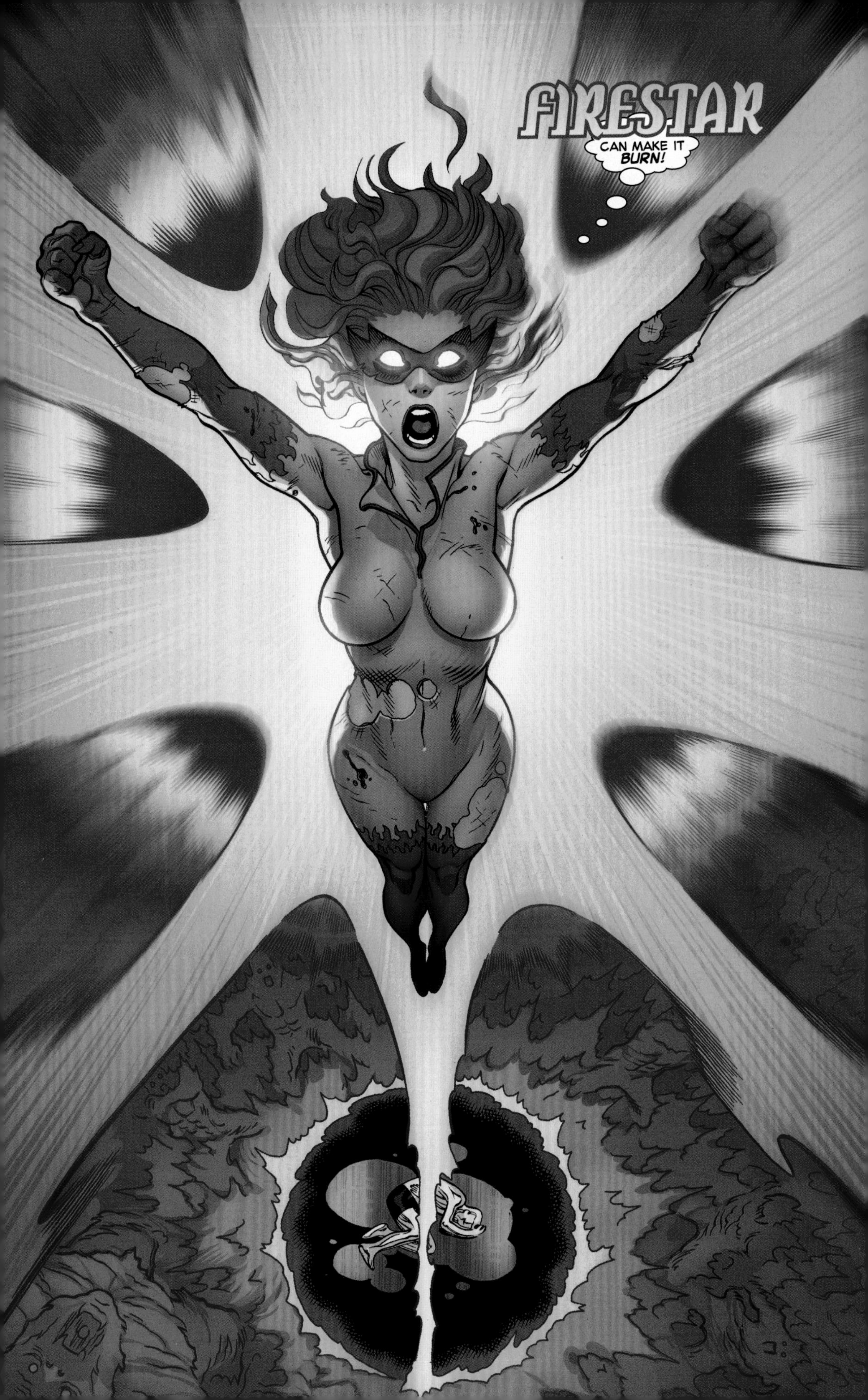
FIRESTAR
CAN MAKE IT BURN!

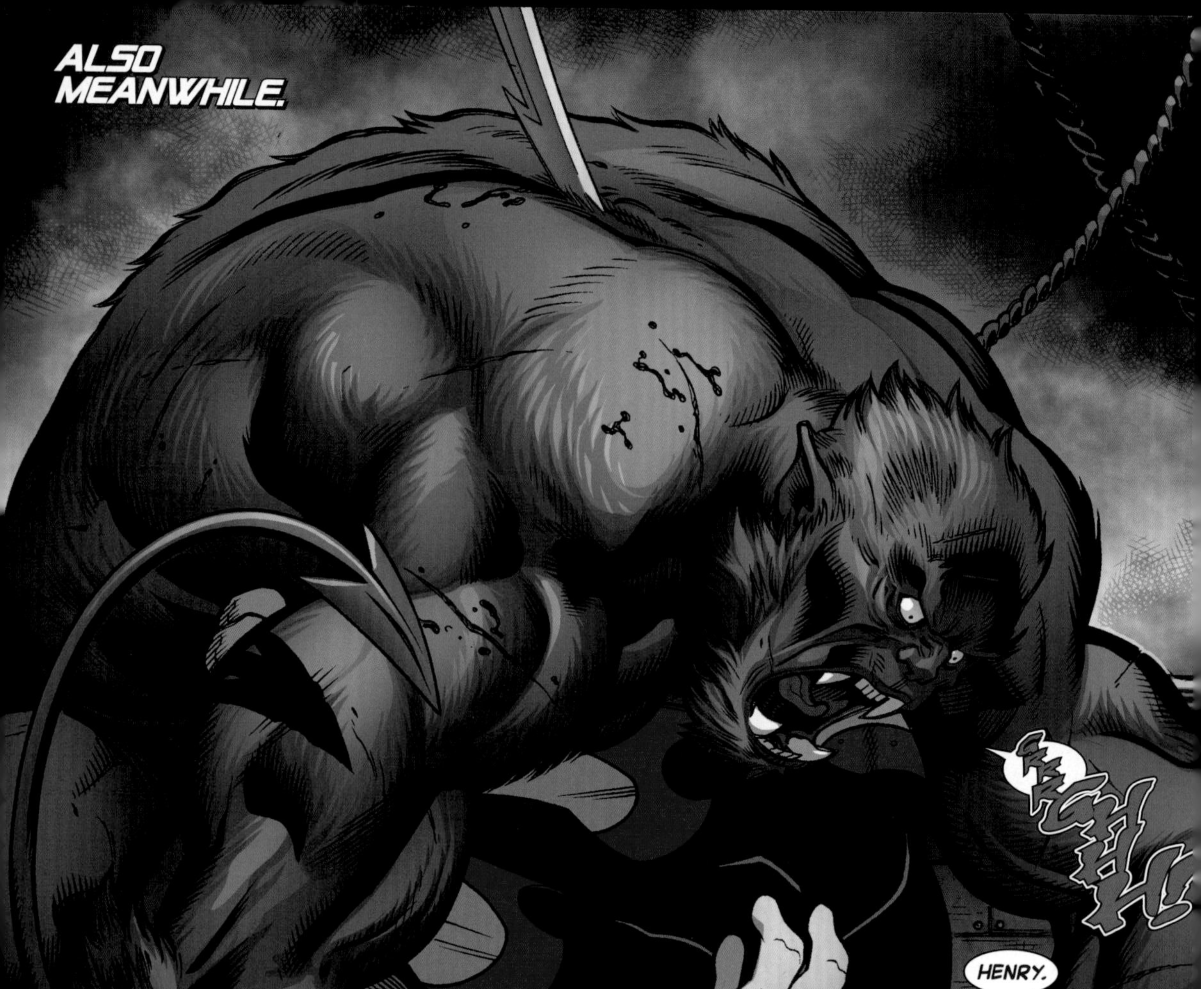
ALSO MEANWHILE.
HENRY.
I'VE MISSED YOU AS WELL, OLD FRIEND.

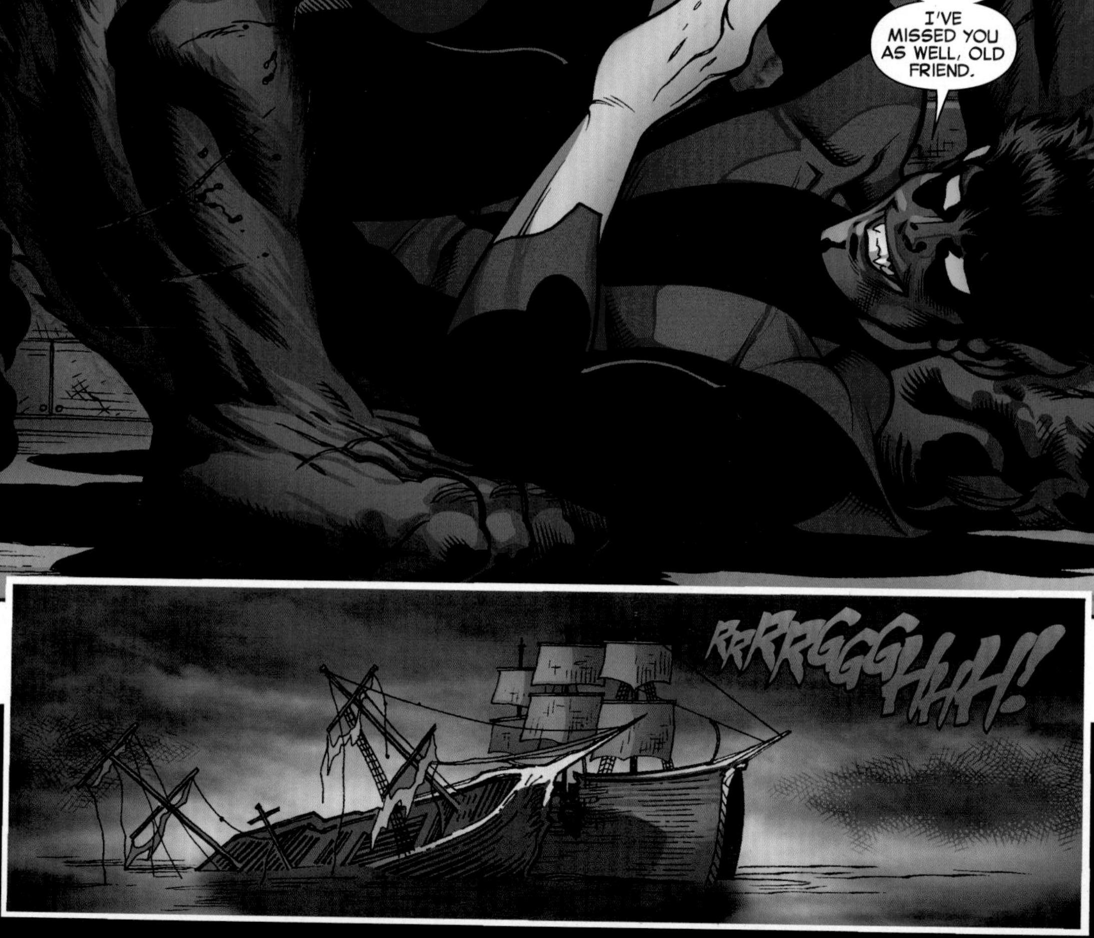
RRRRGGGHHH!

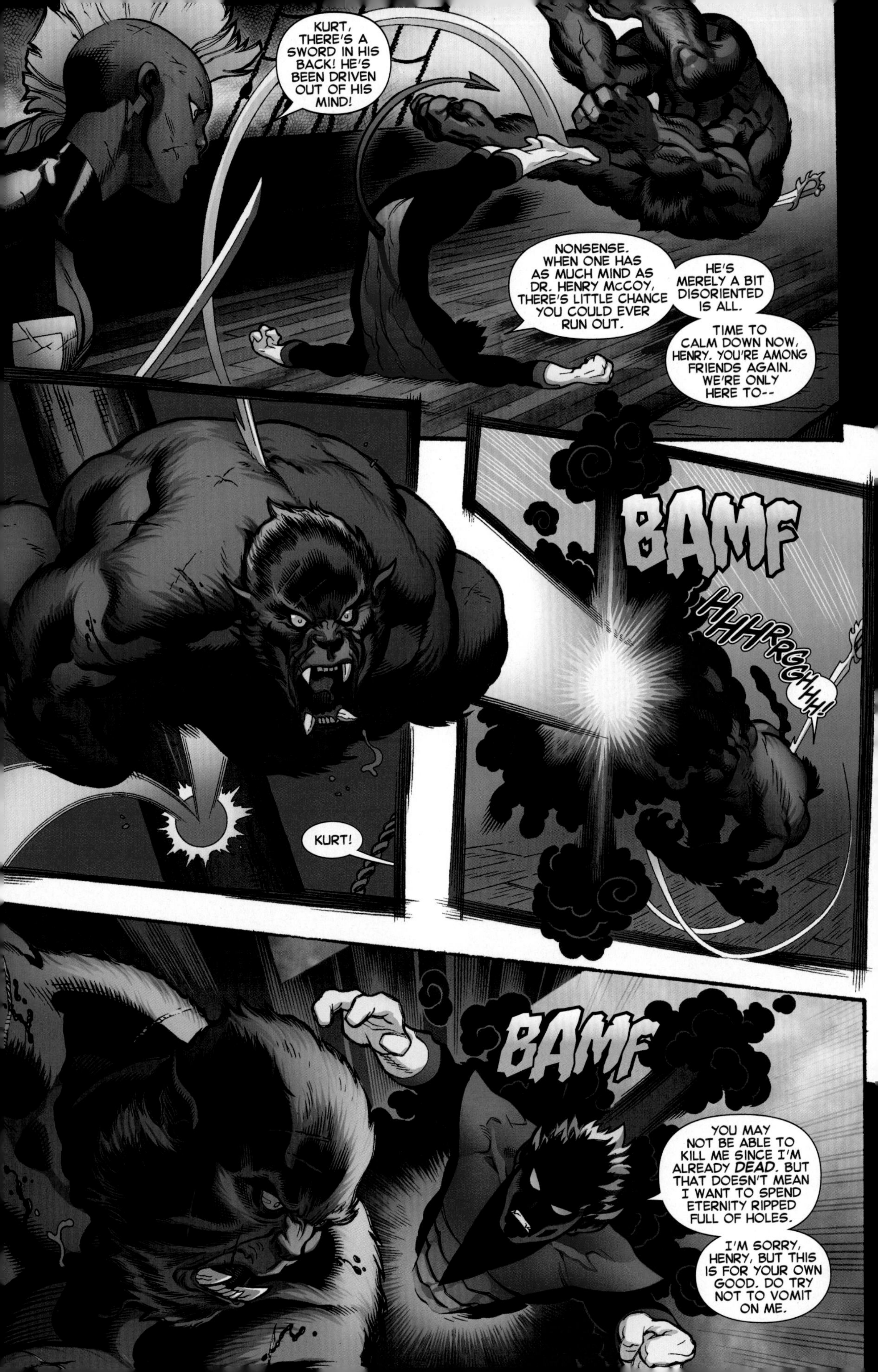
KURT, THERE'S A SWORD IN HIS BACK! HE'S BEEN DRIVEN OUT OF HIS MIND!
NONSENSE. WHEN ONE HAS AS MUCH MIND AS DR. HENRY McCOY, THERE'S LITTLE CHANCE YOU COULD EVER RUN OUT.
HE'S MERELY A BIT DISORIENTED IS ALL.
TIME TO CALM DOWN NOW, HENRY. YOU'RE AMONG FRIENDS AGAIN. WE'RE ONLY HERE TO--
BAMF
HHHRRGHHH!
KURT!
BAMF
YOU MAY NOT BE ABLE TO KILL ME SINCE I'M ALREADY *DEAD*. BUT THAT DOESN'T MEAN I WANT TO SPEND ETERNITY RIPPED FULL OF HOLES.
I'M SORRY, HENRY, BUT THIS IS FOR YOUR OWN GOOD. DO TRY NOT TO VOMIT ON ME.

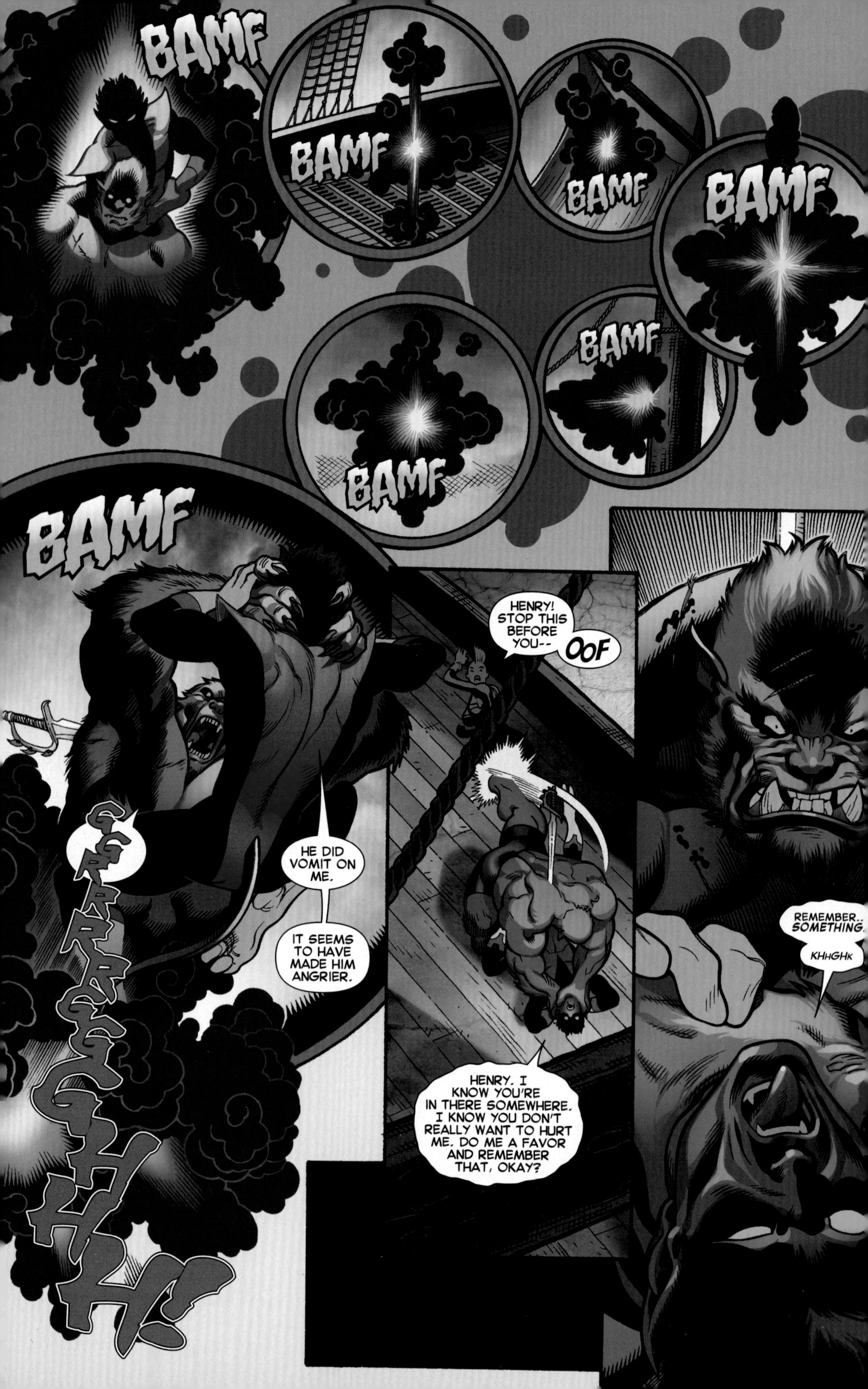
BAMF
BAMF
BAMF
BAMF
BAMF
BAMF
BAMF
GGRRRRGGHHHH!
HE DID VOMIT ON ME.
IT SEEMS TO HAVE MADE HIM ANGRIER.
HENRY! STOP THIS BEFORE YOU--
OOF
HENRY. I KNOW YOU'RE IN THERE SOMEWHERE. I KNOW YOU DON'T REALLY WANT TO HURT ME. DO ME A FAVOR AND REMEMBER THAT, OKAY?
REMEMBER.. SOMETHING.
KHHGHK

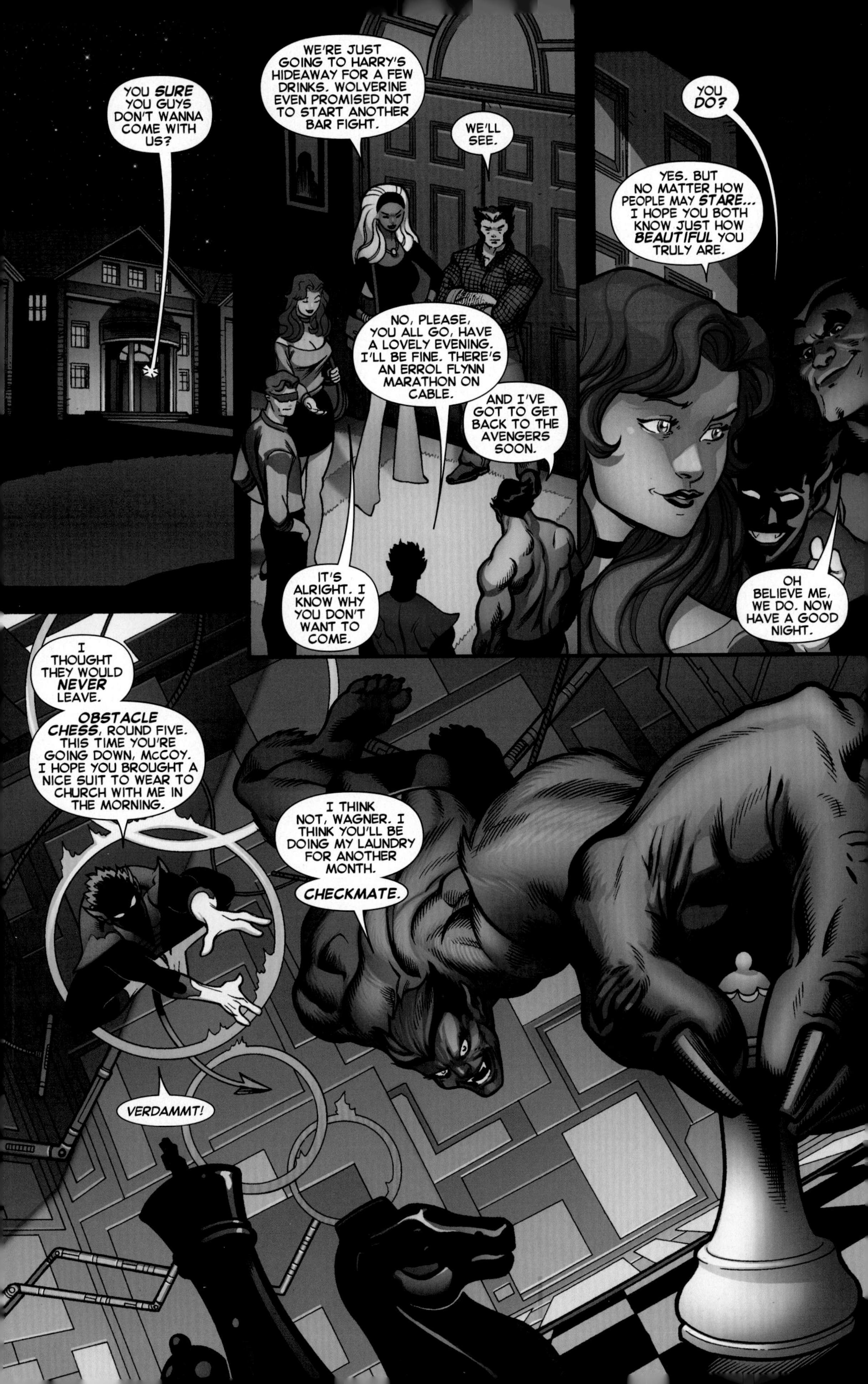
YOU SURE YOU GUYS DON'T WANNA COME WITH US?
WE'RE JUST GOING TO HARRY'S HIDEAWAY FOR A FEW DRINKS. WOLVERINE EVEN PROMISED NOT TO START ANOTHER BAR FIGHT.
WE'LL SEE.
NO, PLEASE, YOU ALL GO, HAVE A LOVELY EVENING. I'LL BE FINE. THERE'S AN ERROL FLYNN MARATHON ON CABLE.
AND I'VE GOT TO GET BACK TO THE AVENGERS SOON.
IT'S ALRIGHT. I KNOW WHY YOU DON'T WANT TO COME.
YOU DO?
YES. BUT NO MATTER HOW PEOPLE MAY STARE... I HOPE YOU BOTH KNOW JUST HOW BEAUTIFUL YOU TRULY ARE.
OH BELIEVE ME, WE DO. NOW HAVE A GOOD NIGHT.
I THOUGHT THEY WOULD NEVER LEAVE.
OBSTACLE CHESS, ROUND FIVE. THIS TIME YOU'RE GOING DOWN, McCOY. I HOPE YOU BROUGHT A NICE SUIT TO WEAR TO CHURCH WITH ME IN THE MORNING.
I THINK NOT, WAGNER. I THINK YOU'LL BE DOING MY LAUNDRY FOR ANOTHER MONTH.
CHECKMATE.
VERDAMMT!

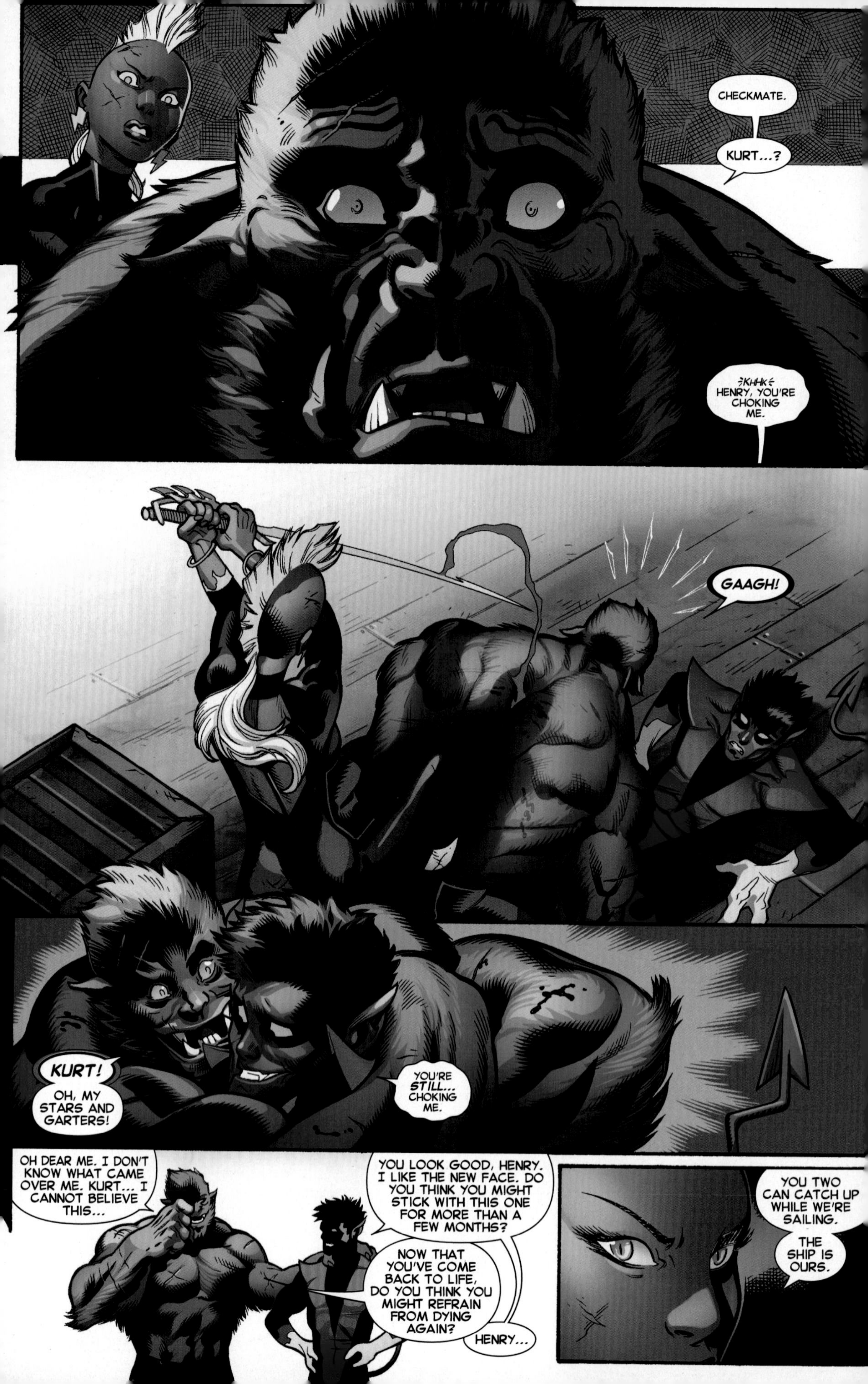

CHECKMATE.
KURT...?
≶KHHK≷ HENRY, YOU'RE CHOKING ME.
GAAGH!
KURT!
OH, MY STARS AND GARTERS!
YOU'RE STILL... CHOKING ME.
OH DEAR ME. I DON'T KNOW WHAT CAME OVER ME. KURT... I CANNOT BELIEVE THIS...
YOU LOOK GOOD, HENRY. I LIKE THE NEW FACE. DO YOU THINK YOU MIGHT STICK WITH THIS ONE FOR MORE THAN A FEW MONTHS?
NOW THAT YOU'VE COME BACK TO LIFE, DO YOU THINK YOU MIGHT REFRAIN FROM DYING AGAIN?
HENRY...
YOU TWO CAN CATCH UP WHILE WE'RE SAILING.
THE SHIP IS OURS.

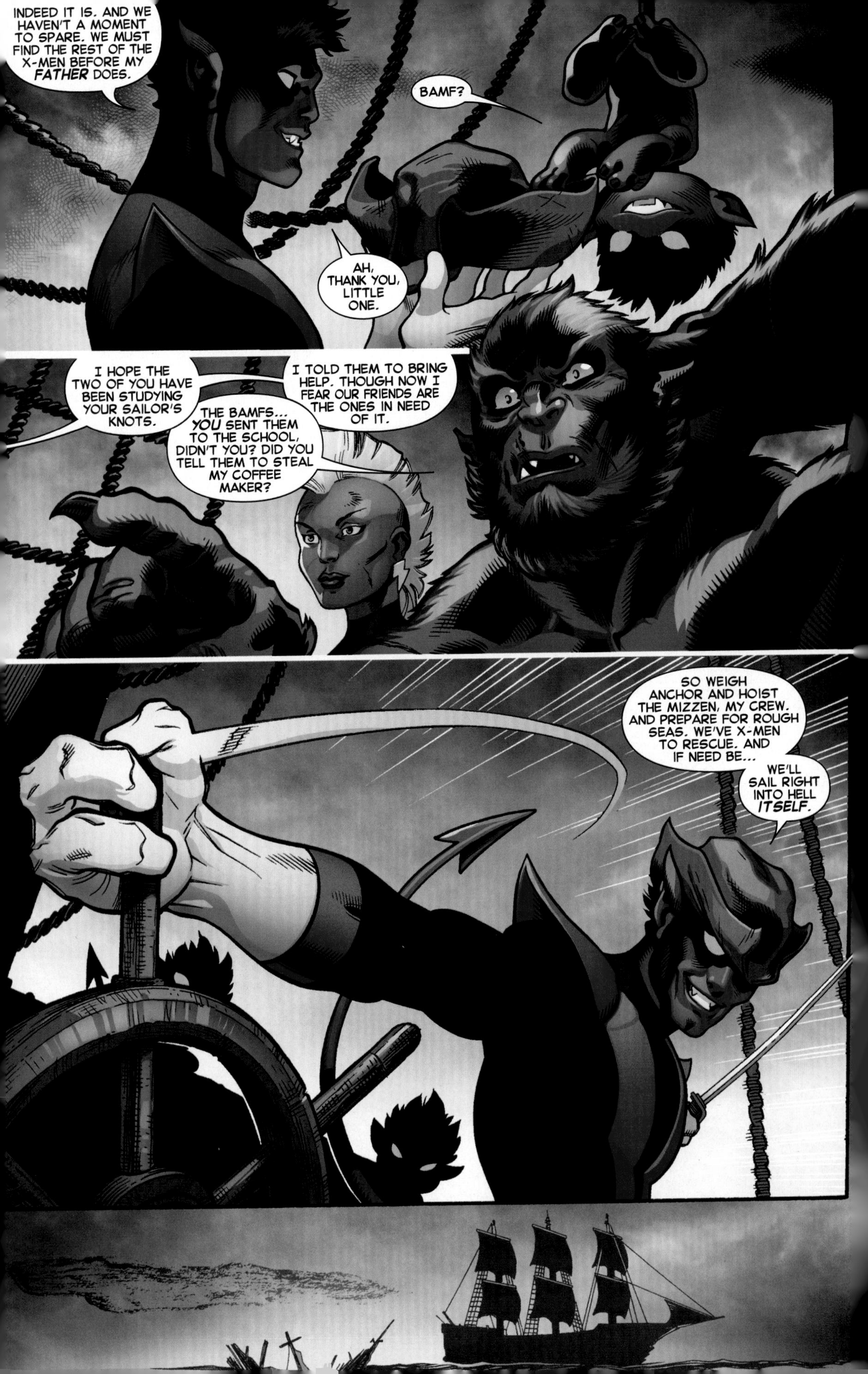
INDEED IT IS. AND WE HAVEN'T A MOMENT TO SPARE. WE MUST FIND THE REST OF THE X-MEN BEFORE MY FATHER DOES.
BAMF?
AH, THANK YOU, LITTLE ONE.
I HOPE THE TWO OF YOU HAVE BEEN STUDYING YOUR SAILOR'S KNOTS.
THE BAMFS... YOU SENT THEM TO THE SCHOOL, DIDN'T YOU? DID YOU TELL THEM TO STEAL MY COFFEE MAKER?
I TOLD THEM TO BRING HELP. THOUGH NOW I FEAR OUR FRIENDS ARE THE ONES IN NEED OF IT.
SO WEIGH ANCHOR AND HOIST THE MIZZEN, MY CREW. AND PREPARE FOR ROUGH SEAS. WE'VE X-MEN TO RESCUE. AND IF NEED BE...
WE'LL SAIL RIGHT INTO HELL ITSELF.

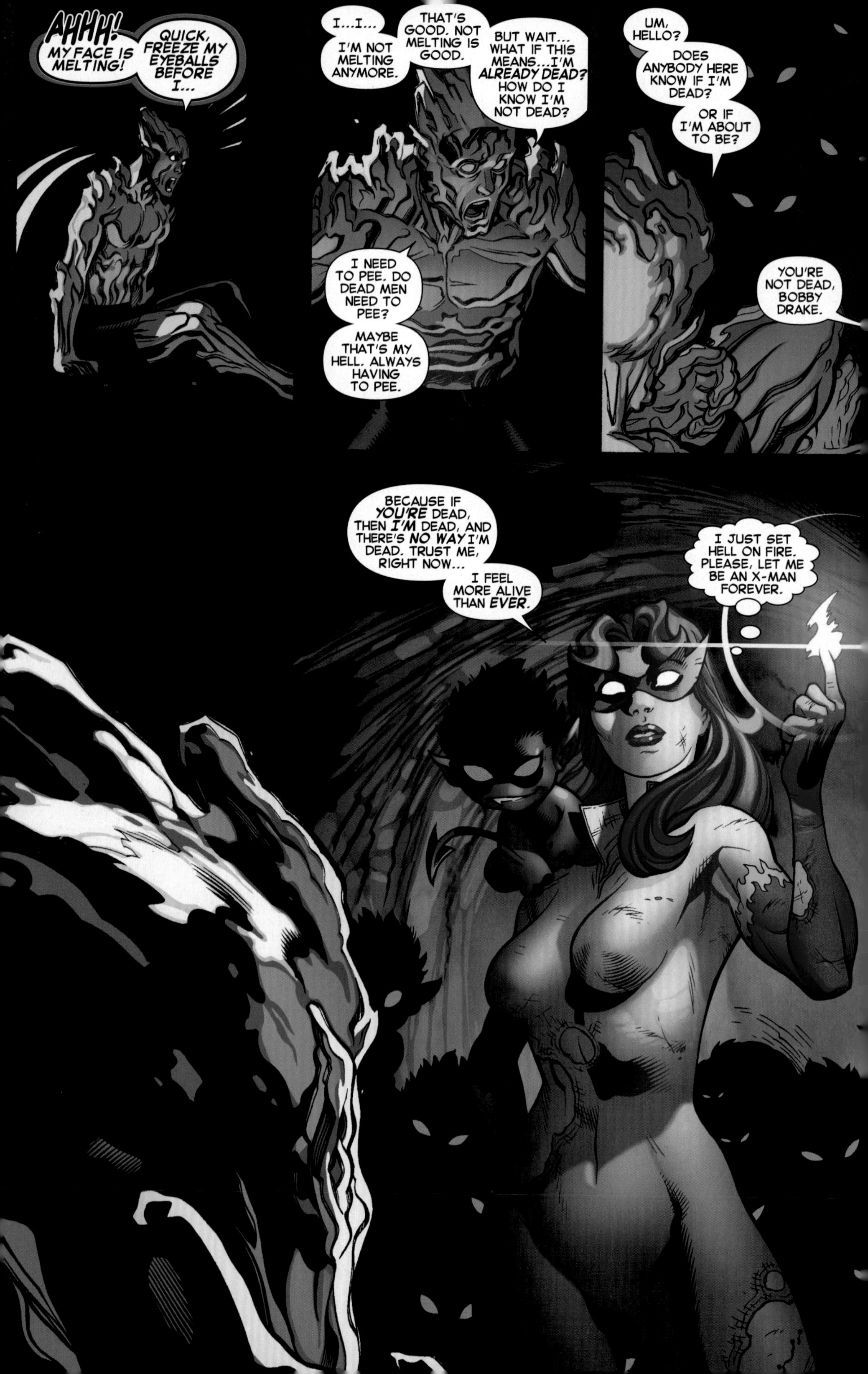
AHHH! MY FACE IS MELTING!
QUICK, FREEZE MY EYEBALLS BEFORE I...
I...I...
I'M NOT MELTING ANYMORE.
THAT'S GOOD. NOT MELTING IS GOOD.
BUT WAIT... WHAT IF THIS MEANS...I'M ALREADY DEAD? HOW DO I KNOW I'M NOT DEAD?
I NEED TO PEE. DO DEAD MEN NEED TO PEE?
MAYBE THAT'S MY HELL. ALWAYS HAVING TO PEE.
UM, HELLO?
DOES ANYBODY HERE KNOW IF I'M DEAD?
OR IF I'M ABOUT TO BE?
YOU'RE NOT DEAD, BOBBY DRAKE.
BECAUSE IF YOU'RE DEAD, THEN I'M DEAD, AND THERE'S NO WAY I'M DEAD. TRUST ME, RIGHT NOW...
I FEEL MORE ALIVE THAN EVER.
I JUST SET HELL ON FIRE. PLEASE, LET ME BE AN X-MAN FOREVER.

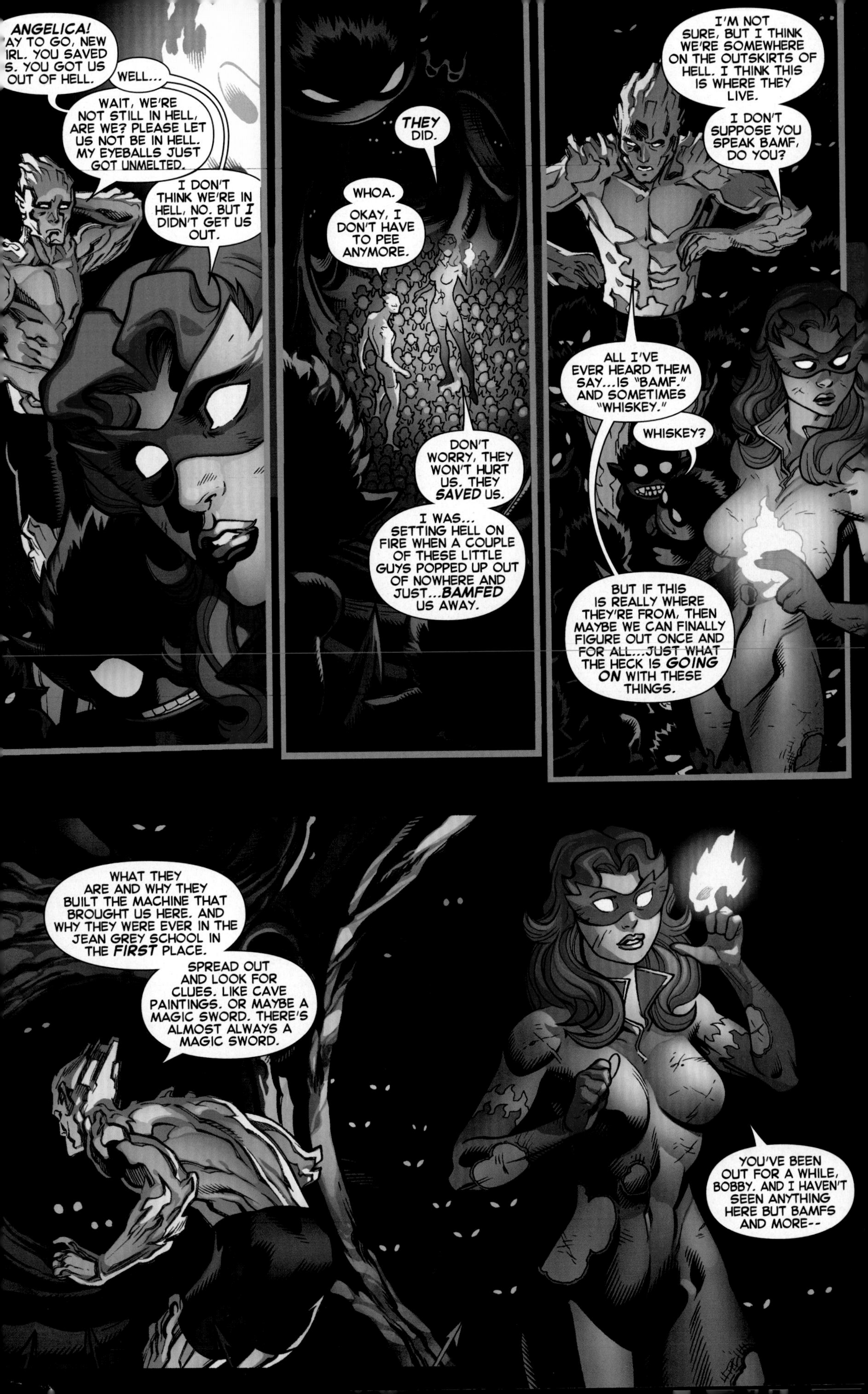
ANGELICA! AY TO GO, NEW IRL. YOU SAVED S. YOU GOT US OUT OF HELL.
WELL...
WAIT, WE'RE NOT STILL IN HELL, ARE WE? PLEASE LET US NOT BE IN HELL. MY EYEBALLS JUST GOT UNMELTED.
I DON'T THINK WE'RE IN HELL, NO. BUT I DIDN'T GET US OUT.
THEY DID.
WHOA.
OKAY, I DON'T HAVE TO PEE ANYMORE.
DON'T WORRY, THEY WON'T HURT US. THEY SAVED US.
I WAS... SETTING HELL ON FIRE WHEN A COUPLE OF THESE LITTLE GUYS POPPED UP OUT OF NOWHERE AND JUST...BAMFED US AWAY.
I'M NOT SURE, BUT I THINK WE'RE SOMEWHERE ON THE OUTSKIRTS OF HELL. I THINK THIS IS WHERE THEY LIVE.
I DON'T SUPPOSE YOU SPEAK BAMF, DO YOU?
ALL I'VE EVER HEARD THEM SAY...IS "BAMF." AND SOMETIMES "WHISKEY."
WHISKEY?
BUT IF THIS IS REALLY WHERE THEY'RE FROM, THEN MAYBE WE CAN FINALLY FIGURE OUT ONCE AND FOR ALL...JUST WHAT THE HECK IS GOING ON WITH THESE THINGS.
WHAT THEY ARE AND WHY THEY BUILT THE MACHINE THAT BROUGHT US HERE. AND WHY THEY WERE EVER IN THE JEAN GREY SCHOOL IN THE FIRST PLACE.
SPREAD OUT AND LOOK FOR CLUES. LIKE CAVE PAINTINGS. OR MAYBE A MAGIC SWORD. THERE'S ALMOST ALWAYS A MAGIC SWORD.
YOU'VE BEEN OUT FOR A WHILE, BOBBY. AND I HAVEN'T SEEN ANYTHING HERE BUT BAMFS AND MORE--

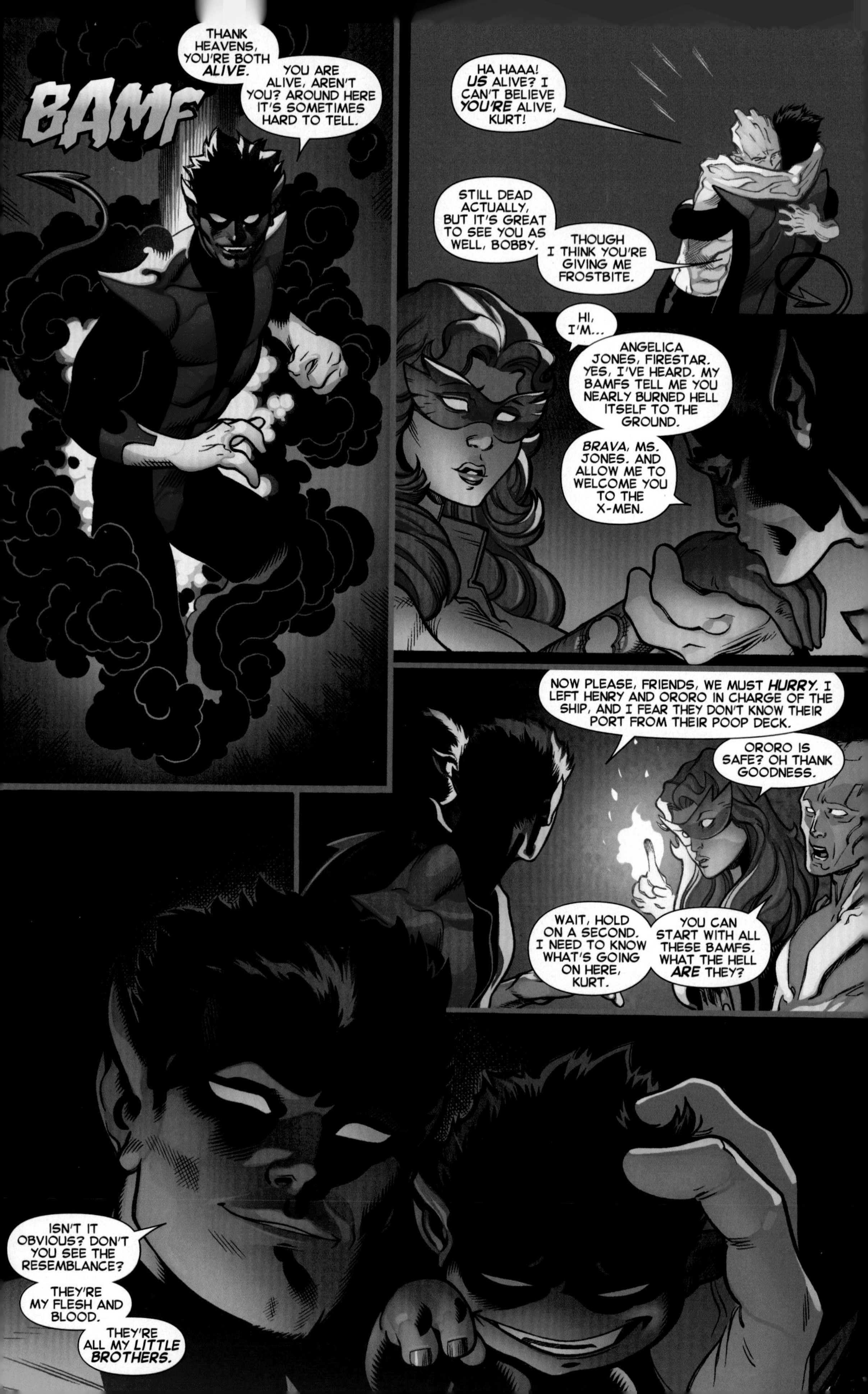
BAMF
THANK HEAVENS, YOU'RE BOTH ALIVE.
YOU ARE ALIVE, AREN'T YOU? AROUND HERE IT'S SOMETIMES HARD TO TELL.
HA HAAA! US ALIVE? I CAN'T BELIEVE YOU'RE ALIVE, KURT!
STILL DEAD ACTUALLY, BUT IT'S GREAT TO SEE YOU AS WELL, BOBBY.
THOUGH I THINK YOU'RE GIVING ME FROSTBITE.
HI, I'M...
ANGELICA JONES, FIRESTAR. YES, I'VE HEARD. MY BAMFS TELL ME YOU NEARLY BURNED HELL ITSELF TO THE GROUND.
BRAVA, MS. JONES. AND ALLOW ME TO WELCOME YOU TO THE X-MEN.
NOW PLEASE, FRIENDS, WE MUST HURRY. I LEFT HENRY AND ORORO IN CHARGE OF THE SHIP, AND I FEAR THEY DON'T KNOW THEIR PORT FROM THEIR POOP DECK.
ORORO IS SAFE? OH THANK GOODNESS.
WAIT, HOLD ON A SECOND. I NEED TO KNOW WHAT'S GOING ON HERE, KURT.
YOU CAN START WITH ALL THESE BAMFS. WHAT THE HELL ARE THEY?
ISN'T IT OBVIOUS? DON'T YOU SEE THE RESEMBLANCE?
THEY'RE MY FLESH AND BLOOD.
THEY'RE ALL MY LITTLE BROTHERS.

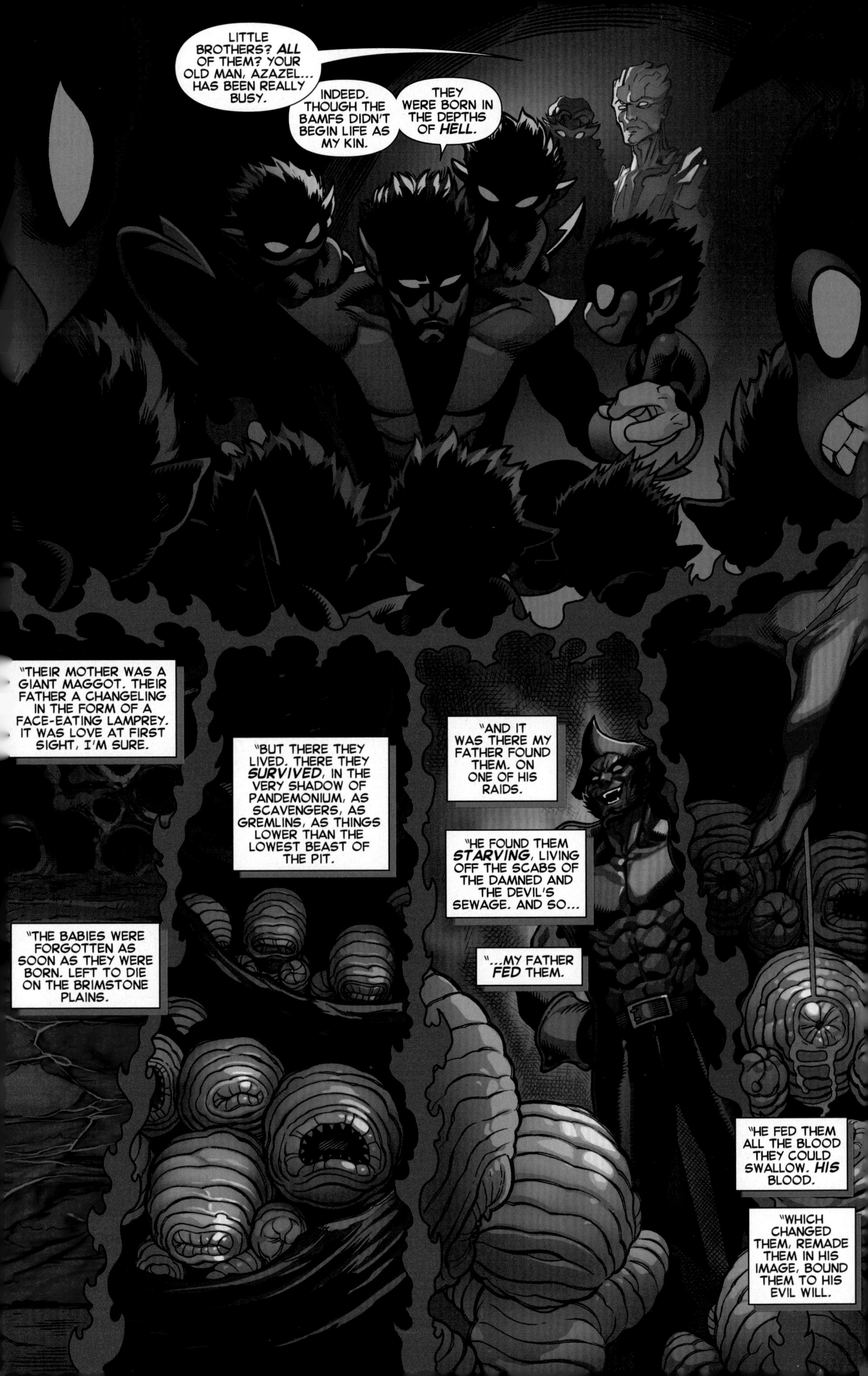
LITTLE BROTHERS? ALL OF THEM? YOUR OLD MAN, AZAZEL... HAS BEEN REALLY BUSY.
INDEED. THOUGH THE BAMFS DIDN'T BEGIN LIFE AS MY KIN.
THEY WERE BORN IN THE DEPTHS OF HELL.
"THEIR MOTHER WAS A GIANT MAGGOT. THEIR FATHER A CHANGELING IN THE FORM OF A FACE-EATING LAMPREY. IT WAS LOVE AT FIRST SIGHT, I'M SURE.
"THE BABIES WERE FORGOTTEN AS SOON AS THEY WERE BORN. LEFT TO DIE ON THE BRIMSTONE PLAINS.
"BUT THERE THEY LIVED. THERE THEY SURVIVED, IN THE VERY SHADOW OF PANDEMONIUM, AS SCAVENGERS, AS GREMLINS, AS THINGS LOWER THAN THE LOWEST BEAST OF THE PIT.
"AND IT WAS THERE MY FATHER FOUND THEM. ON ONE OF HIS RAIDS.
"HE FOUND THEM STARVING, LIVING OFF THE SCABS OF THE DAMNED AND THE DEVIL'S SEWAGE. AND SO...
"...MY FATHER FED THEM.
"HE FED THEM ALL THE BLOOD THEY COULD SWALLOW. HIS BLOOD.
"WHICH CHANGED THEM, REMADE THEM IN HIS IMAGE, BOUND THEM TO HIS EVIL WILL.

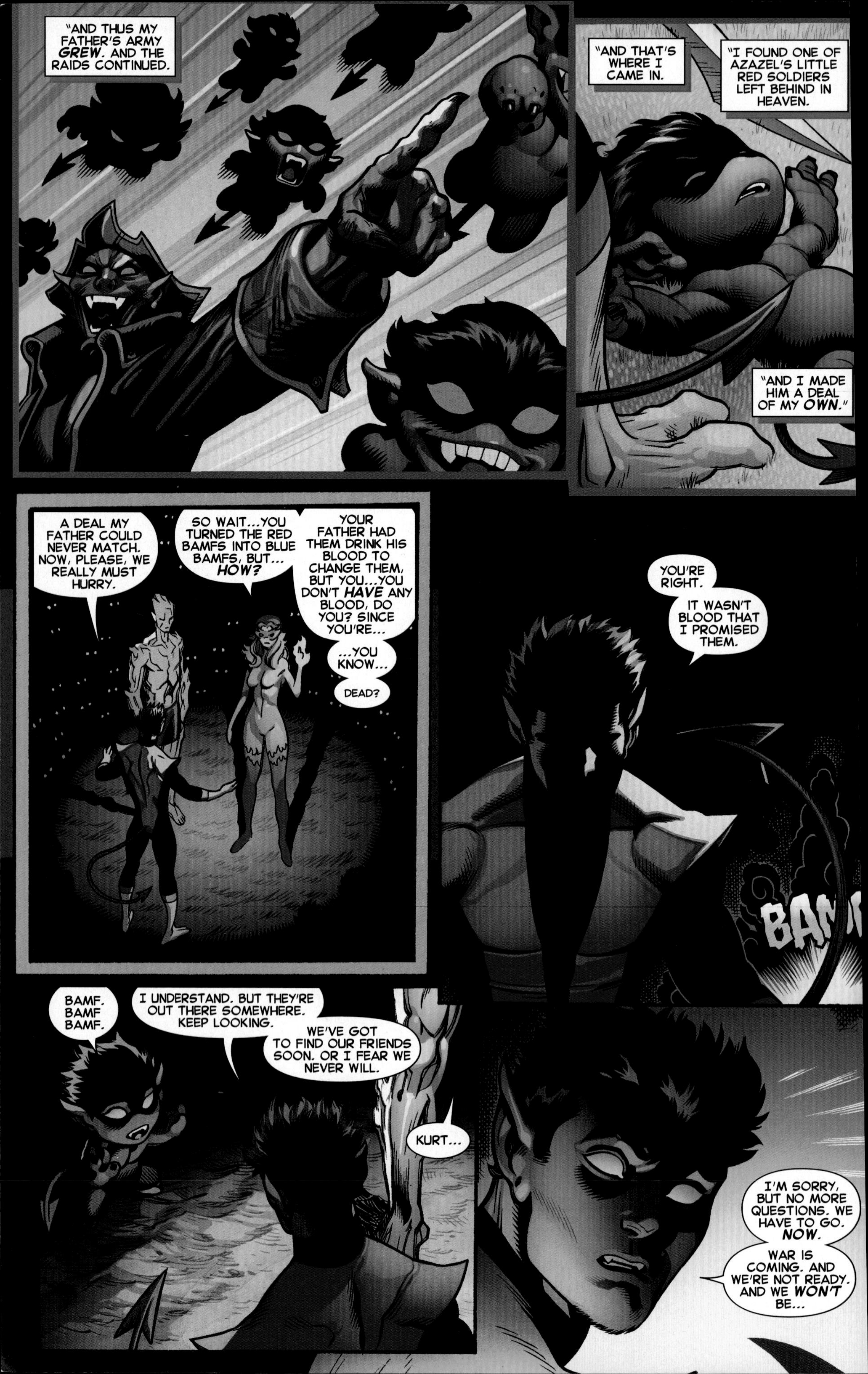
"AND THUS MY FATHER'S ARMY GREW. AND THE RAIDS CONTINUED.
"AND THAT'S WHERE I CAME IN.
"I FOUND ONE OF AZAZEL'S LITTLE RED SOLDIERS LEFT BEHIND IN HEAVEN.
"AND I MADE HIM A DEAL OF MY OWN."
A DEAL MY FATHER COULD NEVER MATCH. NOW, PLEASE, WE REALLY MUST HURRY.
SO WAIT...YOU TURNED THE RED BAMFS INTO BLUE BAMFS, BUT... HOW?
YOUR FATHER HAD THEM DRINK HIS BLOOD TO CHANGE THEM, BUT YOU...YOU DON'T HAVE ANY BLOOD, DO YOU? SINCE YOU'RE...
...YOU KNOW...
DEAD?
YOU'RE RIGHT.
IT WASN'T BLOOD THAT I PROMISED THEM.
BAMF. BAMF BAMF.
I UNDERSTAND. BUT THEY'RE OUT THERE SOMEWHERE. KEEP LOOKING.
WE'VE GOT TO FIND OUR FRIENDS SOON. OR I FEAR WE NEVER WILL.
KURT...
I'M SORRY, BUT NO MORE QUESTIONS. WE HAVE TO GO. NOW.
WAR IS COMING. AND WE'RE NOT READY. AND WE WON'T BE...

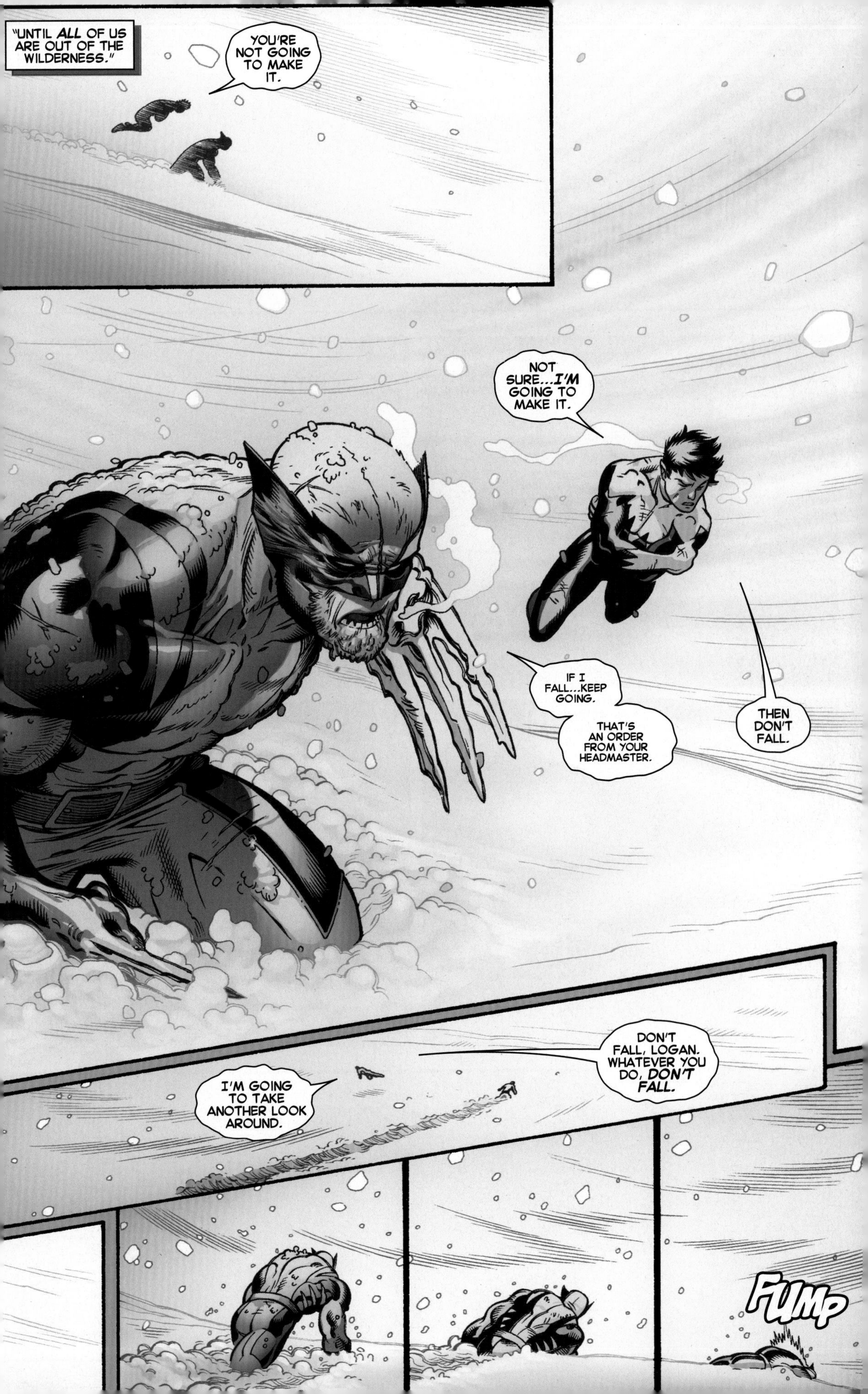
"UNTIL ALL OF US ARE OUT OF THE WILDERNESS."
YOU'RE NOT GOING TO MAKE IT.
NOT SURE...I'M GOING TO MAKE IT.
IF I FALL...KEEP GOING.
THAT'S AN ORDER FROM YOUR HEADMASTER.
THEN DON'T FALL.
DON'T FALL, LOGAN. WHATEVER YOU DO, DON'T FALL.
I'M GOING TO TAKE ANOTHER LOOK AROUND.
FUMP

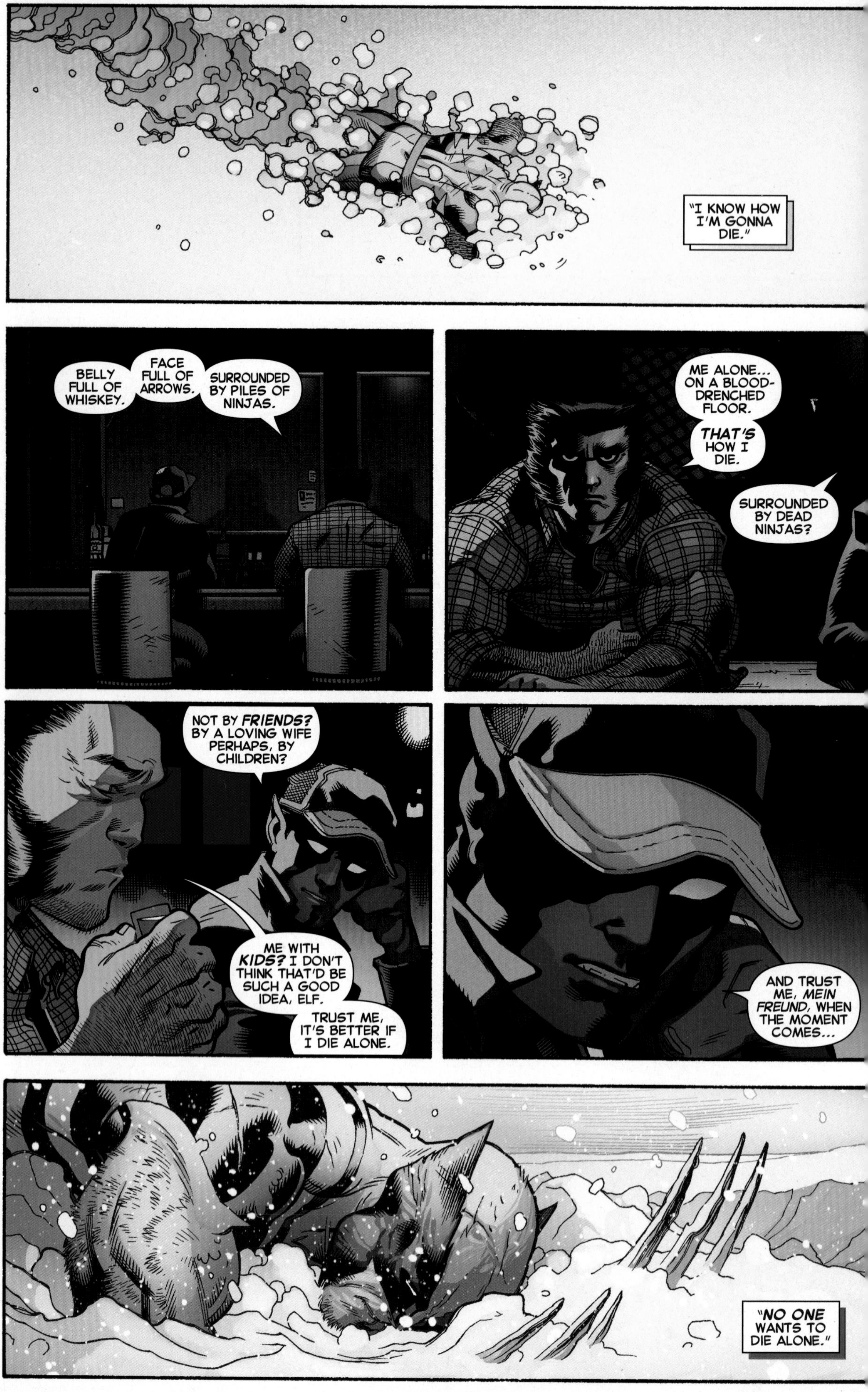
"I KNOW HOW I'M GONNA DIE."
BELLY FULL OF WHISKEY.
FACE FULL OF ARROWS.
SURROUNDED BY PILES OF NINJAS.
ME ALONE... ON A BLOOD-DRENCHED FLOOR.
THAT'S HOW I DIE.
SURROUNDED BY DEAD NINJAS?
NOT BY FRIENDS? BY A LOVING WIFE PERHAPS, BY CHILDREN?
ME WITH KIDS? I DON'T THINK THAT'D BE SUCH A GOOD IDEA, ELF.
TRUST ME, IT'S BETTER IF I DIE ALONE.
AND TRUST ME, MEIN FREUND, WHEN THE MOMENT COMES...
"NO ONE WANTS TO DIE ALONE."

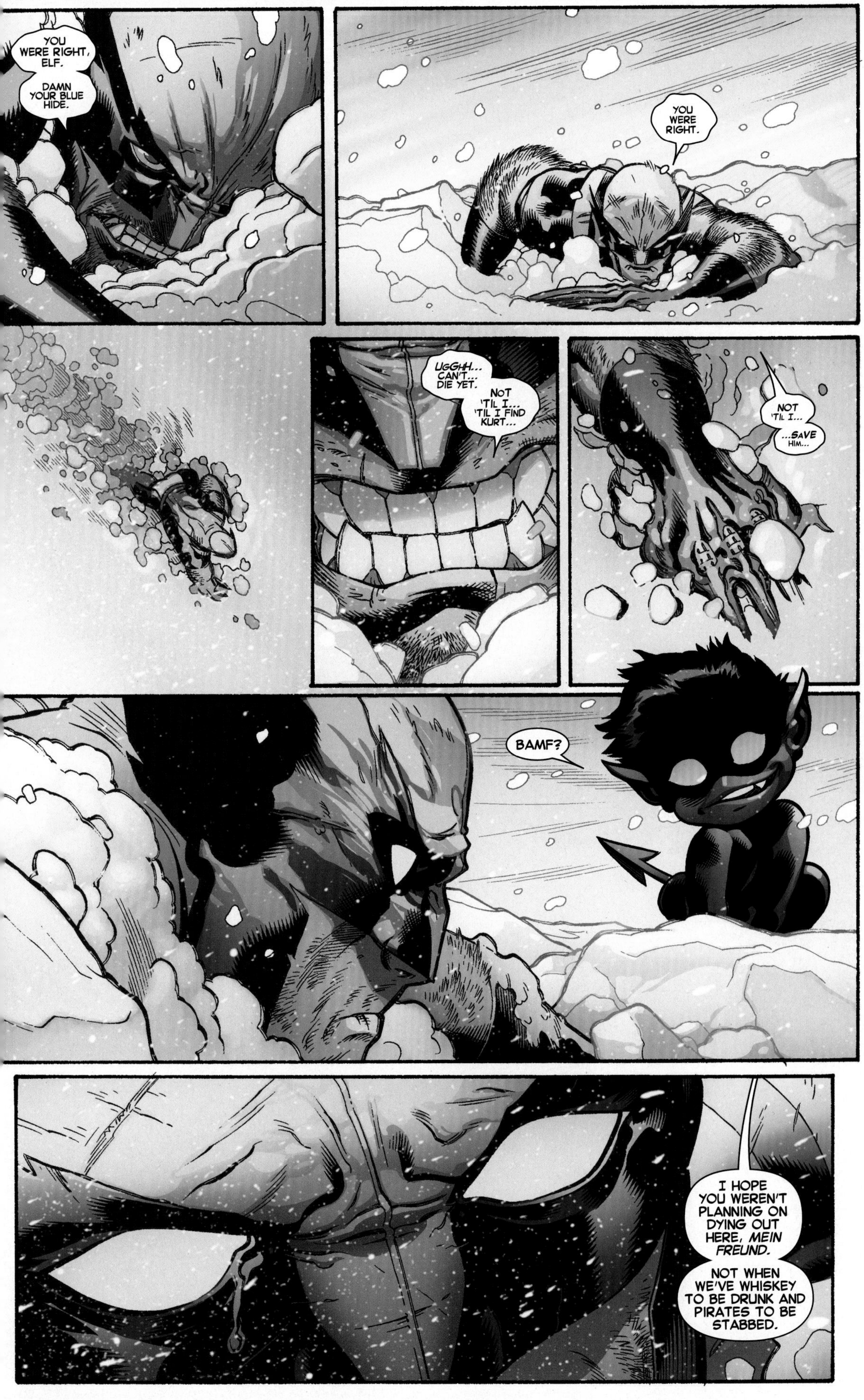
YOU WERE RIGHT, ELF.
DAMN YOUR BLUE HIDE.
YOU WERE RIGHT.
UGGHH... CAN'T... DIE YET.
NOT 'TIL I... 'TIL I FIND KURT...
NOT 'TIL I...
...SAVE HIM...
BAMF?
I HOPE YOU WEREN'T PLANNING ON DYING OUT HERE, *MEIN FREUND.*
NOT WHEN WE'VE WHISKEY TO BE DRUNK AND PIRATES TO BE STABBED.

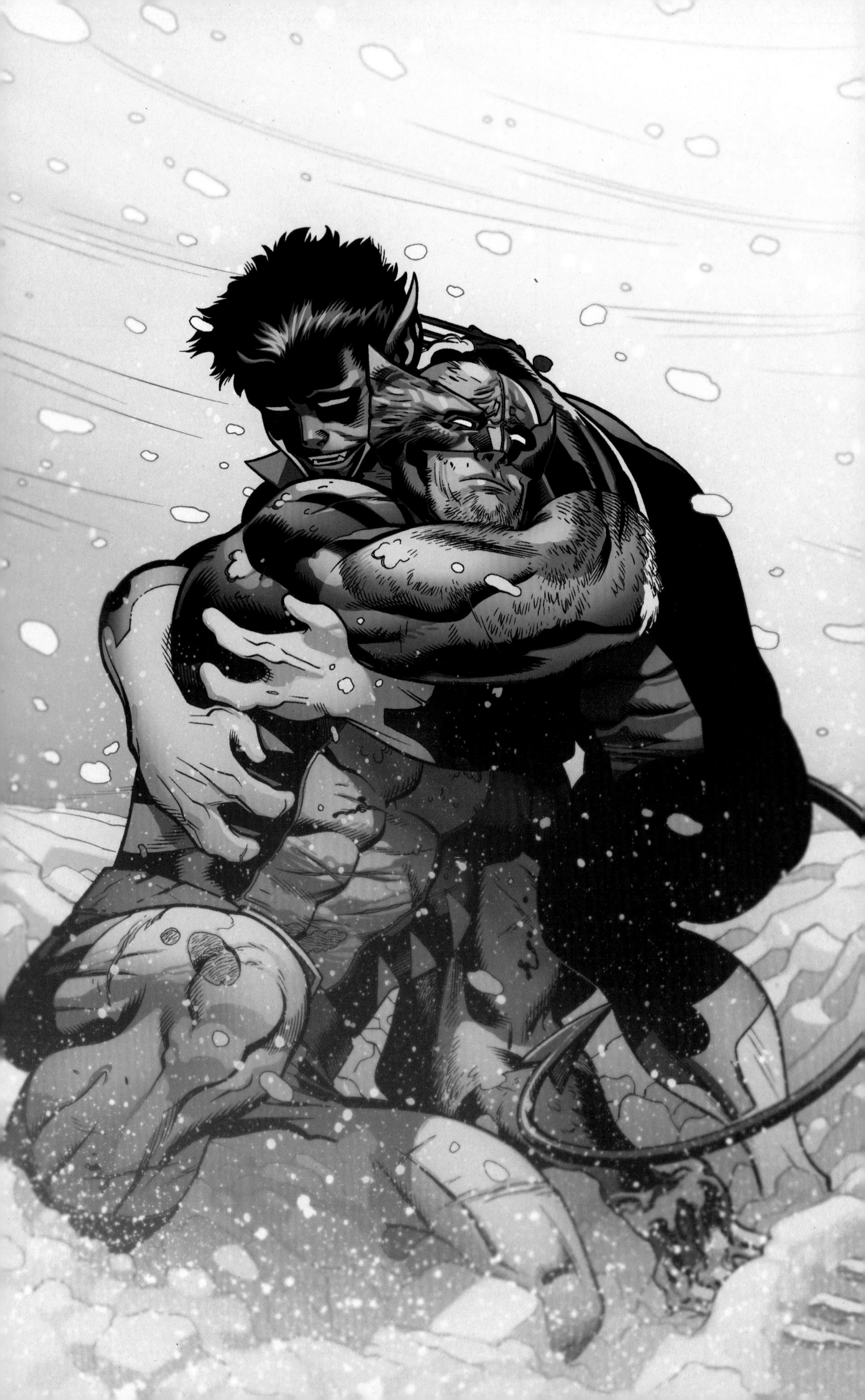

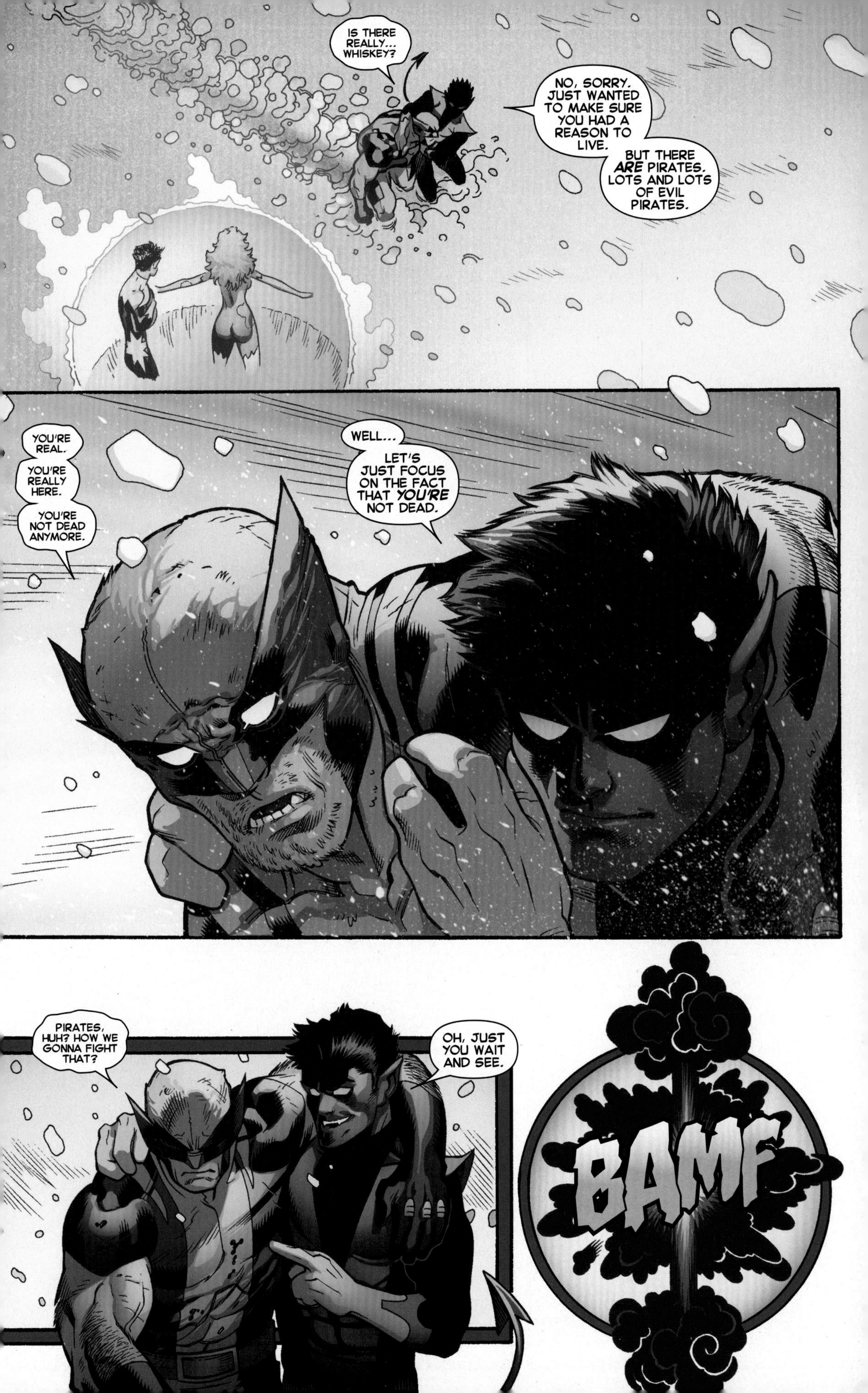
IS THERE REALLY... WHISKEY?
NO, SORRY. JUST WANTED TO MAKE SURE YOU HAD A REASON TO LIVE.
BUT THERE *ARE* PIRATES. LOTS AND LOTS OF EVIL PIRATES.
YOU'RE REAL.
YOU'RE REALLY HERE.
YOU'RE NOT DEAD ANYMORE.
WELL...
LET'S JUST FOCUS ON THE FACT THAT *YOU'RE* NOT DEAD.
PIRATES, HUH? HOW WE GONNA FIGHT THAT?
OH, JUST YOU WAIT AND SEE.
BAMF

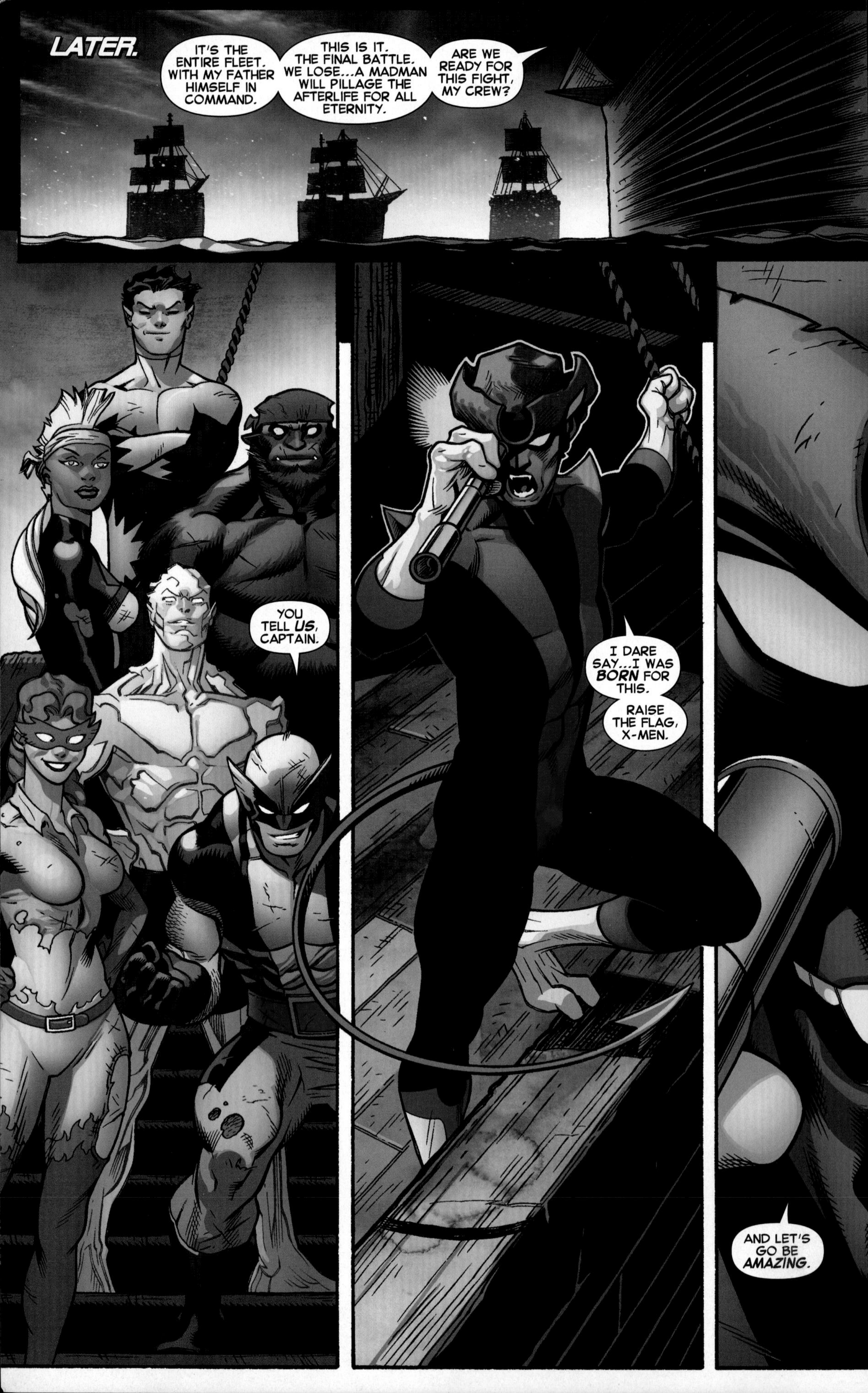
LATER.
IT'S THE ENTIRE FLEET. WITH MY FATHER HIMSELF IN COMMAND.
THIS IS IT. THE FINAL BATTLE. WE LOSE...A MADMAN WILL PILLAGE THE AFTERLIFE FOR ALL ETERNITY.
ARE WE READY FOR THIS FIGHT, MY CREW?
YOU TELL *US*, CAPTAIN.
I DARE SAY...I WAS *BORN* FOR THIS.
RAISE THE FLAG, X-MEN.
AND LET'S GO BE *AMAZING*.

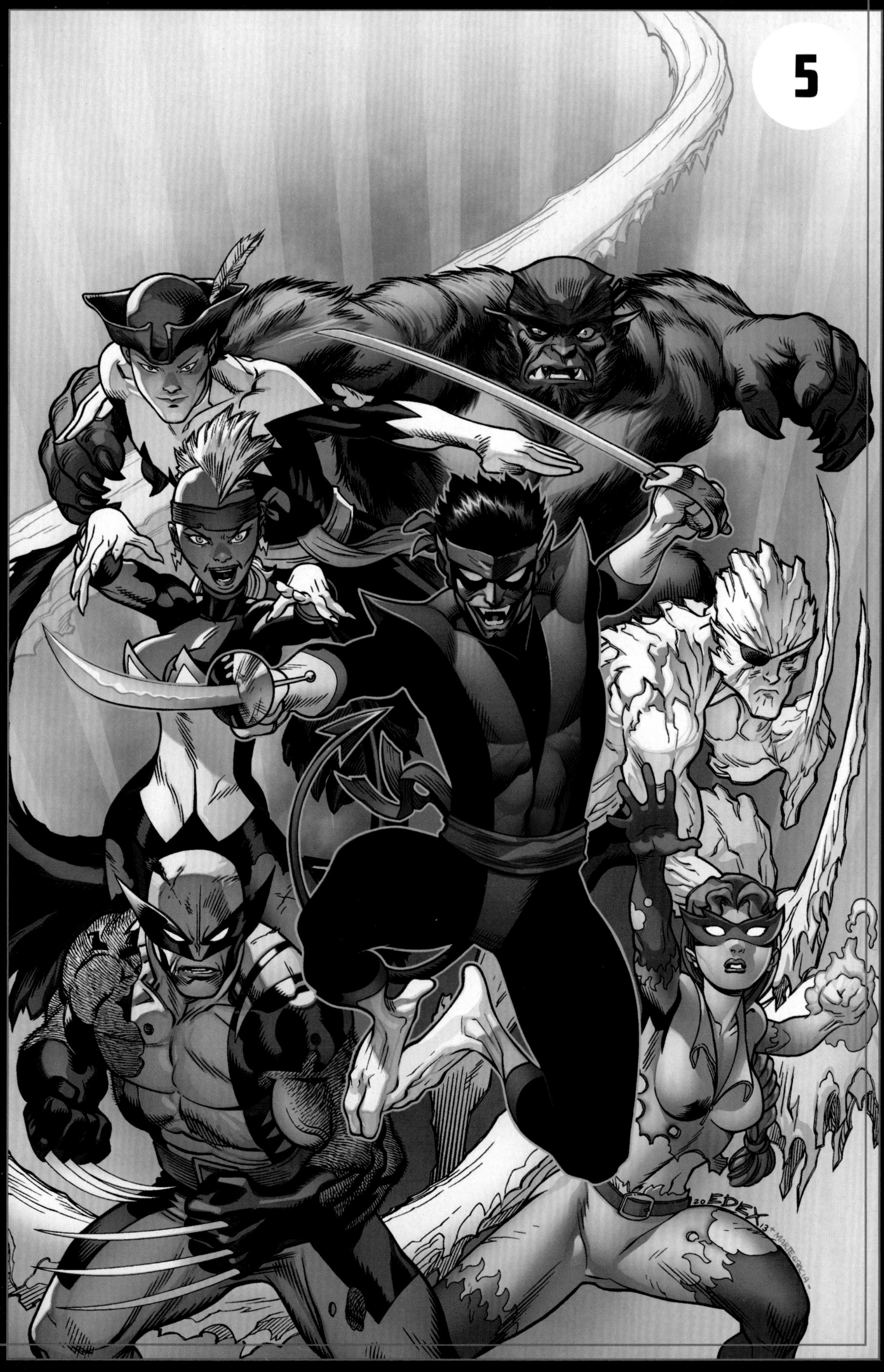
5

THE QUEST FOR NIGHTCRAWLER PART 5

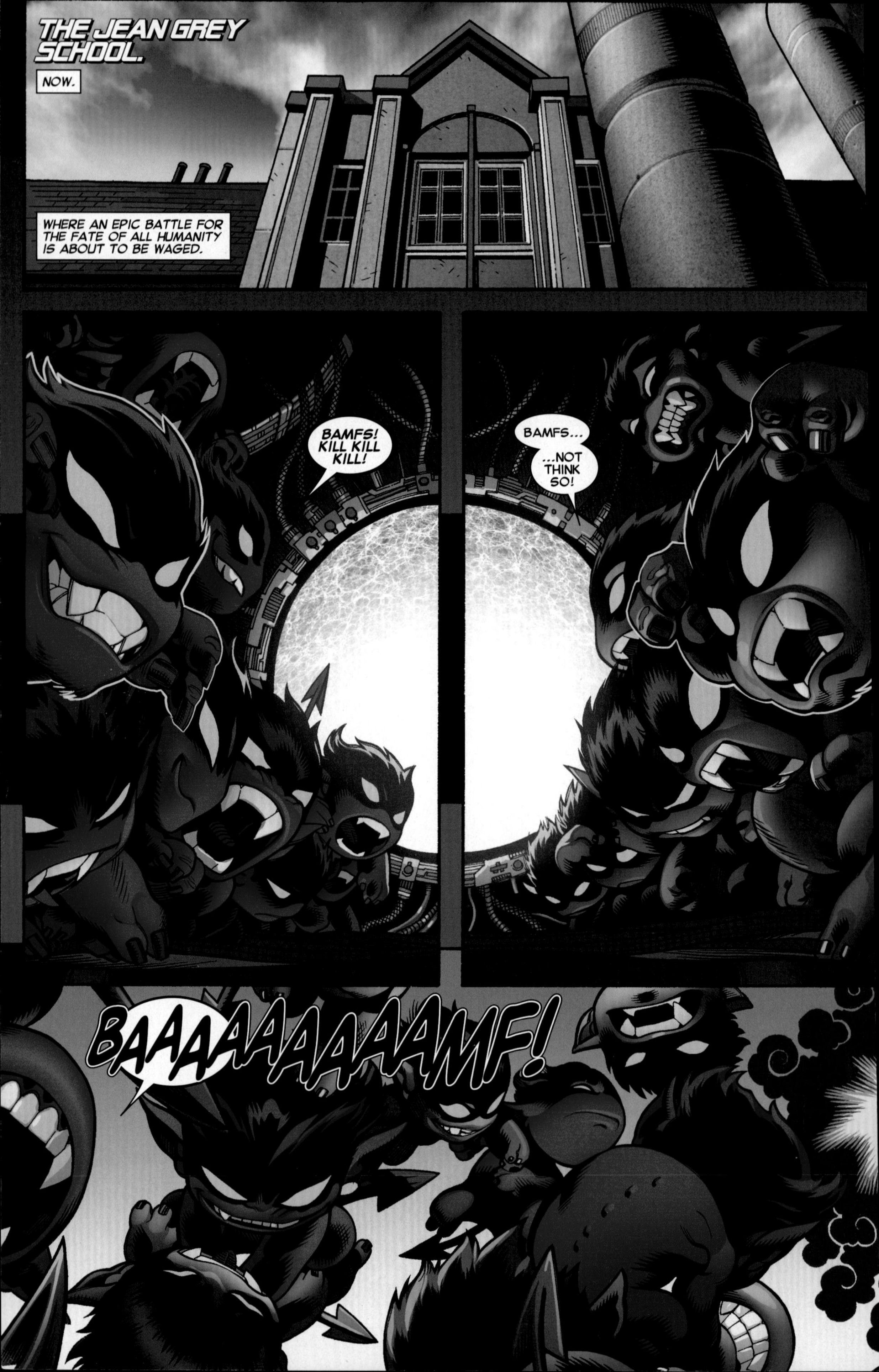
THE JEAN GREY SCHOOL.
NOW.
WHERE AN EPIC BATTLE FOR THE FATE OF ALL HUMANITY IS ABOUT TO BE WAGED.
BAMFS! KILL KILL KILL!
BAMFS...
...NOT THINK SO!
BAAAAAAAAAMF!

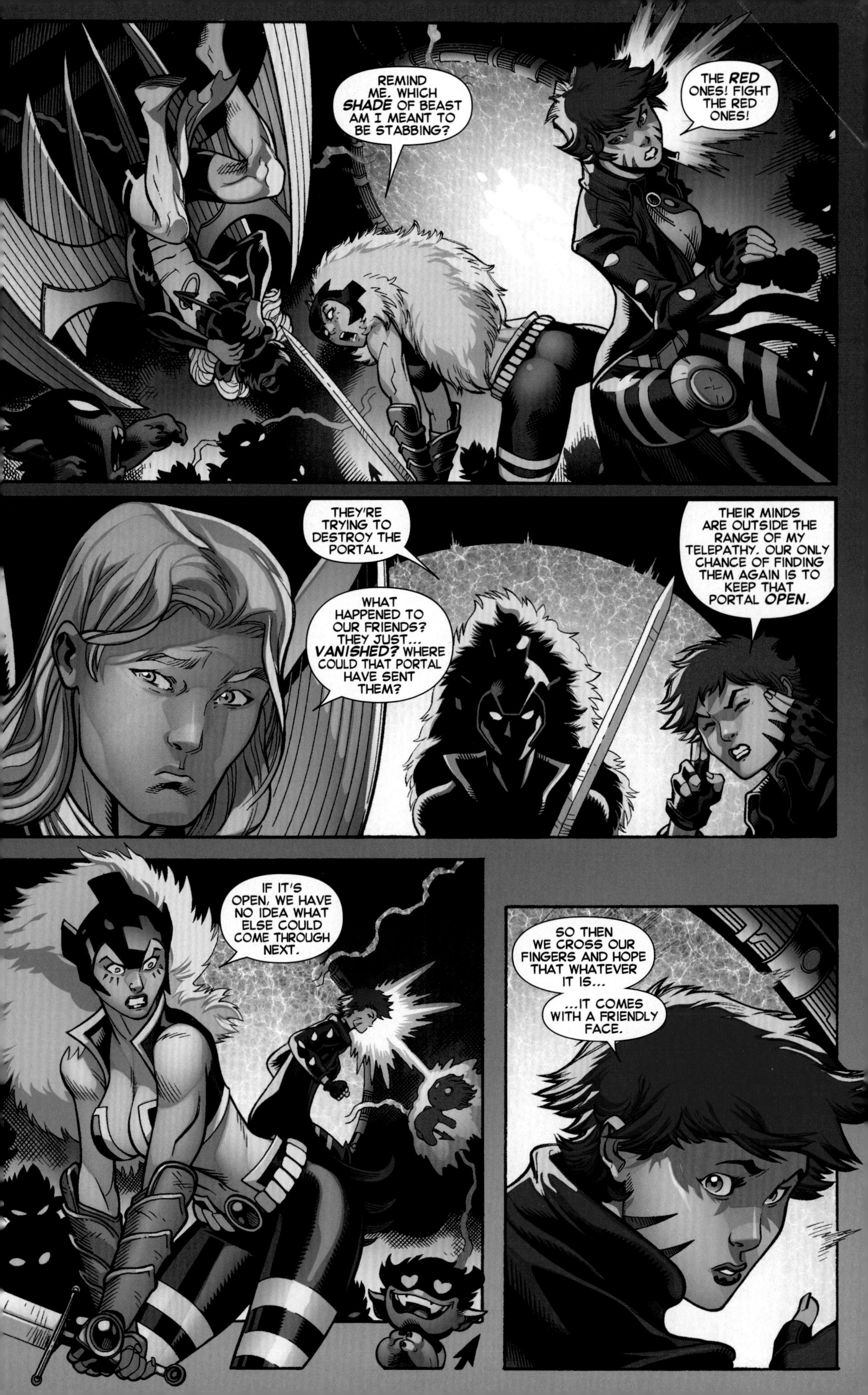

REMIND ME. WHICH SHADE OF BEAST AM I MEANT TO BE STABBING?
THE RED ONES! FIGHT THE RED ONES!
THEY'RE TRYING TO DESTROY THE PORTAL.
WHAT HAPPENED TO OUR FRIENDS? THEY JUST... VANISHED? WHERE COULD THAT PORTAL HAVE SENT THEM?
THEIR MINDS ARE OUTSIDE THE RANGE OF MY TELEPATHY. OUR ONLY CHANCE OF FINDING THEM AGAIN IS TO KEEP THAT PORTAL OPEN.
IF IT'S OPEN, WE HAVE NO IDEA WHAT ELSE COULD COME THROUGH NEXT.
SO THEN WE CROSS OUR FINGERS AND HOPE THAT WHATEVER IT IS...
...IT COMES WITH A FRIENDLY FACE.

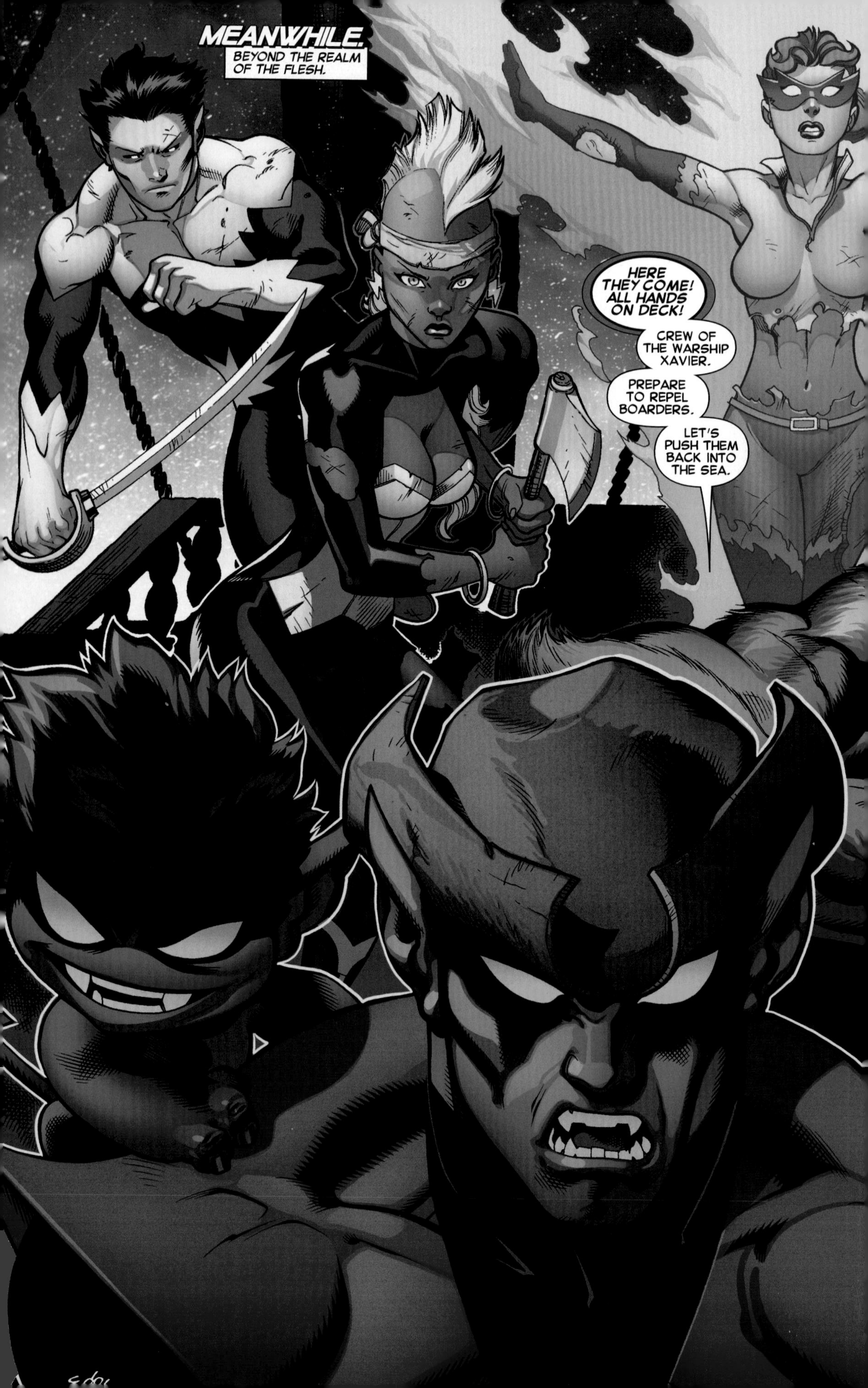
MEANWHILE.
BEYOND THE REALM OF THE FLESH.
HERE THEY COME! ALL HANDS ON DECK!
CREW OF THE WARSHIP XAVIER.
PREPARE TO REPEL BOARDERS.
LET'S PUSH THEM BACK INTO THE SEA.

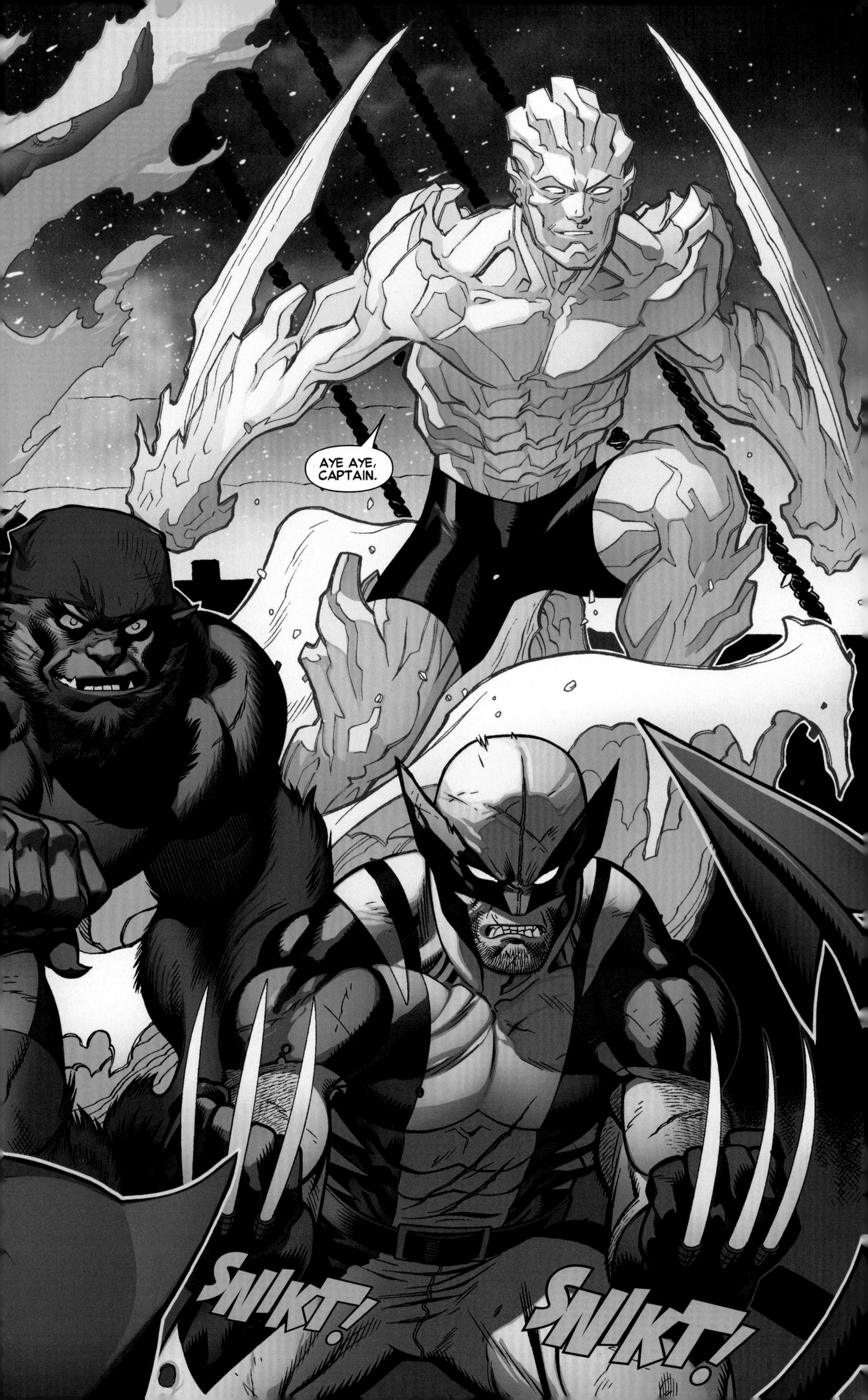
AYE AYE, CAPTAIN.
SNIKT!
SNIKT!

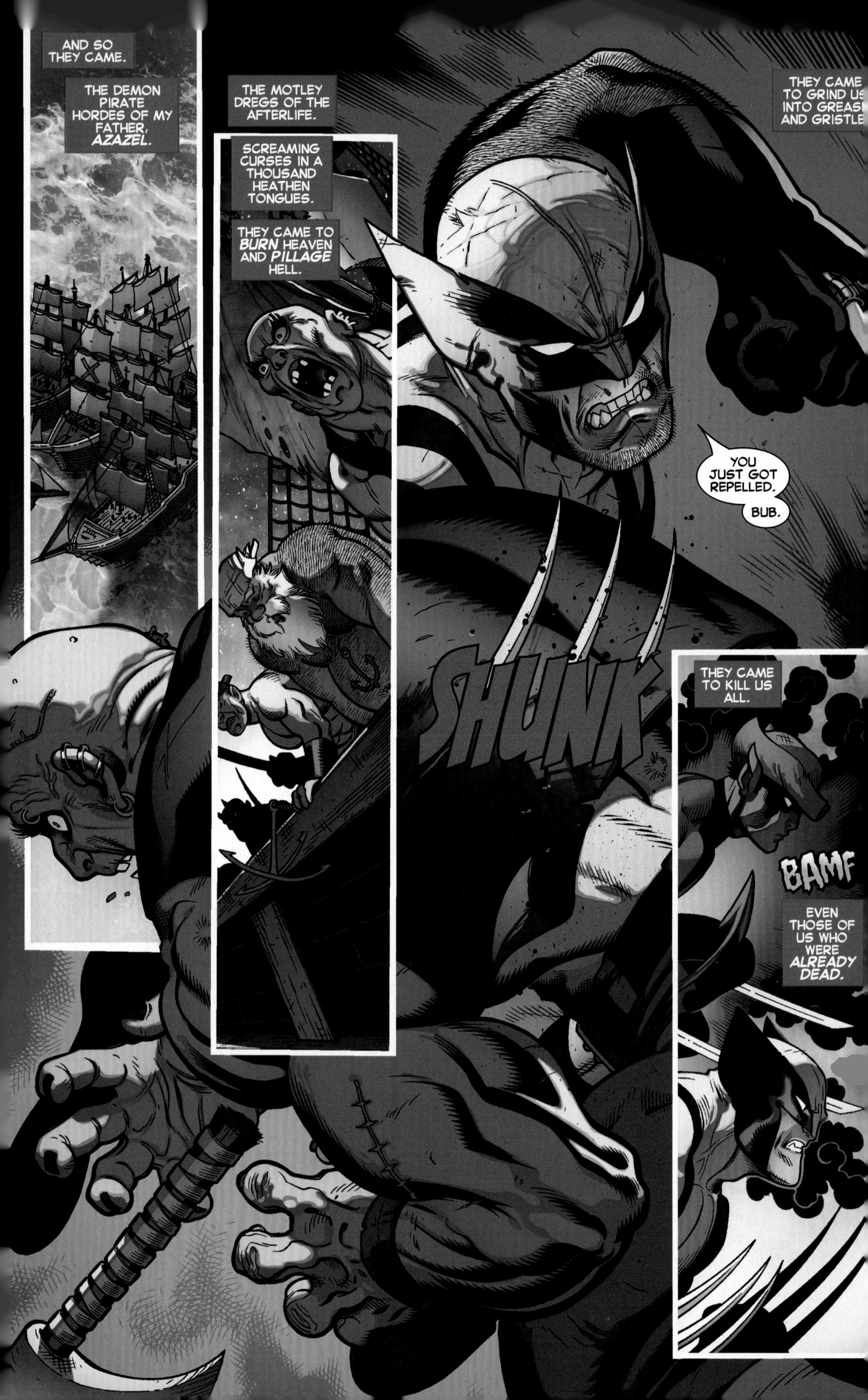

AND SO THEY CAME.
THE DEMON PIRATE HORDES OF MY FATHER, *AZAZEL*.
THE MOTLEY DREGS OF THE AFTERLIFE.
SCREAMING CURSES IN A THOUSAND HEATHEN TONGUES.
THEY CAME TO *BURN* HEAVEN AND *PILLAGE* HELL.
THEY CAME TO GRIND US INTO GREAS AND GRISTLE
YOU JUST GOT REPELLED.
BUB.
SHUNK
THEY CAME TO KILL US ALL.
BAMF
EVEN THOSE OF US WHO WERE *ALREADY DEAD*.

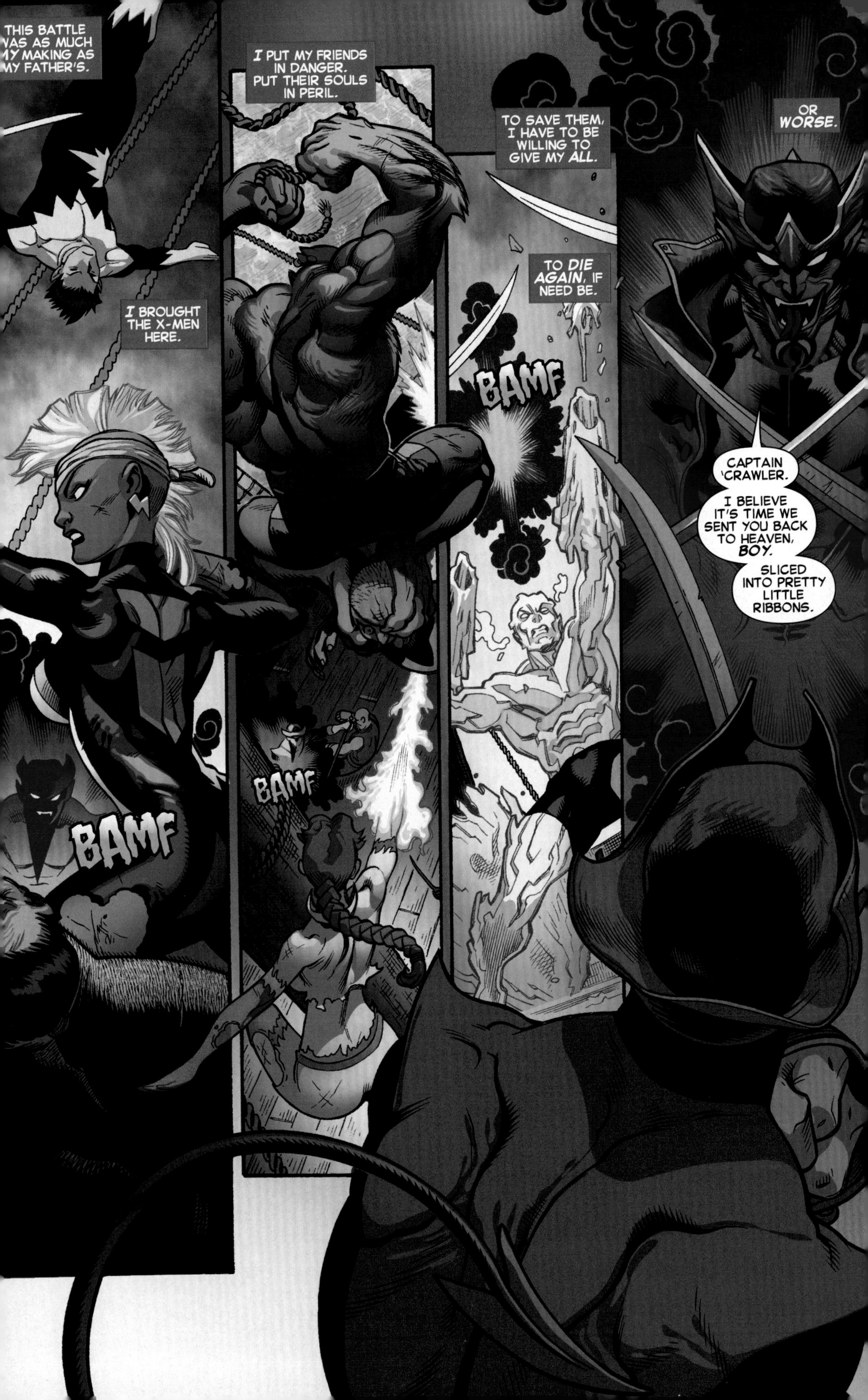
THIS BATTLE WAS AS MUCH MY MAKING AS MY FATHER'S.
I BROUGHT THE X-MEN HERE.
I PUT MY FRIENDS IN DANGER. PUT THEIR SOULS IN PERIL.
TO SAVE THEM, I HAVE TO BE WILLING TO GIVE MY ALL.
TO DIE AGAIN, IF NEED BE.
OR WORSE.
BAMF
BAMF
BAMF
CAPTAIN 'CRAWLER.
I BELIEVE IT'S TIME WE SENT YOU BACK TO HEAVEN, BOY.
SLICED INTO PRETTY LITTLE RIBBONS.

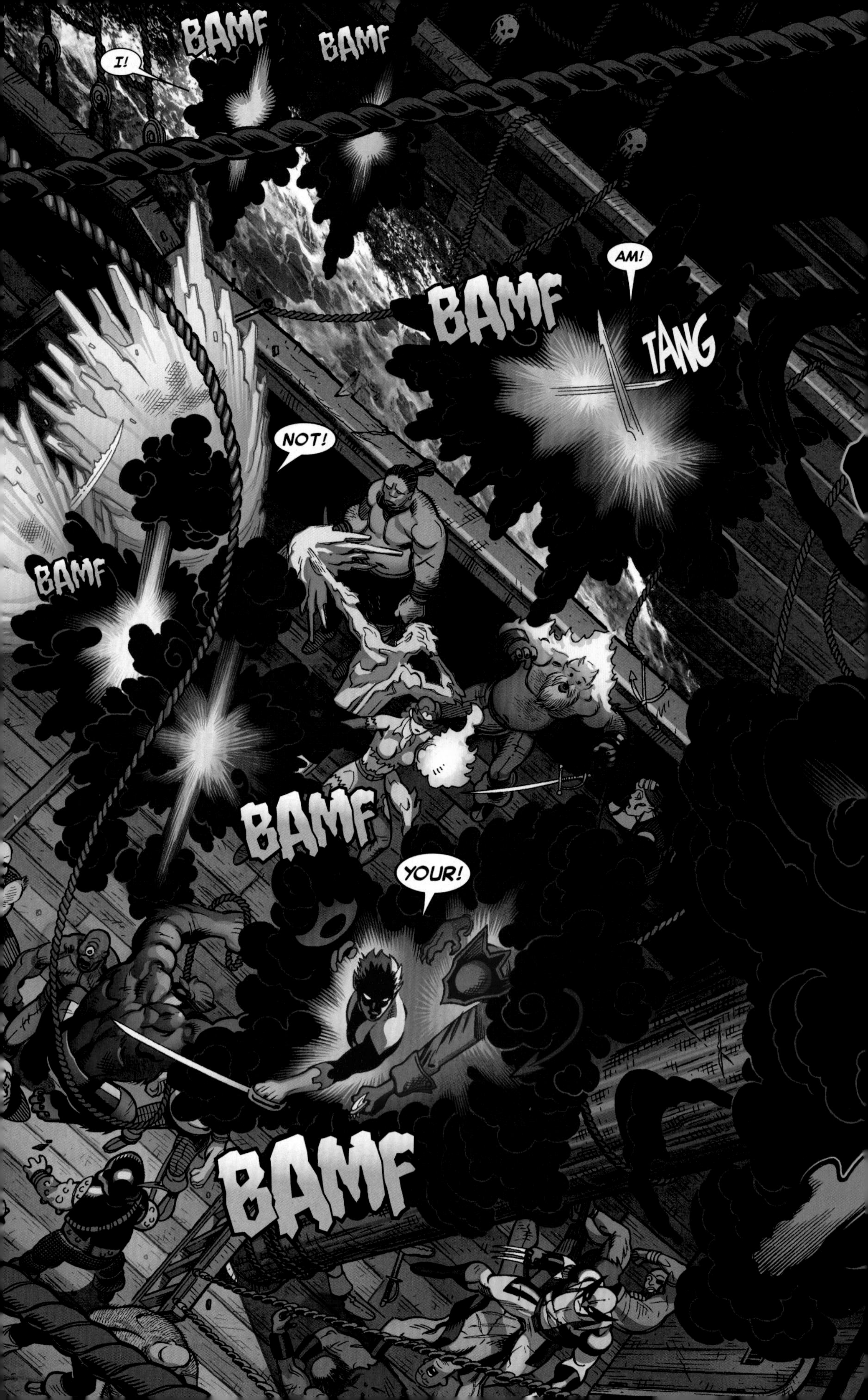
BAMF
BAMF
I!
BAMF
AM!
TANG
NOT!
BAMF
BAMF
YOUR!
BAMF

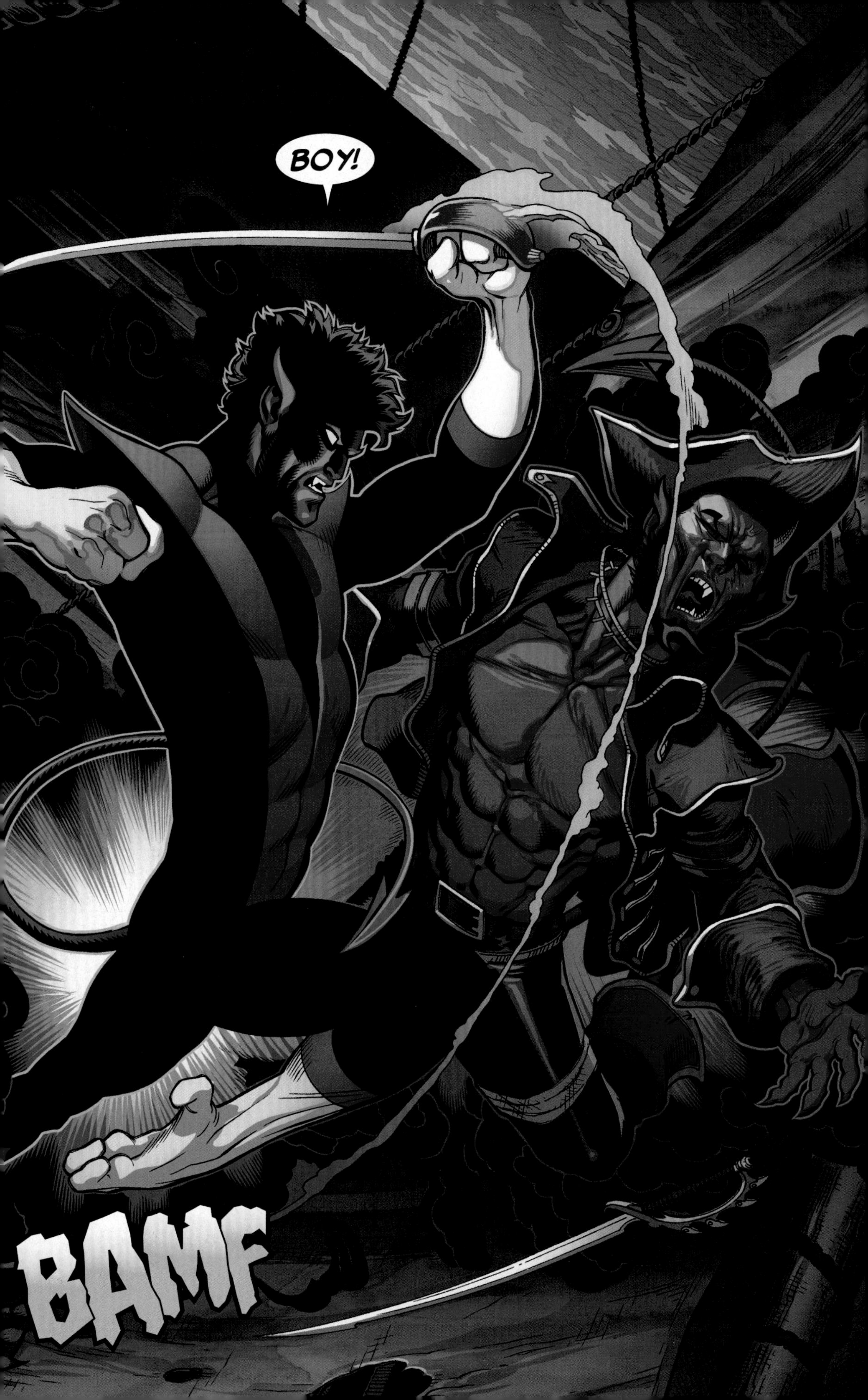
BOY!
BAMF

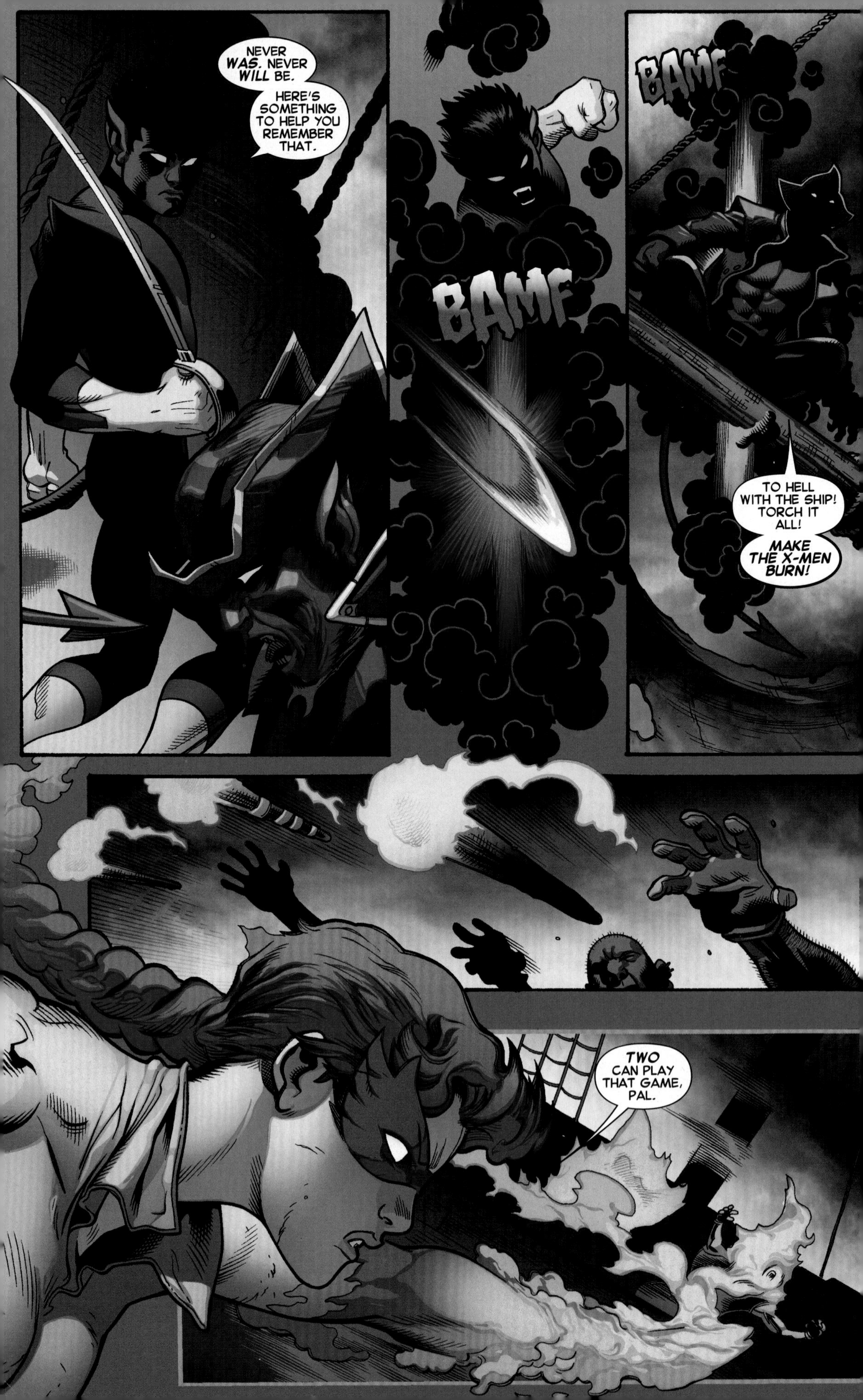
NEVER WAS. NEVER WILL BE.
HERE'S SOMETHING TO HELP YOU REMEMBER THAT.
BAMF
BAMF
TO HELL WITH THE SHIP! TORCH IT ALL!
MAKE THE X-MEN BURN!
TWO CAN PLAY THAT GAME, PAL.

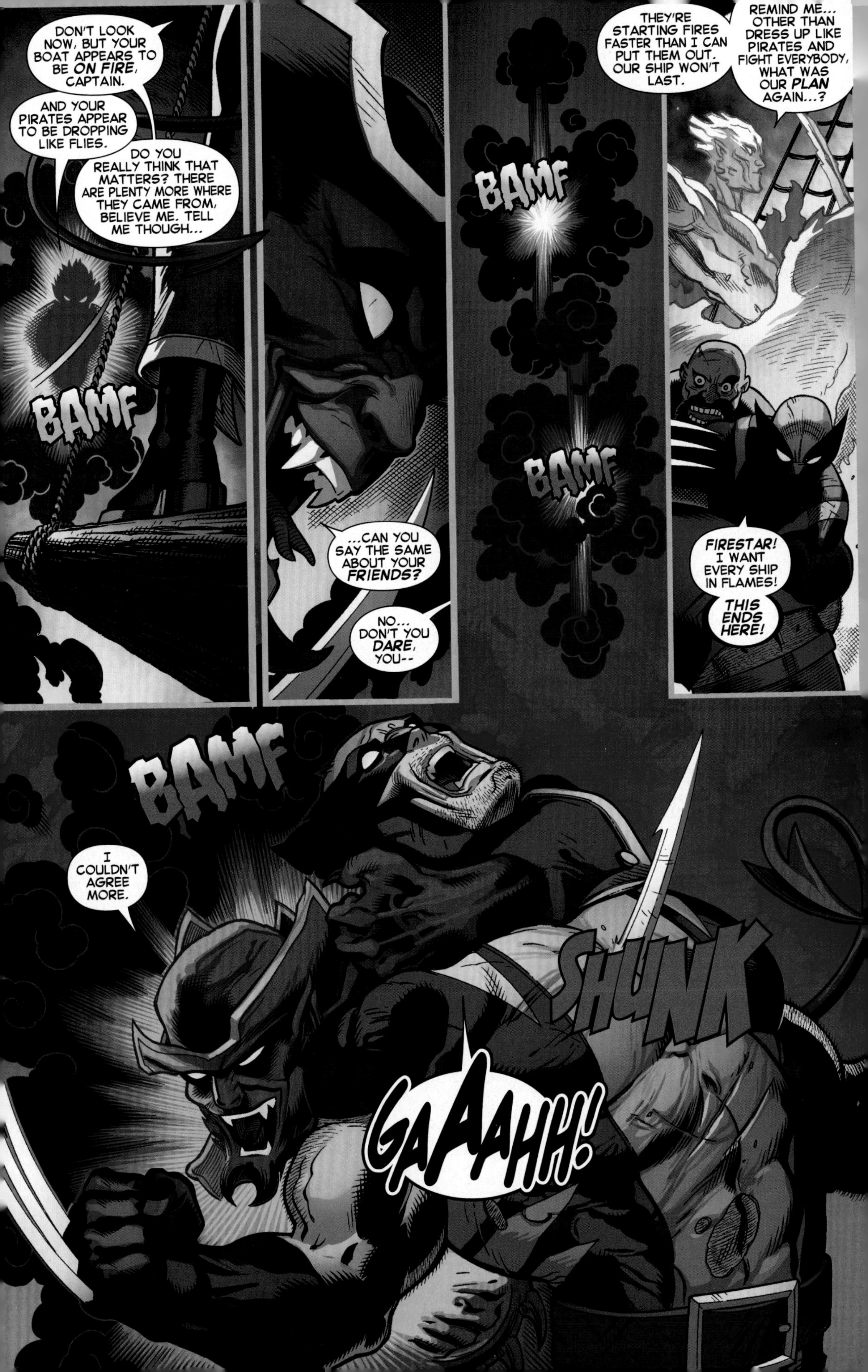

DON'T LOOK NOW, BUT YOUR BOAT APPEARS TO BE ON FIRE, CAPTAIN.
AND YOUR PIRATES APPEAR TO BE DROPPING LIKE FLIES.
DO YOU REALLY THINK THAT MATTERS? THERE ARE PLENTY MORE WHERE THEY CAME FROM, BELIEVE ME. TELL ME THOUGH...
BAMF
...CAN YOU SAY THE SAME ABOUT YOUR FRIENDS?
NO... DON'T YOU DARE, YOU--
BAMF
BAMF
THEY'RE STARTING FIRES FASTER THAN I CAN PUT THEM OUT. OUR SHIP WON'T LAST.
REMIND ME... OTHER THAN DRESS UP LIKE PIRATES AND FIGHT EVERYBODY, WHAT WAS OUR PLAN AGAIN...?
FIRESTAR! I WANT EVERY SHIP IN FLAMES!
THIS ENDS HERE!
BAMF
I COULDN'T AGREE MORE.
SHUNK
GAAAHH!

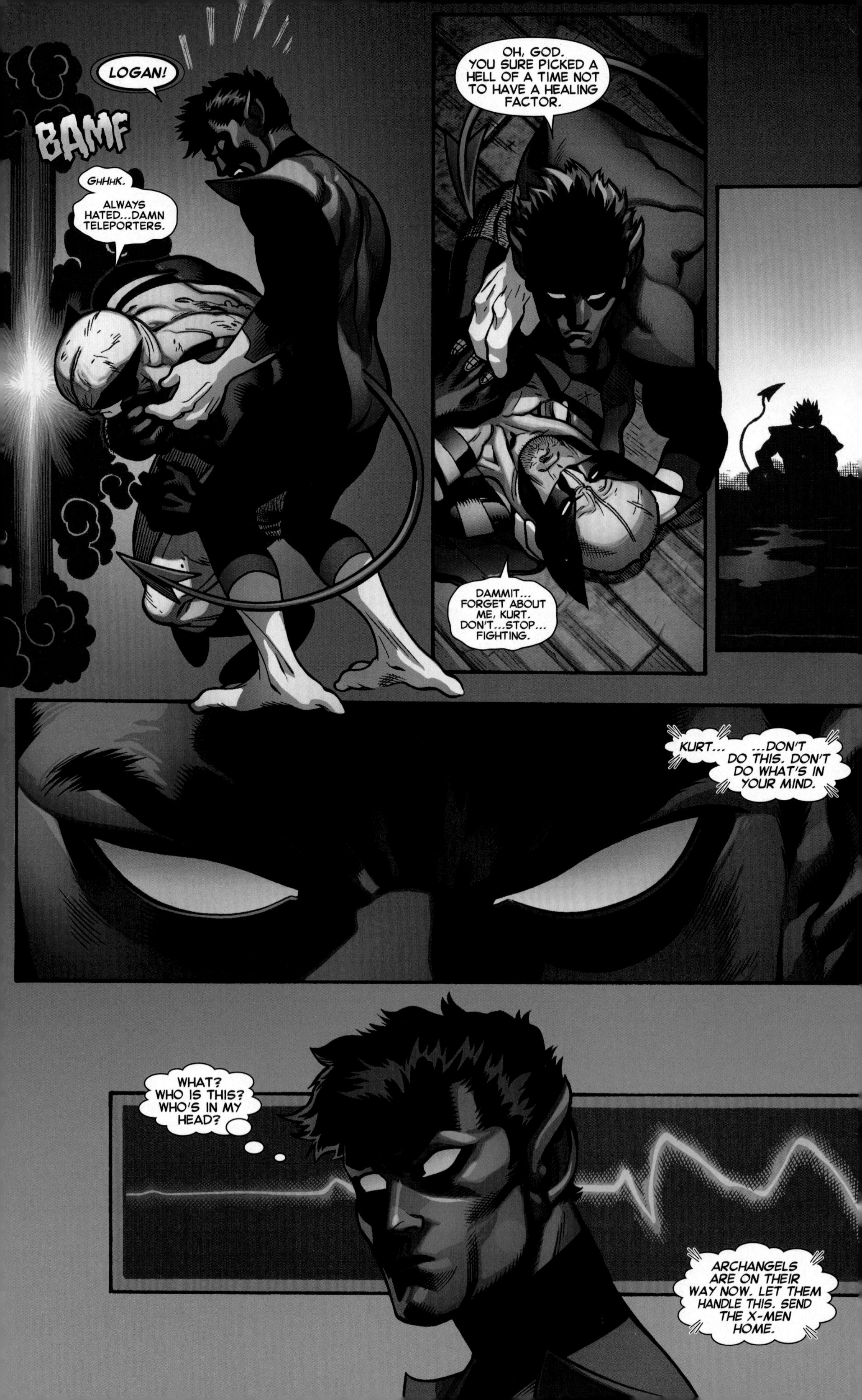
LOGAN!
BAMF
GHHHK.
ALWAYS HATED...DAMN TELEPORTERS.
OH, GOD. YOU SURE PICKED A HELL OF A TIME NOT TO HAVE A HEALING FACTOR.
DAMMIT... FORGET ABOUT ME, KURT. DON'T...STOP... FIGHTING.
KURT...
...DON'T DO THIS. DON'T DO WHAT'S IN YOUR MIND.
WHAT? WHO IS THIS? WHO'S IN MY HEAD?
ARCHANGELS ARE ON THEIR WAY NOW. LET THEM HANDLE THIS. SEND THE X-MEN HOME.

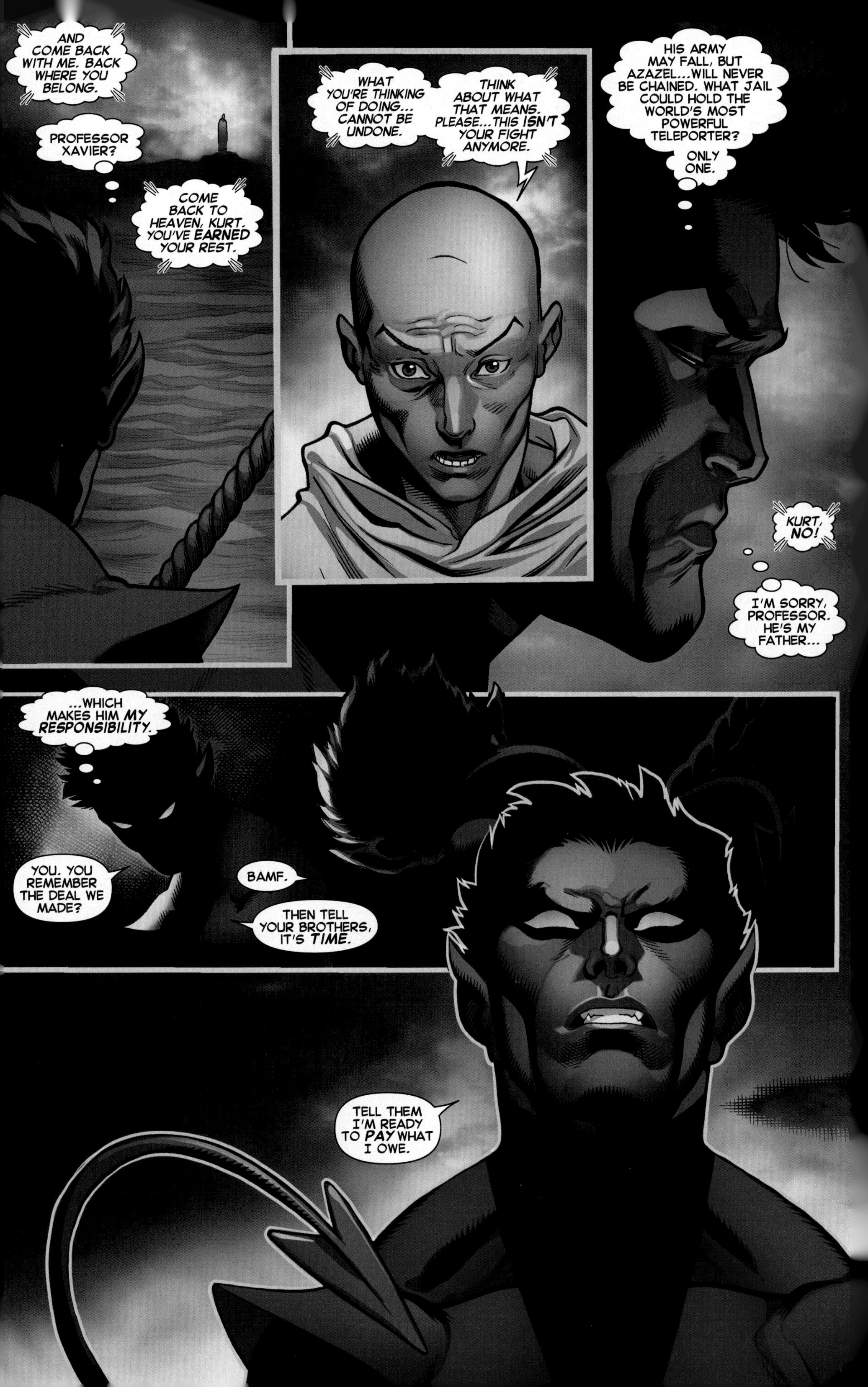
AND COME BACK WITH ME. BACK WHERE YOU BELONG.
PROFESSOR XAVIER?
COME BACK TO HEAVEN, KURT. YOU'VE EARNED YOUR REST.
WHAT YOU'RE THINKING OF DOING... CANNOT BE UNDONE.
THINK ABOUT WHAT THAT MEANS. PLEASE...THIS ISN'T YOUR FIGHT ANYMORE.
HIS ARMY MAY FALL, BUT AZAZEL...WILL NEVER BE CHAINED. WHAT JAIL COULD HOLD THE WORLD'S MOST POWERFUL TELEPORTER?
ONLY ONE.
KURT, NO!
I'M SORRY, PROFESSOR. HE'S MY FATHER...
...WHICH MAKES HIM MY RESPONSIBILITY.
YOU. YOU REMEMBER THE DEAL WE MADE?
BAMF.
THEN TELL YOUR BROTHERS, IT'S TIME.
TELL THEM I'M READY TO PAY WHAT I OWE.

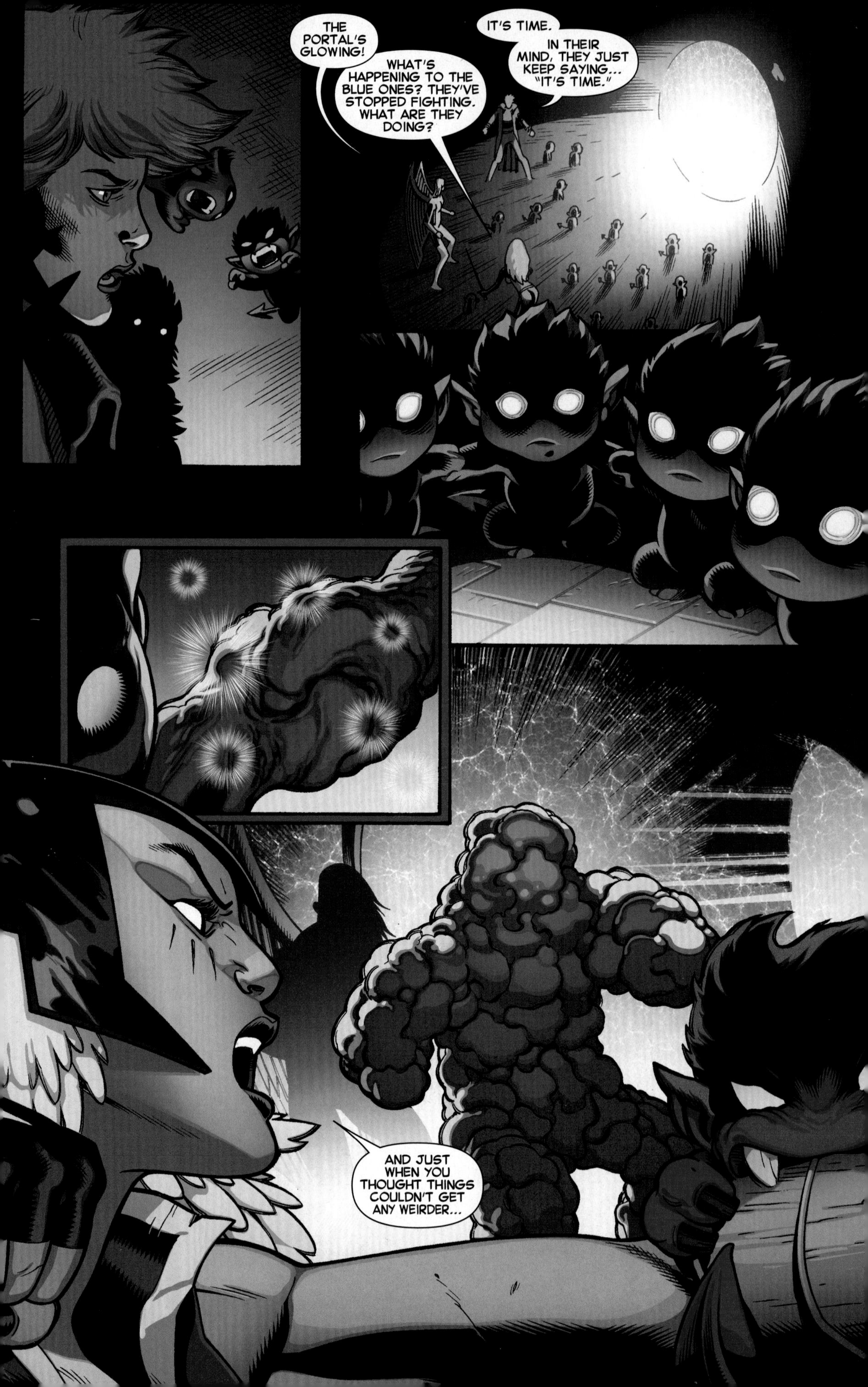
THE PORTAL'S GLOWING!
WHAT'S HAPPENING TO THE BLUE ONES? THEY'VE STOPPED FIGHTING. WHAT ARE THEY DOING?
IT'S TIME.
IN THEIR MIND, THEY JUST KEEP SAYING... "IT'S TIME."
AND JUST WHEN YOU THOUGHT THINGS COULDN'T GET ANY WEIRDER...

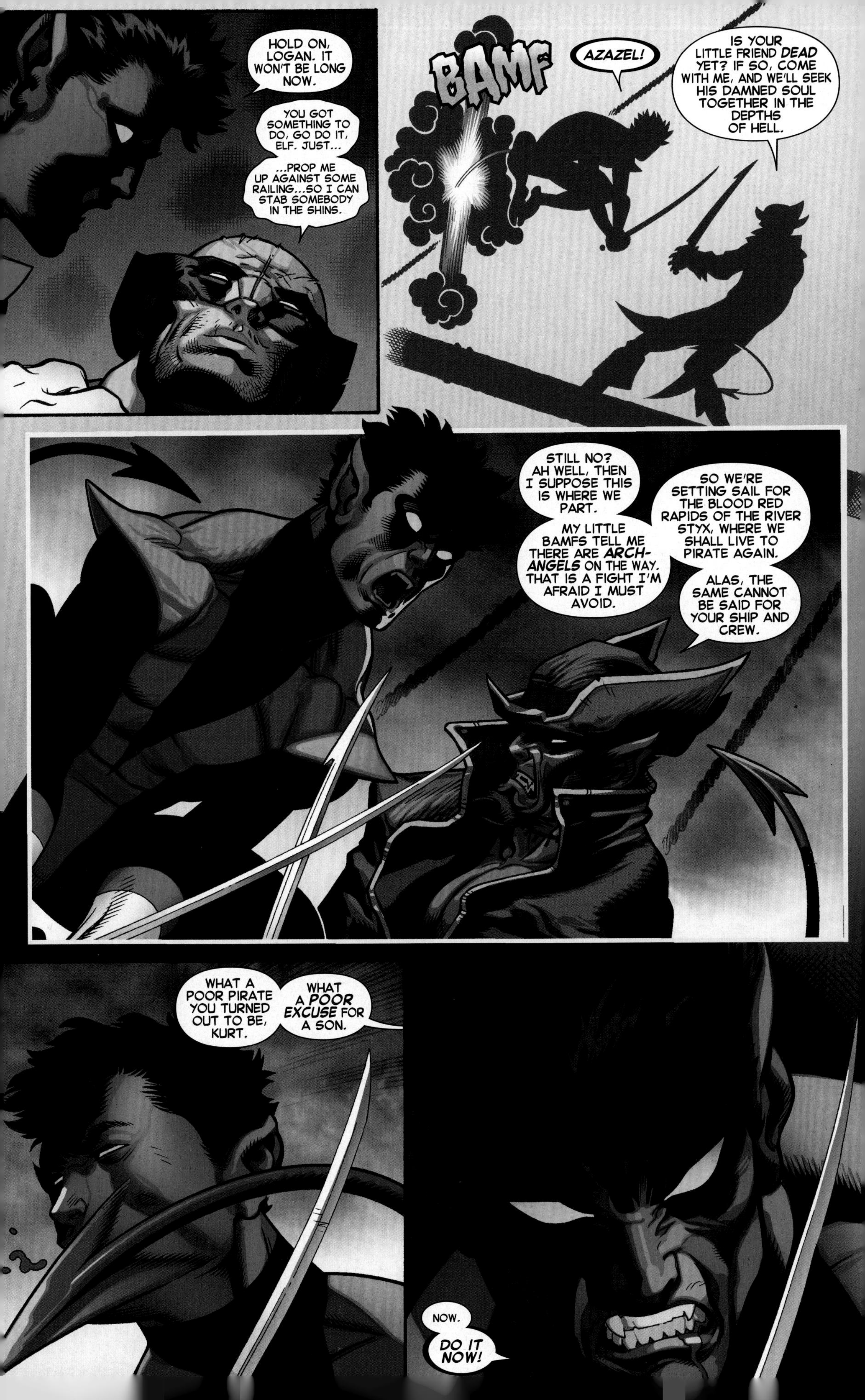
HOLD ON, LOGAN. IT WON'T BE LONG NOW.
YOU GOT SOMETHING TO DO, GO DO IT, ELF. JUST...
...PROP ME UP AGAINST SOME RAILING...SO I CAN STAB SOMEBODY IN THE SHINS.
BAMF
AZAZEL!
IS YOUR LITTLE FRIEND DEAD YET? IF SO, COME WITH ME, AND WE'LL SEEK HIS DAMNED SOUL TOGETHER IN THE DEPTHS OF HELL.
STILL NO? AH WELL, THEN I SUPPOSE THIS IS WHERE WE PART.
MY LITTLE BAMFS TELL ME THERE ARE ARCH-ANGELS ON THE WAY. THAT IS A FIGHT I'M AFRAID I MUST AVOID.
SO WE'RE SETTING SAIL FOR THE BLOOD RED RAPIDS OF THE RIVER STYX, WHERE WE SHALL LIVE TO PIRATE AGAIN.
ALAS, THE SAME CANNOT BE SAID FOR YOUR SHIP AND CREW.
WHAT A POOR PIRATE YOU TURNED OUT TO BE, KURT.
WHAT A POOR EXCUSE FOR A SON.
NOW.
DO IT NOW!

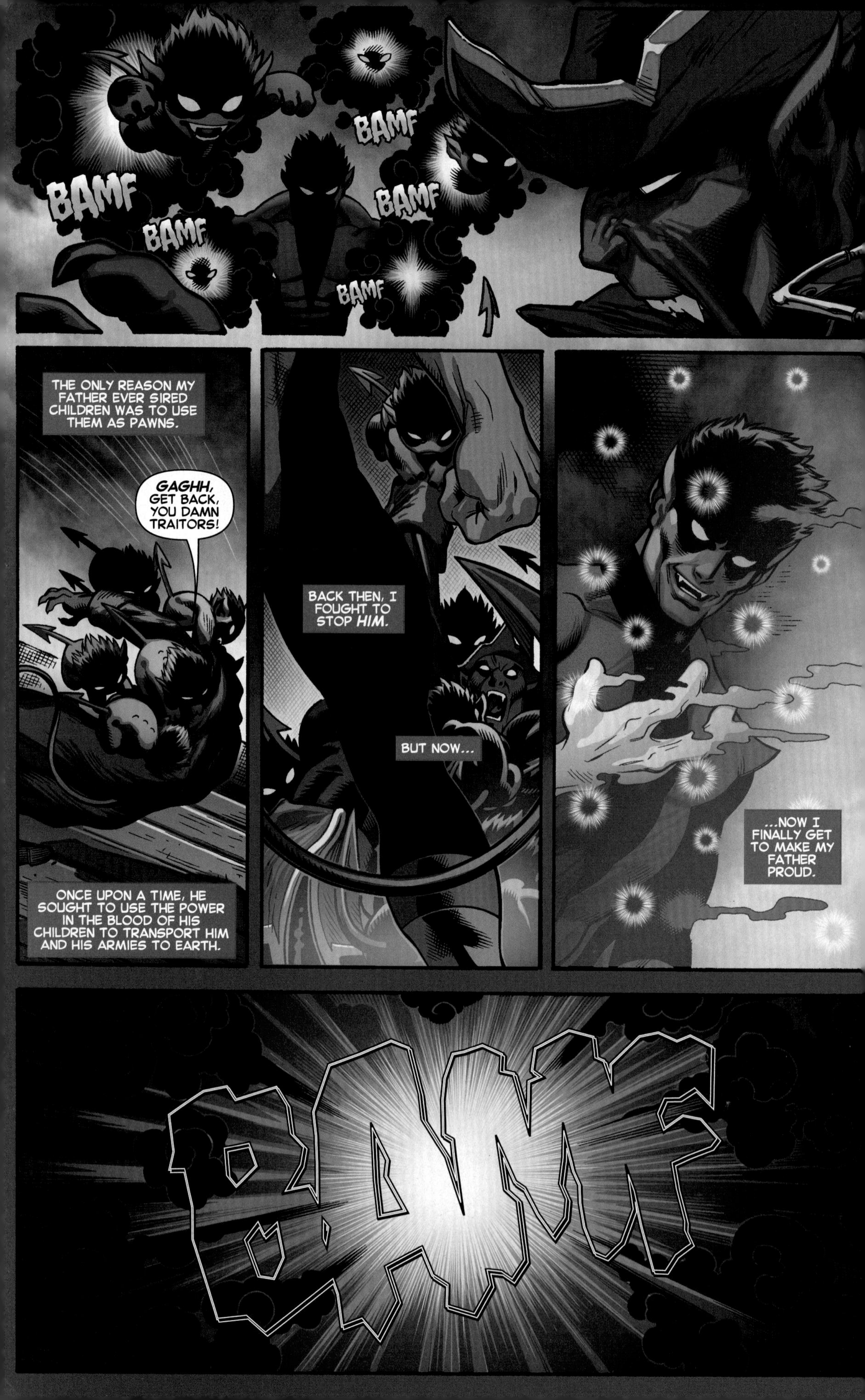

BAMF
BAMF
BAMF
BAMF
BAMF
BAMF
THE ONLY REASON MY FATHER EVER SIRED CHILDREN WAS TO USE THEM AS PAWNS.
GAGHH, GET BACK, YOU DAMN TRAITORS!
ONCE UPON A TIME, HE SOUGHT TO USE THE POWER IN THE BLOOD OF HIS CHILDREN TO TRANSPORT HIM AND HIS ARMIES TO EARTH.
BACK THEN, I FOUGHT TO STOP HIM.
BUT NOW...
...NOW I FINALLY GET TO MAKE MY FATHER PROUD.
BAMF

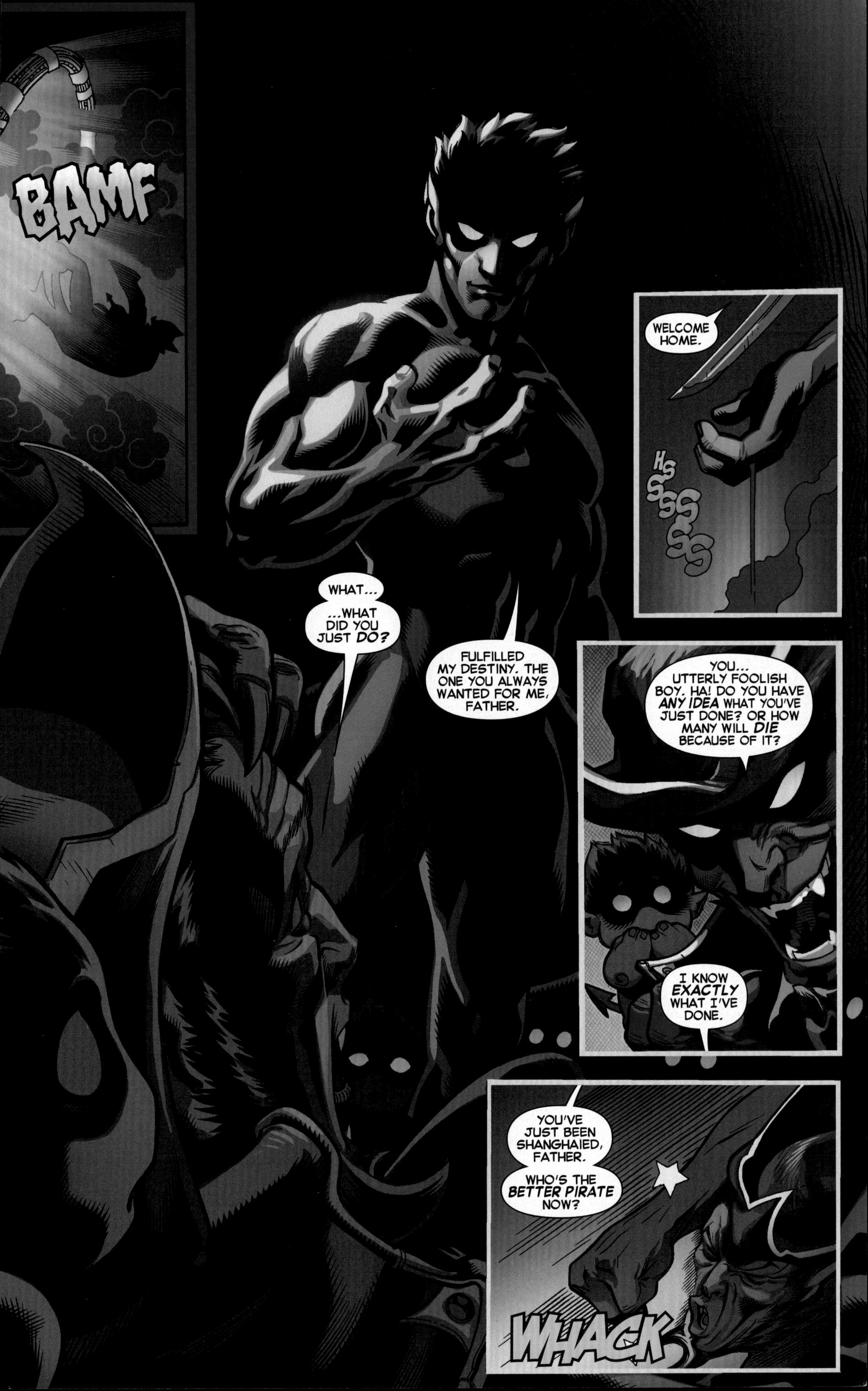
BAMF
WHAT...
...WHAT DID YOU JUST DO?
FULFILLED MY DESTINY. THE ONE YOU ALWAYS WANTED FOR ME, FATHER.
WELCOME HOME.
HSSSSSS
YOU... UTTERLY FOOLISH BOY. HA! DO YOU HAVE ANY IDEA WHAT YOU'VE JUST DONE? OR HOW MANY WILL DIE BECAUSE OF IT?
I KNOW EXACTLY WHAT I'VE DONE.
YOU'VE JUST BEEN SHANGHAIED, FATHER.
WHO'S THE BETTER PIRATE NOW?
WHACK

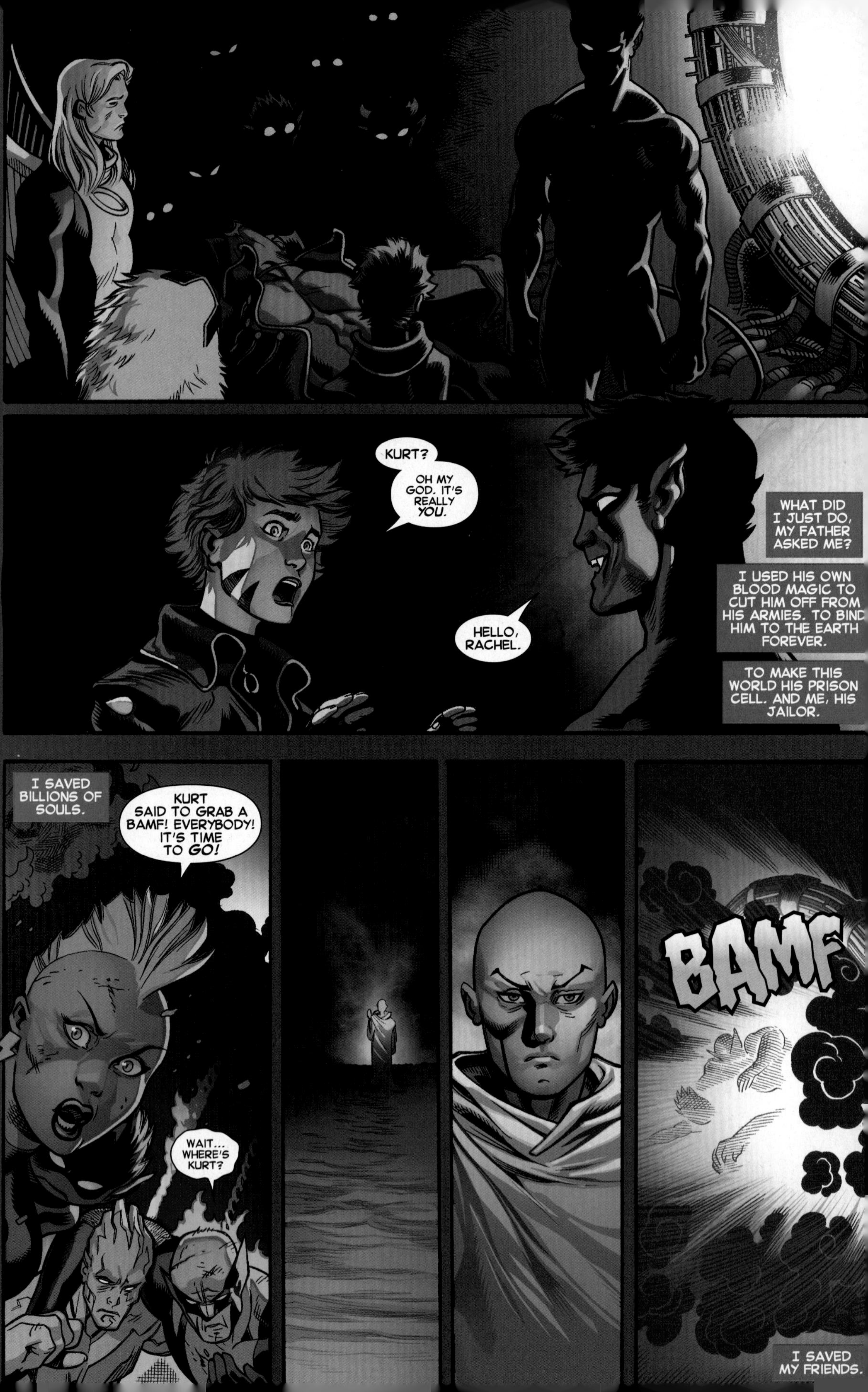
KURT?
OH MY GOD. IT'S REALLY YOU.
HELLO, RACHEL.
WHAT DID I JUST DO, MY FATHER ASKED ME?
I USED HIS OWN BLOOD MAGIC TO CUT HIM OFF FROM HIS ARMIES. TO BIND HIM TO THE EARTH FOREVER.
TO MAKE THIS WORLD HIS PRISON CELL. AND ME, HIS JAILOR.
I SAVED BILLIONS OF SOULS.
KURT SAID TO GRAB A BAMF! EVERYBODY! IT'S TIME TO GO!
WAIT... WHERE'S KURT?
BAMF
I SAVED MY FRIENDS.

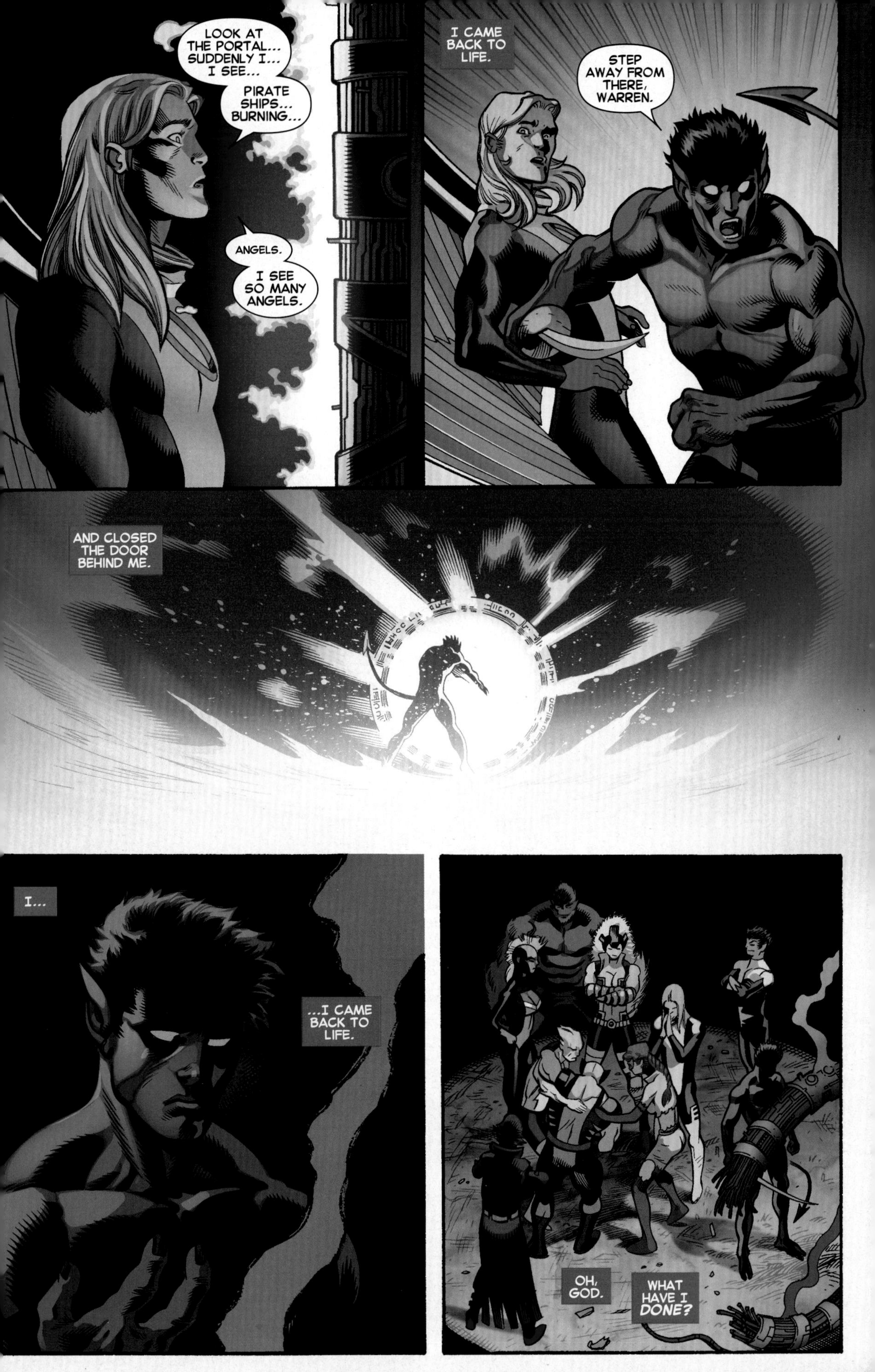

LOOK AT THE PORTAL... SUDDENLY I... I SEE...
PIRATE SHIPS... BURNING...
ANGELS.
I SEE SO MANY ANGELS.
I CAME BACK TO LIFE.
STEP AWAY FROM THERE, WARREN.
AND CLOSED THE DOOR BEHIND ME.
I...
...I CAME BACK TO LIFE.
OH, GOD.
WHAT HAVE I DONE?

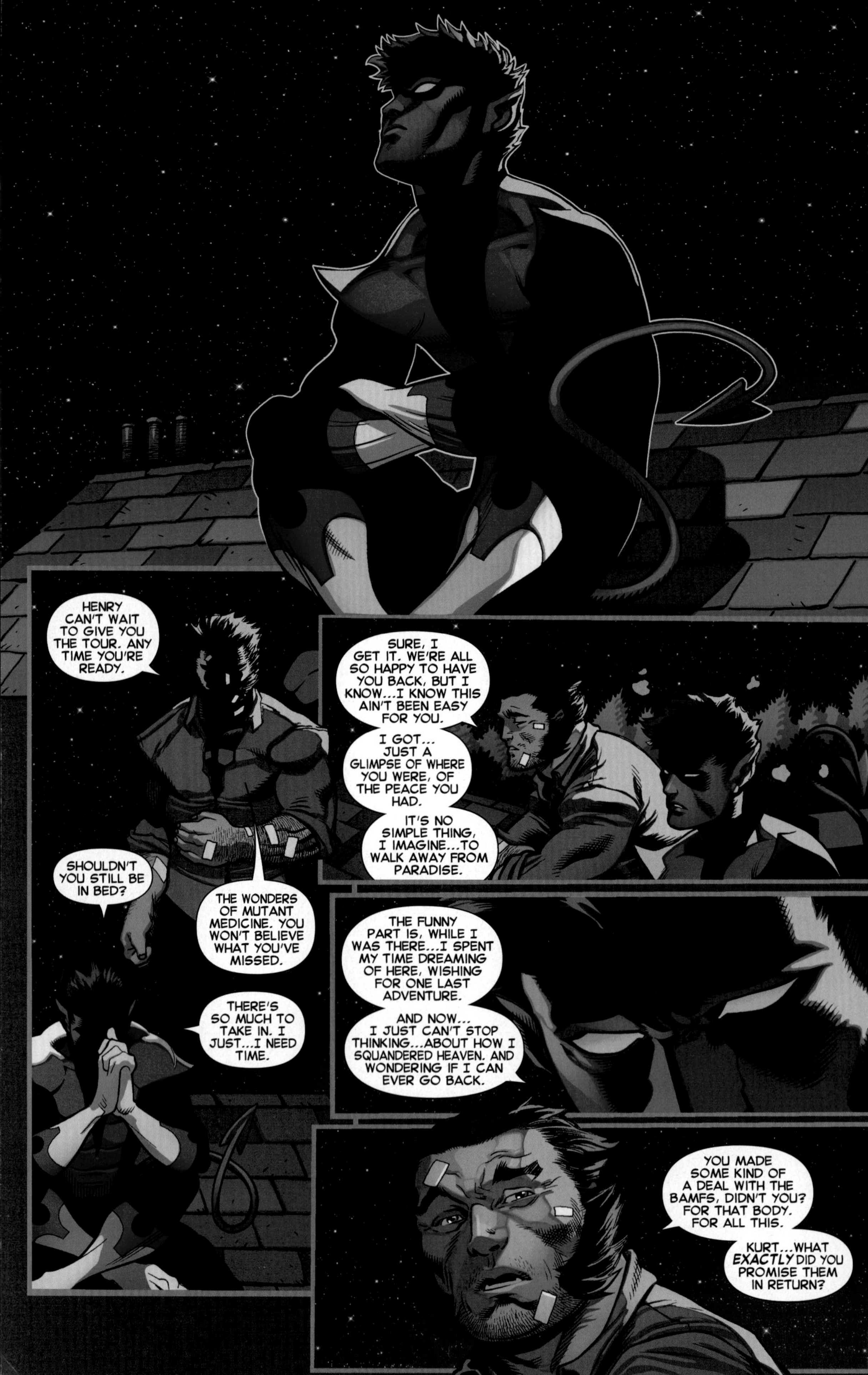
HENRY CAN'T WAIT TO GIVE YOU THE TOUR. ANY TIME YOU'RE READY.
SHOULDN'T YOU STILL BE IN BED?
THE WONDERS OF MUTANT MEDICINE. YOU WON'T BELIEVE WHAT YOU'VE MISSED.
THERE'S SO MUCH TO TAKE IN. I JUST...I NEED TIME.
SURE, I GET IT. WE'RE ALL SO HAPPY TO HAVE YOU BACK, BUT I KNOW...I KNOW THIS AIN'T BEEN EASY FOR YOU.
I GOT... JUST A GLIMPSE OF WHERE YOU WERE, OF THE PEACE YOU HAD.
IT'S NO SIMPLE THING, I IMAGINE...TO WALK AWAY FROM PARADISE.
THE FUNNY PART IS, WHILE I WAS THERE...I SPENT MY TIME DREAMING OF HERE, WISHING FOR ONE LAST ADVENTURE.
AND NOW... I JUST CAN'T STOP THINKING...ABOUT HOW I SQUANDERED HEAVEN. AND WONDERING IF I CAN EVER GO BACK.
YOU MADE SOME KIND OF A DEAL WITH THE BAMFS, DIDN'T YOU? FOR THAT BODY. FOR ALL THIS.
KURT...WHAT *EXACTLY* DID YOU PROMISE THEM IN RETURN?

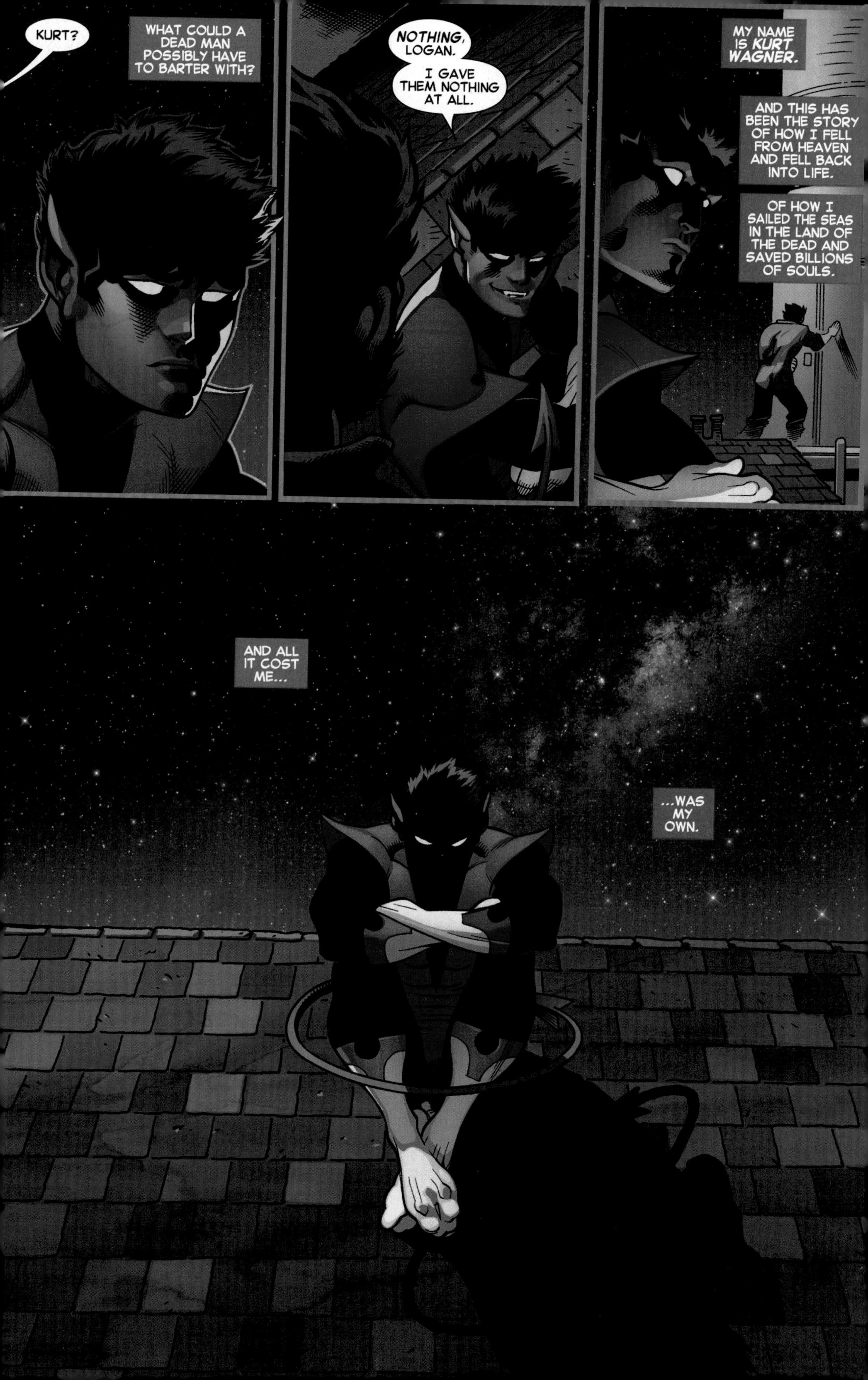
KURT?
WHAT COULD A DEAD MAN POSSIBLY HAVE TO BARTER WITH?
NOTHING, LOGAN.
I GAVE THEM NOTHING AT ALL.
MY NAME IS KURT WAGNER.
AND THIS HAS BEEN THE STORY OF HOW I FELL FROM HEAVEN AND FELL BACK INTO LIFE.
OF HOW I SAILED THE SEAS IN THE LAND OF THE DEAD AND SAVED BILLIONS OF SOULS.
AND ALL IT COST ME...
...WAS MY OWN.

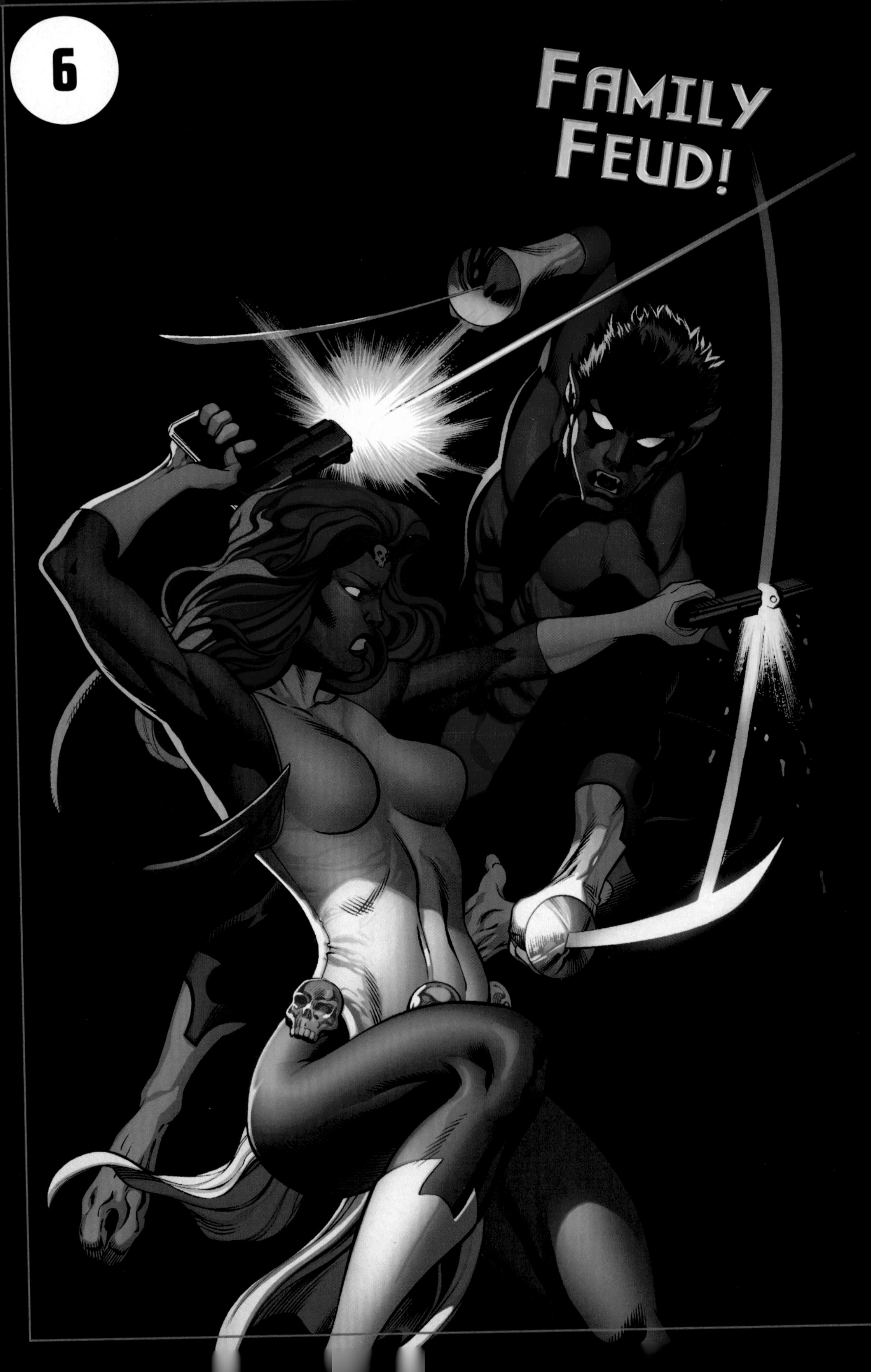
6
FAMILY FEUD!

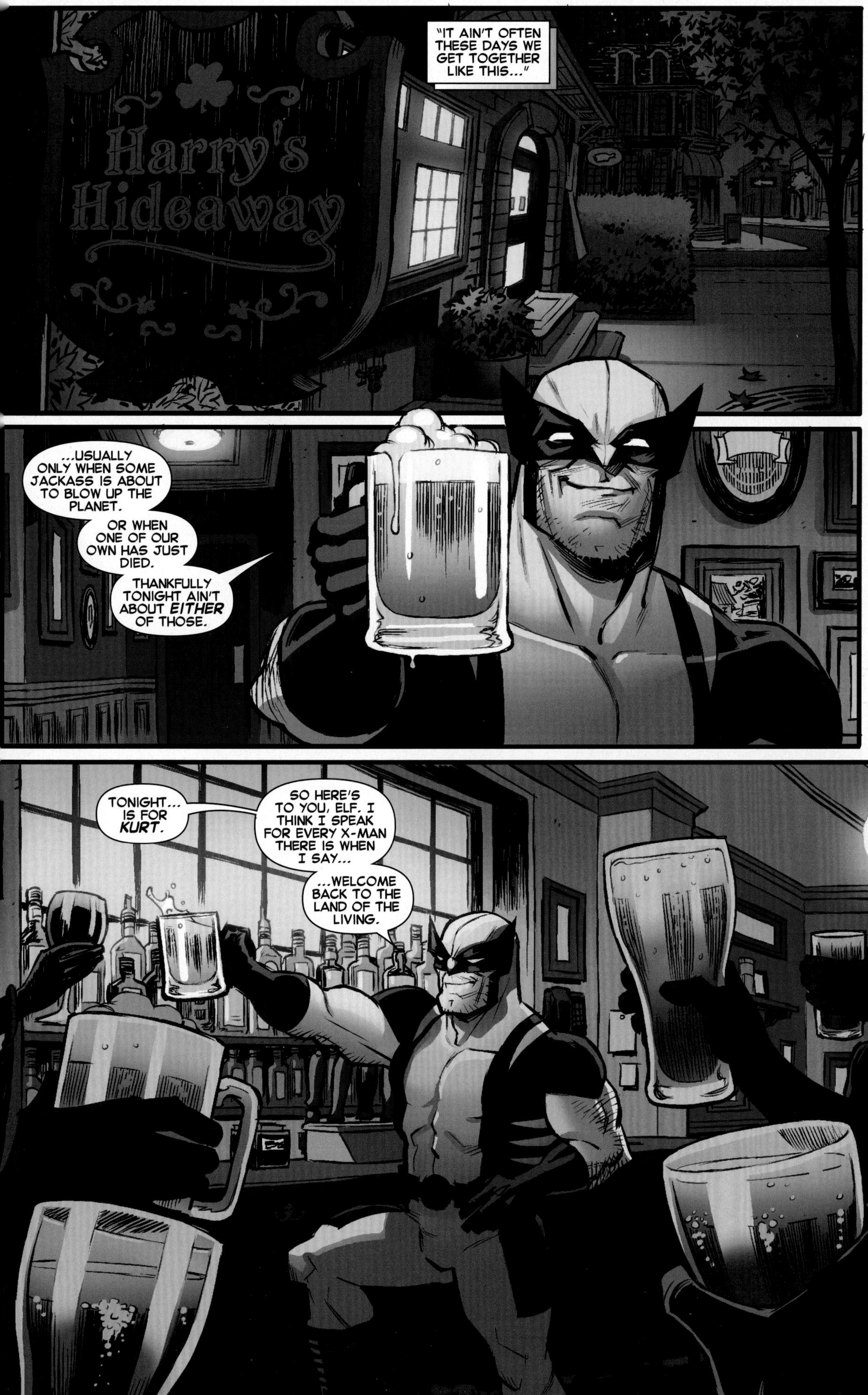

Harry's Hideaway
"IT AIN'T OFTEN THESE DAYS WE GET TOGETHER LIKE THIS..."
...USUALLY ONLY WHEN SOME JACKASS IS ABOUT TO BLOW UP THE PLANET.
OR WHEN ONE OF OUR OWN HAS JUST DIED.
THANKFULLY TONIGHT AIN'T ABOUT *EITHER* OF THOSE.
TONIGHT... IS FOR *KURT*.
SO HERE'S TO YOU, ELF. I THINK I SPEAK FOR EVERY X-MAN THERE IS WHEN I SAY...
...WELCOME BACK TO THE LAND OF THE LIVING.

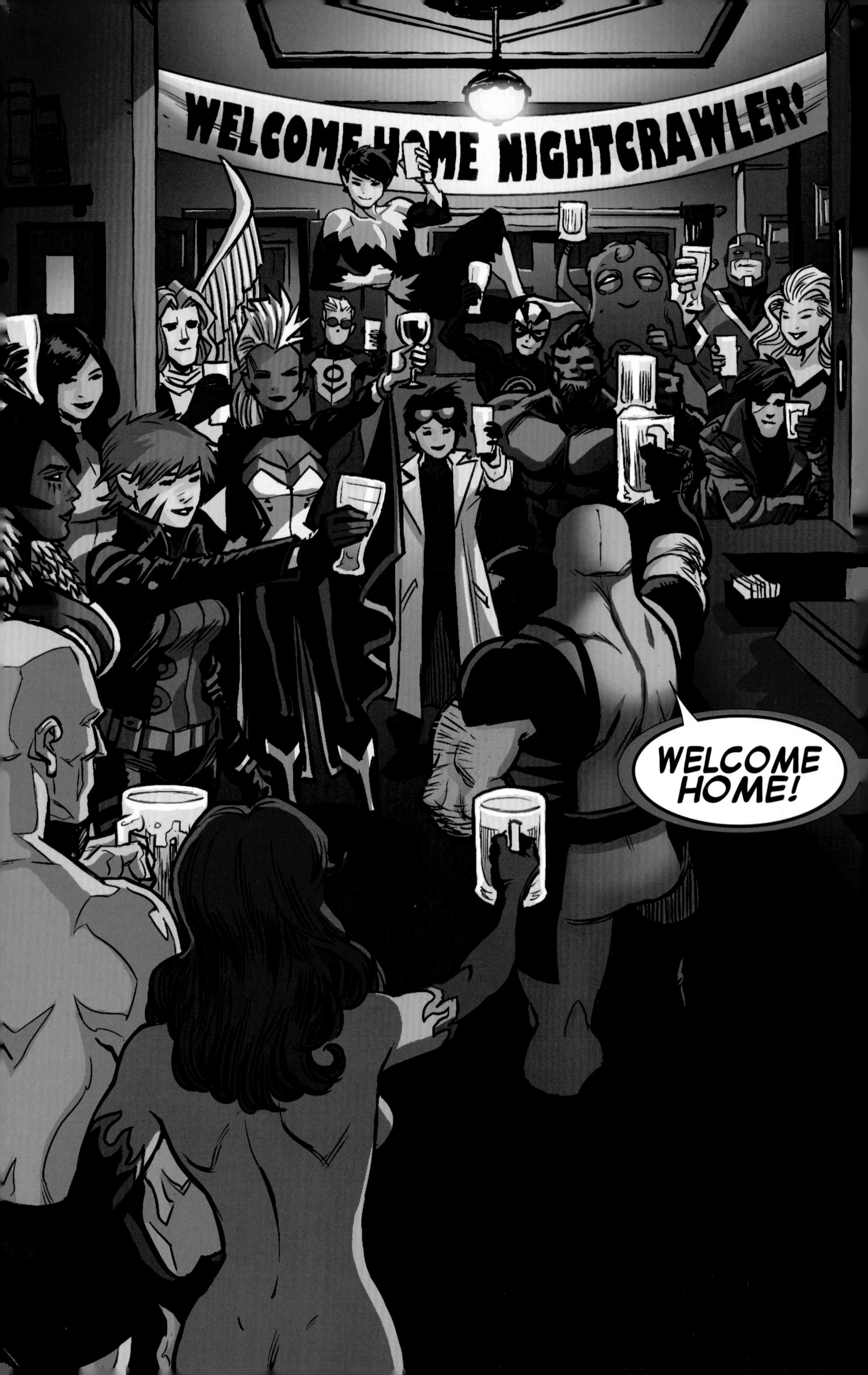
WELCOME HOME NIGHTCRAWLER!
WELCOME HOME!

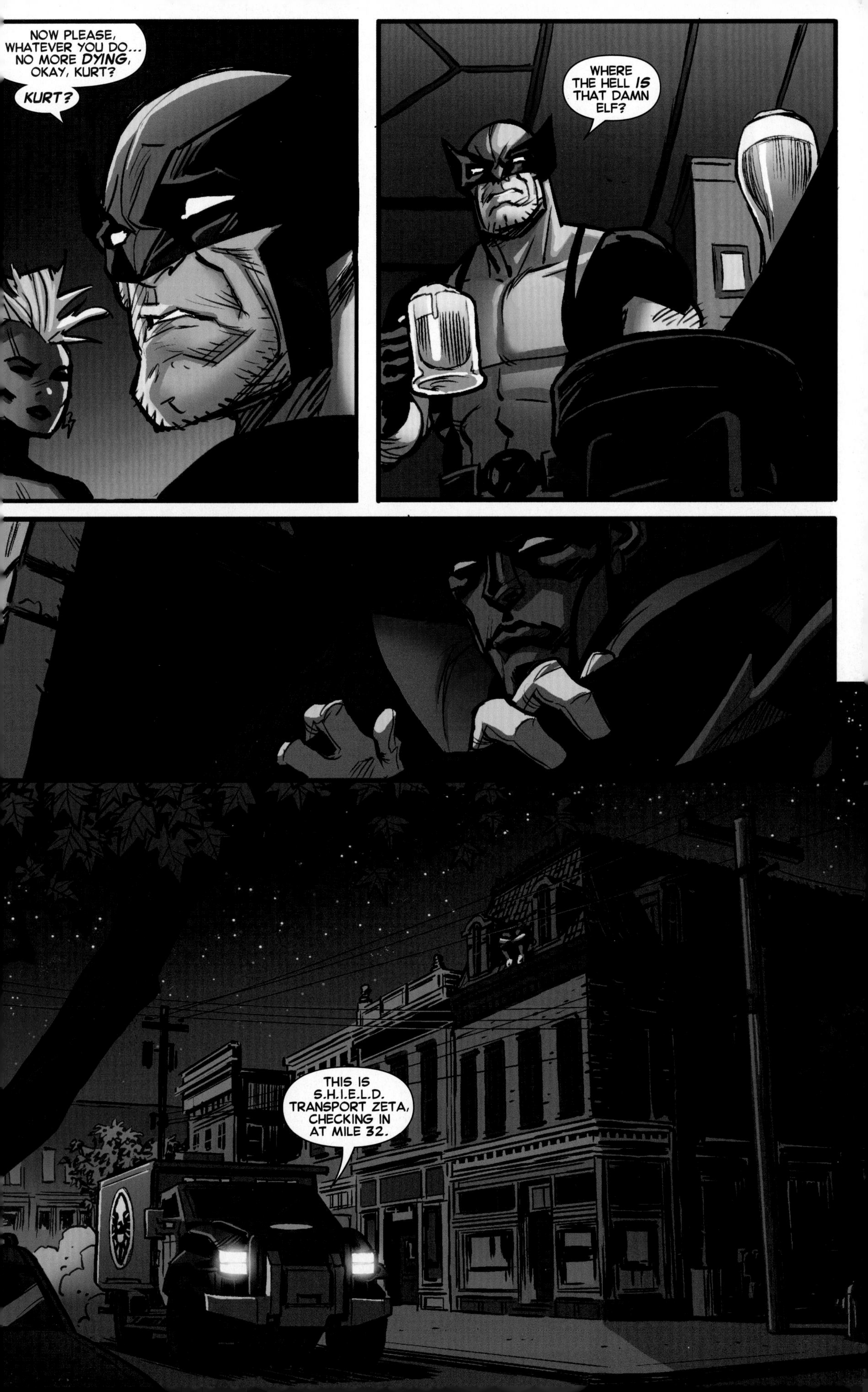
NOW PLEASE, WHATEVER YOU DO... NO MORE DYING, OKAY, KURT?
KURT?
WHERE THE HELL IS THAT DAMN ELF?
THIS IS S.H.I.E.L.D. TRANSPORT ZETA, CHECKING IN AT MILE 32.

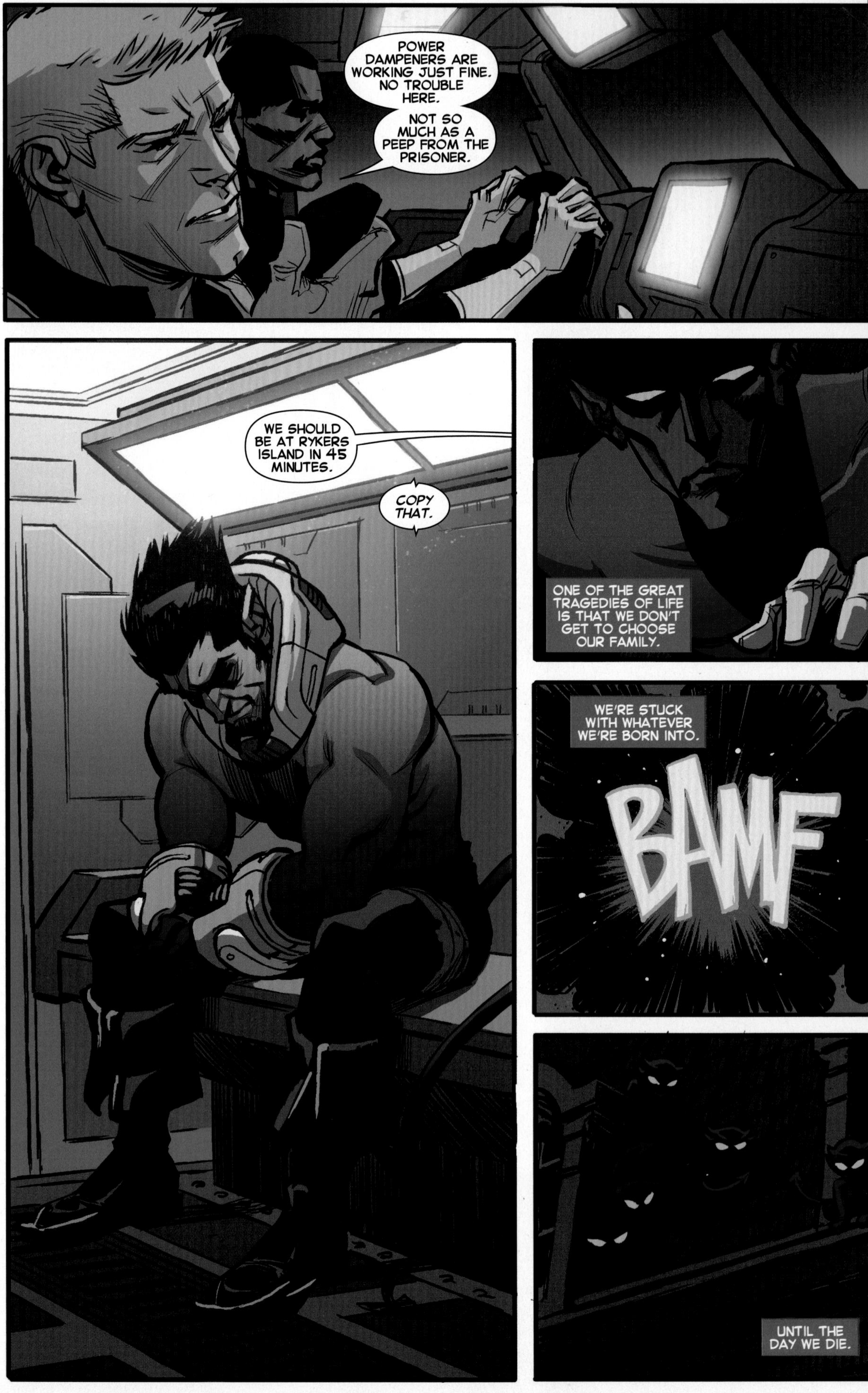
POWER DAMPENERS ARE WORKING JUST FINE. NO TROUBLE HERE.
NOT SO MUCH AS A PEEP FROM THE PRISONER.
WE SHOULD BE AT RYKERS ISLAND IN 45 MINUTES.
COPY THAT.
ONE OF THE GREAT TRAGEDIES OF LIFE IS THAT WE DON'T GET TO CHOOSE OUR FAMILY.
WE'RE STUCK WITH WHATEVER WE'RE BORN INTO.
BAMF
UNTIL THE DAY WE DIE.

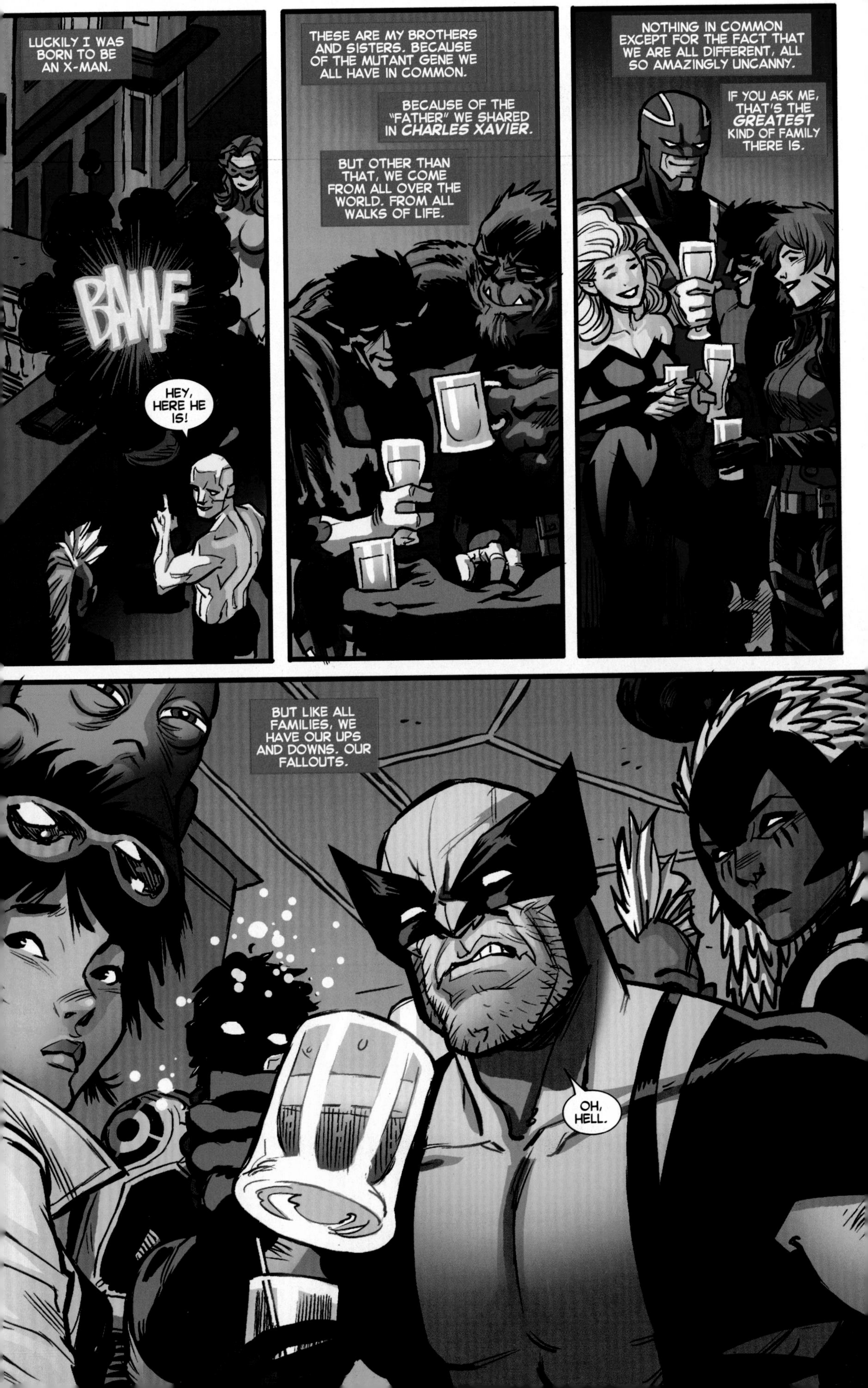
LUCKILY I WAS BORN TO BE AN X-MAN.
BAMF
HEY, HERE HE IS!
THESE ARE MY BROTHERS AND SISTERS. BECAUSE OF THE MUTANT GENE WE ALL HAVE IN COMMON.
BECAUSE OF THE "FATHER" WE SHARED IN CHARLES XAVIER.
BUT OTHER THAN THAT, WE COME FROM ALL OVER THE WORLD. FROM ALL WALKS OF LIFE.
NOTHING IN COMMON EXCEPT FOR THE FACT THAT WE ARE ALL DIFFERENT, ALL SO AMAZINGLY UNCANNY.
IF YOU ASK ME, THAT'S THE GREATEST KIND OF FAMILY THERE IS.
BUT LIKE ALL FAMILIES, WE HAVE OUR UPS AND DOWNS. OUR FALLOUTS.
OH, HELL.

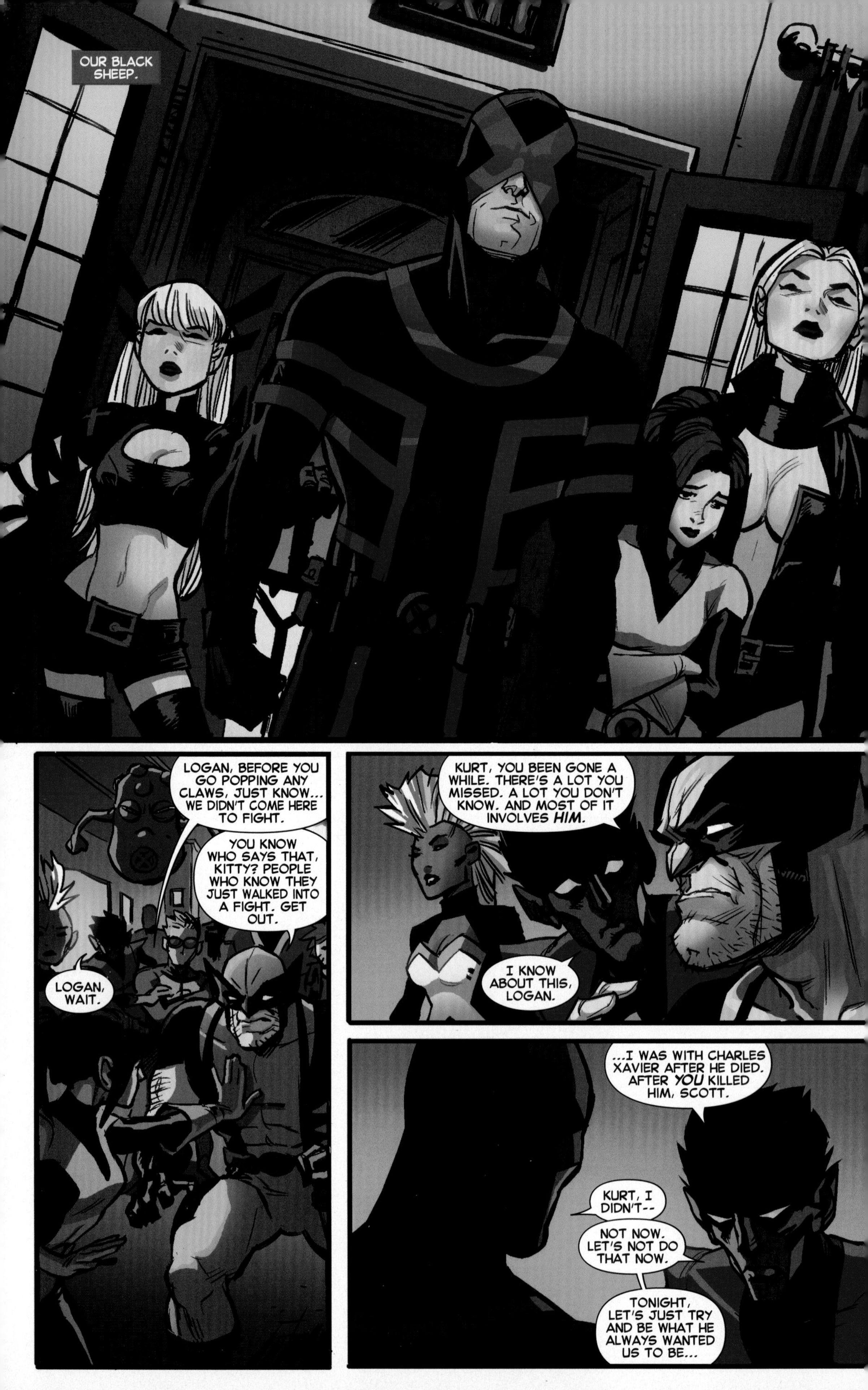

OUR BLACK SHEEP.
LOGAN, BEFORE YOU GO POPPING ANY CLAWS, JUST KNOW... WE DIDN'T COME HERE TO FIGHT.
YOU KNOW WHO SAYS THAT, KITTY? PEOPLE WHO KNOW THEY JUST WALKED INTO A FIGHT. GET OUT.
LOGAN, WAIT.
KURT, YOU BEEN GONE A WHILE. THERE'S A LOT YOU MISSED. A LOT YOU DON'T KNOW. AND MOST OF IT INVOLVES HIM.
I KNOW ABOUT THIS, LOGAN.
...I WAS WITH CHARLES XAVIER AFTER HE DIED. AFTER YOU KILLED HIM, SCOTT.
KURT, I DIDN'T--
NOT NOW. LET'S NOT DO THAT NOW.
TONIGHT, LET'S JUST TRY AND BE WHAT HE ALWAYS WANTED US TO BE...

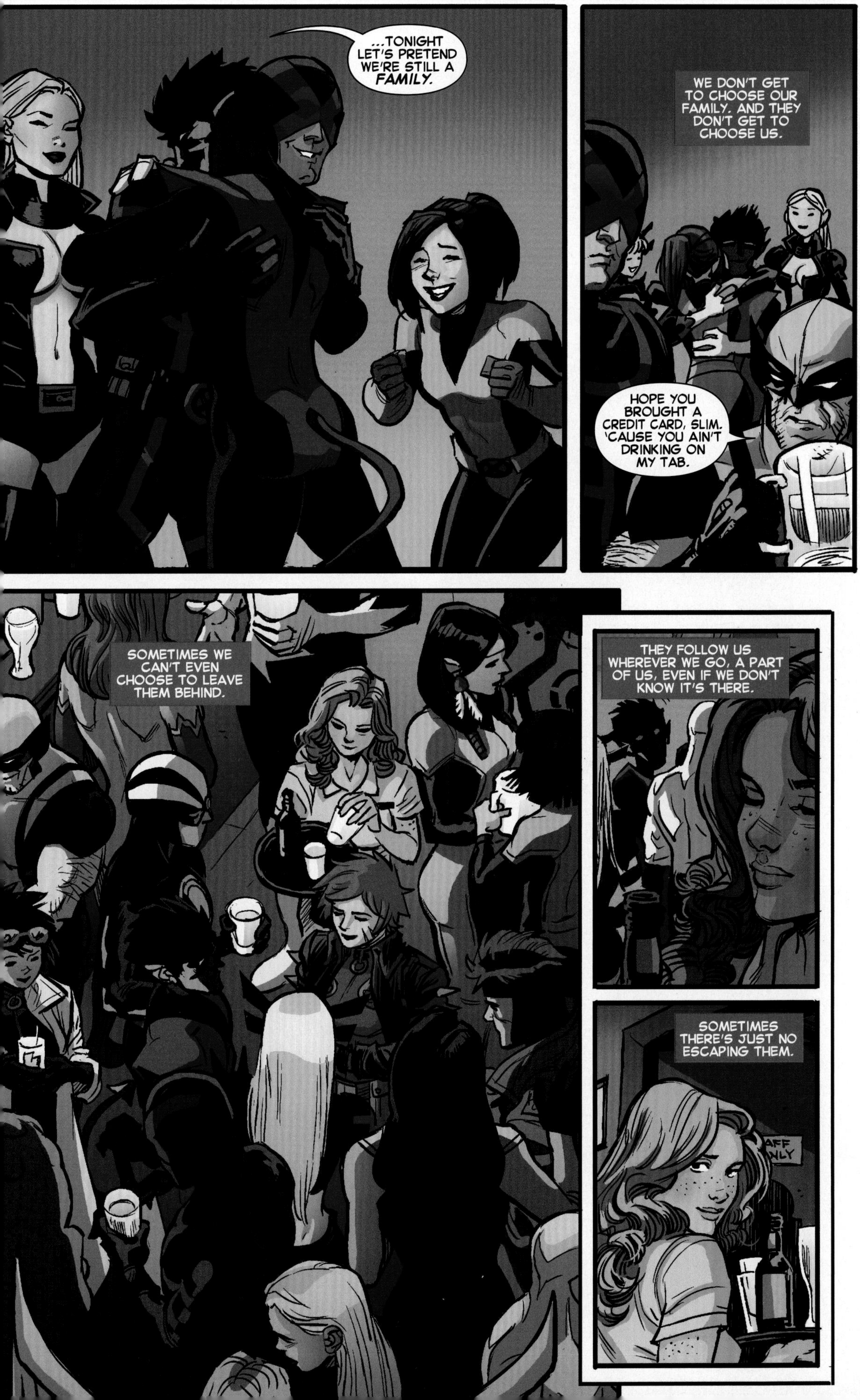
...TONIGHT LET'S PRETEND WE'RE STILL A FAMILY.
WE DON'T GET TO CHOOSE OUR FAMILY. AND THEY DON'T GET TO CHOOSE US.
HOPE YOU BROUGHT A CREDIT CARD, SLIM. 'CAUSE YOU AIN'T DRINKING ON MY TAB.
SOMETIMES WE CAN'T EVEN CHOOSE TO LEAVE THEM BEHIND.
THEY FOLLOW US WHEREVER WE GO, A PART OF US, EVEN IF WE DON'T KNOW IT'S THERE.
SOMETIMES THERE'S JUST NO ESCAPING THEM.

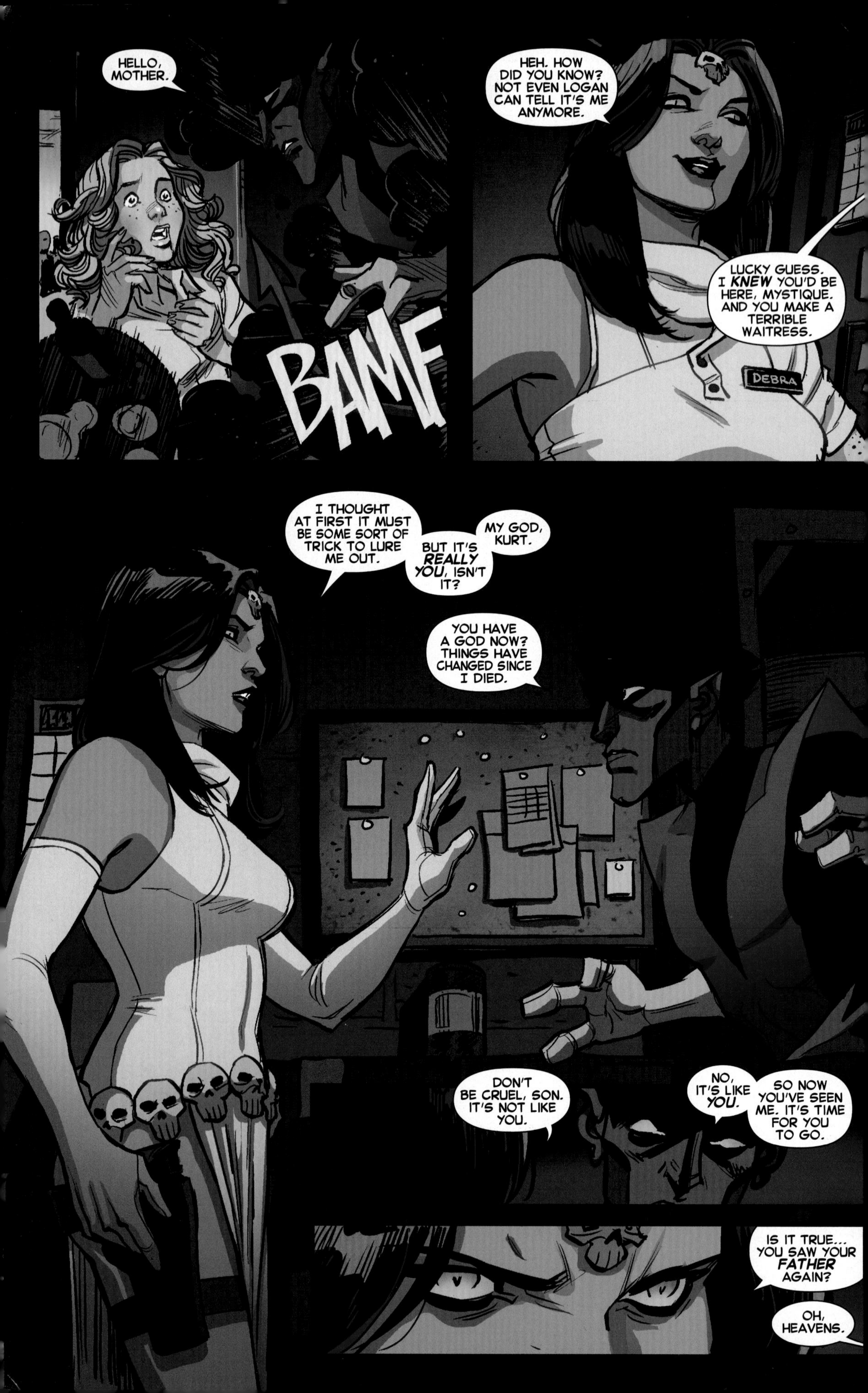
HELLO, MOTHER.
BAMF
HEH. HOW DID YOU KNOW? NOT EVEN LOGAN CAN TELL IT'S ME ANYMORE.
LUCKY GUESS. I KNEW YOU'D BE HERE, MYSTIQUE. AND YOU MAKE A TERRIBLE WAITRESS.
DEBRA
I THOUGHT AT FIRST IT MUST BE SOME SORT OF TRICK TO LURE ME OUT.
BUT IT'S REALLY YOU, ISN'T IT?
MY GOD, KURT.
YOU HAVE A GOD NOW? THINGS HAVE CHANGED SINCE I DIED.
DON'T BE CRUEL, SON. IT'S NOT LIKE YOU.
NO, IT'S LIKE YOU.
SO NOW YOU'VE SEEN ME. IT'S TIME FOR YOU TO GO.
IS IT TRUE... YOU SAW YOUR FATHER AGAIN?
OH, HEAVENS.

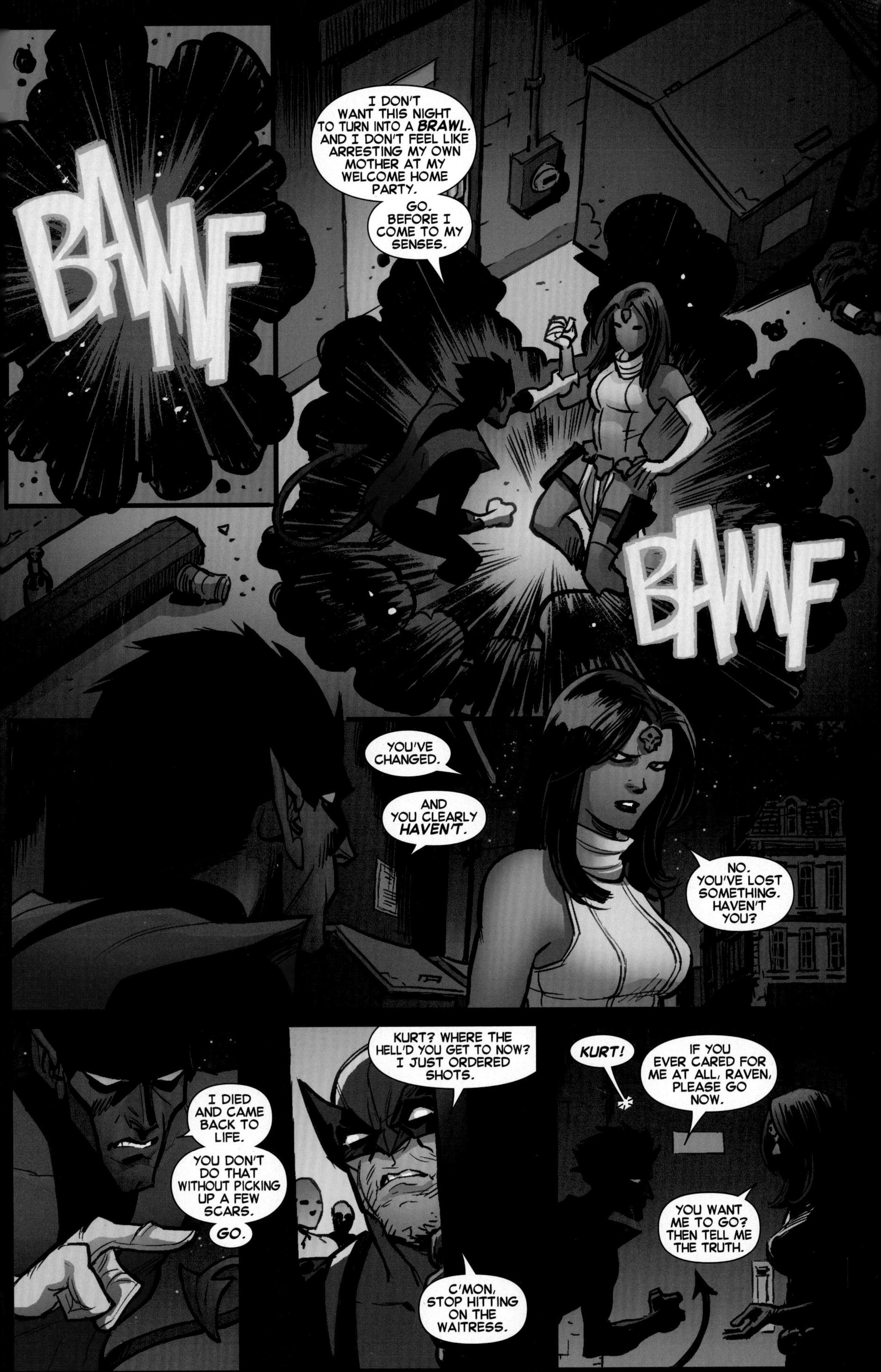
BAMF
I DON'T WANT THIS NIGHT TO TURN INTO A BRAWL. AND I DON'T FEEL LIKE ARRESTING MY OWN MOTHER AT MY WELCOME HOME PARTY.
GO. BEFORE I COME TO MY SENSES.
BAMF
YOU'VE CHANGED.
AND YOU CLEARLY HAVEN'T.
NO. YOU'VE LOST SOMETHING. HAVEN'T YOU?
I DIED AND CAME BACK TO LIFE.
YOU DON'T DO THAT WITHOUT PICKING UP A FEW SCARS.
GO.
KURT? WHERE THE HELL'D YOU GET TO NOW? I JUST ORDERED SHOTS.
C'MON, STOP HITTING ON THE WAITRESS.
KURT!
IF YOU EVER CARED FOR ME AT ALL, RAVEN, PLEASE GO NOW.
YOU WANT ME TO GO? THEN TELL ME THE TRUTH.

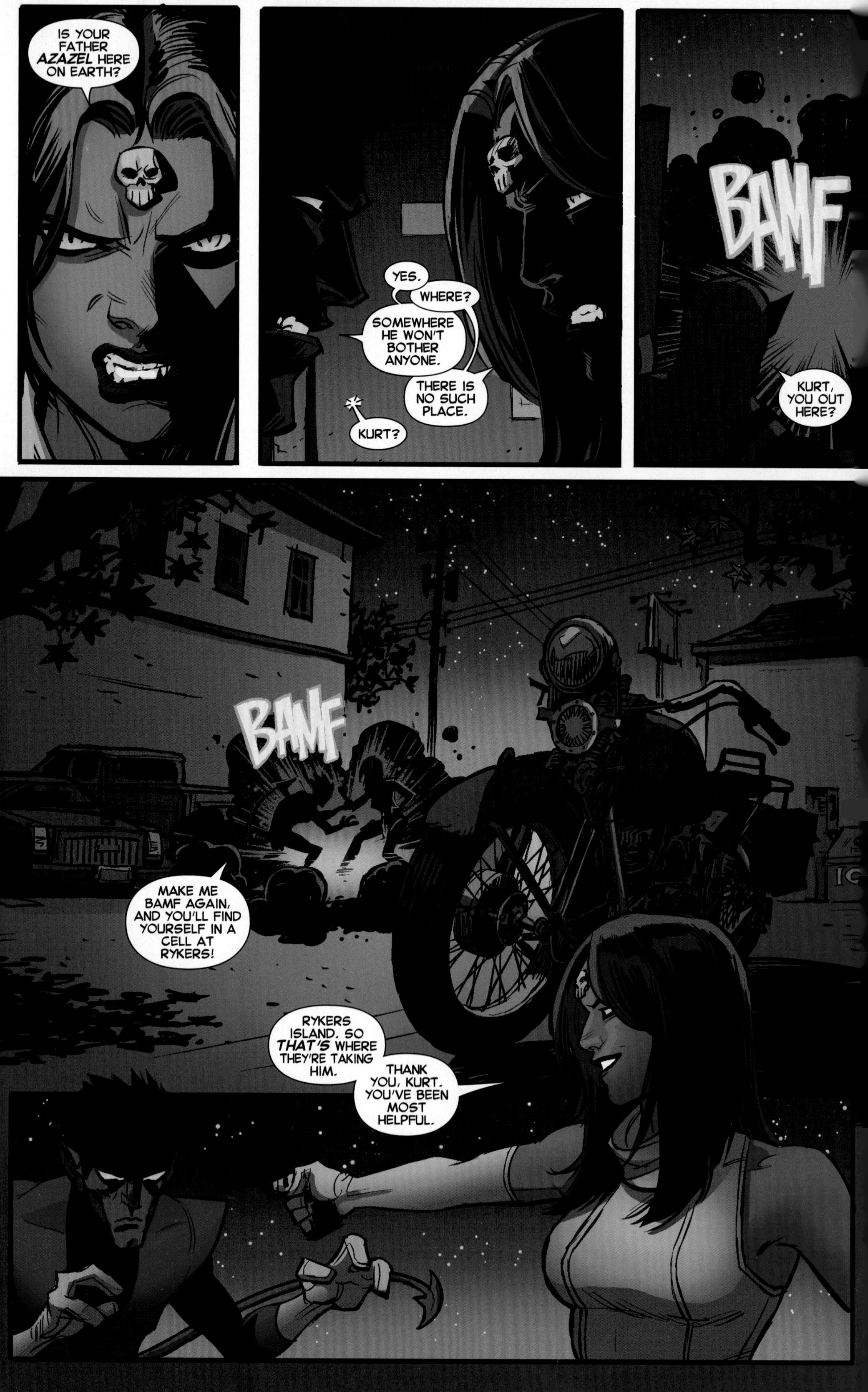
IS YOUR FATHER AZAZEL HERE ON EARTH?
YES.
WHERE?
SOMEWHERE HE WON'T BOTHER ANYONE.
THERE IS NO SUCH PLACE.
KURT?
BAMF
KURT, YOU OUT HERE?
BAMF
MAKE ME BAMF AGAIN, AND YOU'LL FIND YOURSELF IN A CELL AT RYKERS!
RYKERS ISLAND. SO THAT'S WHERE THEY'RE TAKING HIM.
THANK YOU, KURT. YOU'VE BEEN MOST HELPFUL.

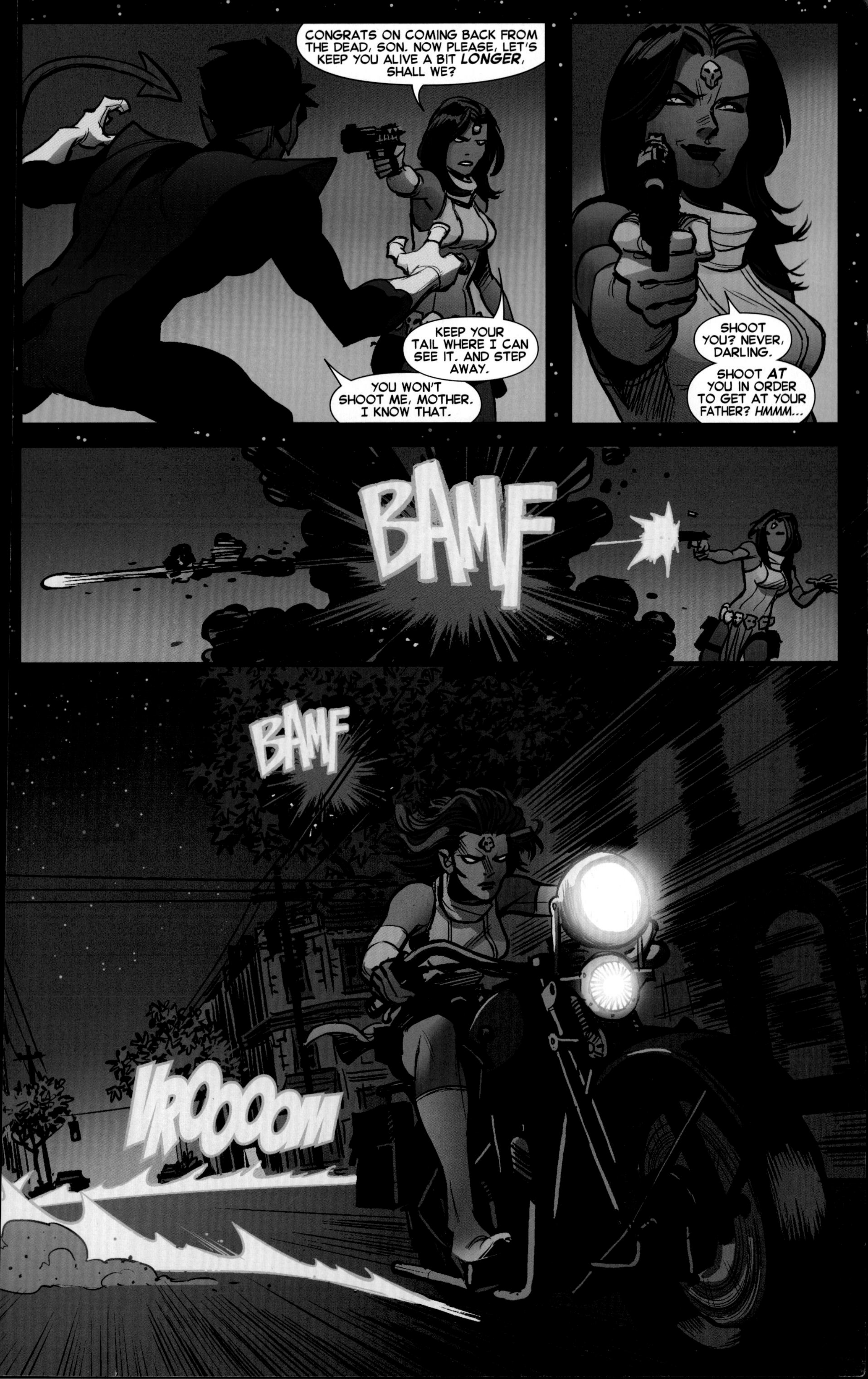
CONGRATS ON COMING BACK FROM THE DEAD, SON. NOW PLEASE, LET'S KEEP YOU ALIVE A BIT LONGER, SHALL WE?
KEEP YOUR TAIL WHERE I CAN SEE IT. AND STEP AWAY.
YOU WON'T SHOOT ME, MOTHER. I KNOW THAT.
SHOOT YOU? NEVER, DARLING.
SHOOT AT YOU IN ORDER TO GET AT YOUR FATHER? HMMM...
BAMF
BAMF
VROOOOOM

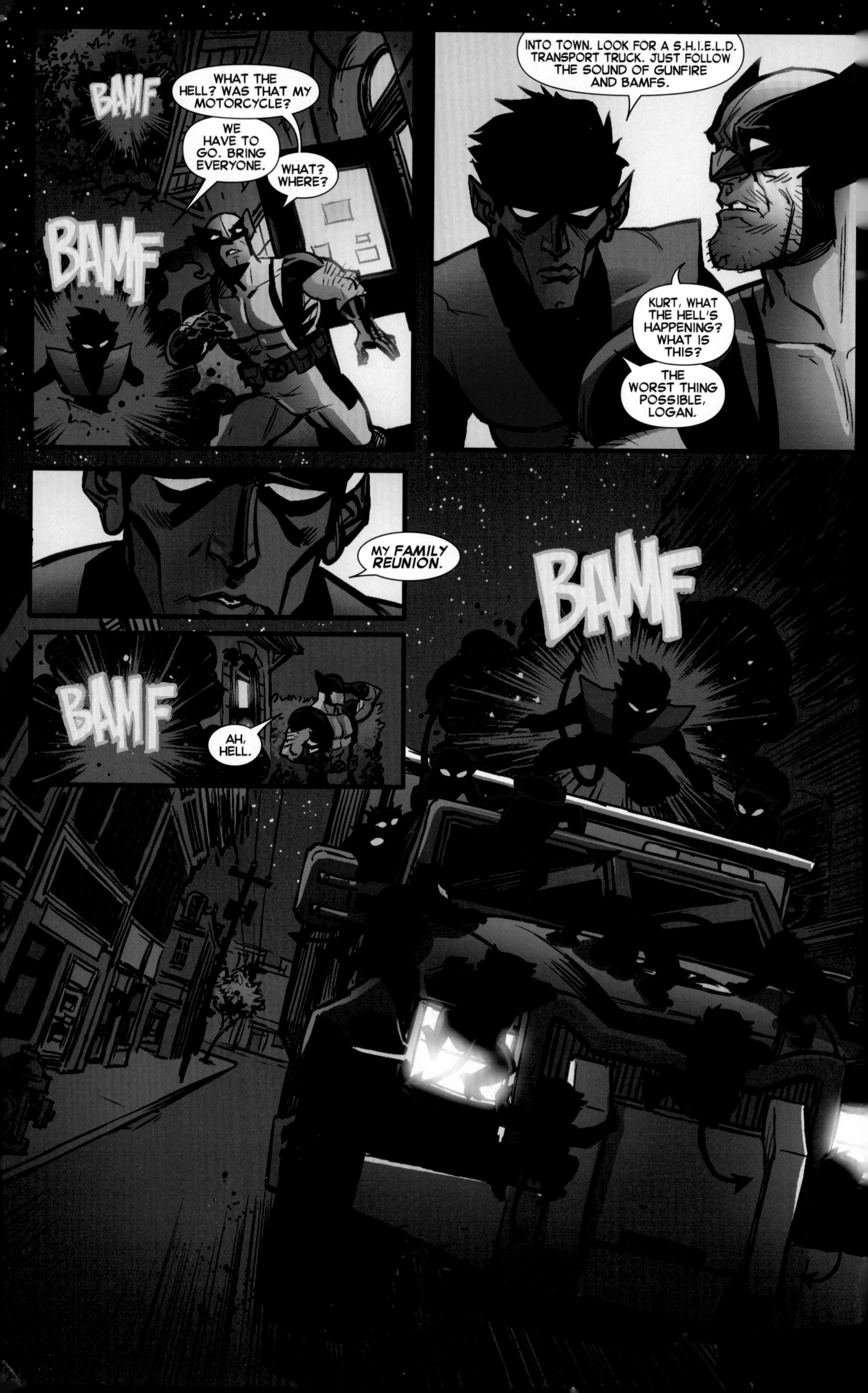
BAMF
WHAT THE HELL? WAS THAT MY MOTORCYCLE?
WE HAVE TO GO. BRING EVERYONE.
WHAT? WHERE?
BAMF
INTO TOWN. LOOK FOR A S.H.I.E.L.D. TRANSPORT TRUCK. JUST FOLLOW THE SOUND OF GUNFIRE AND BAMFS.
KURT, WHAT THE HELL'S HAPPENING? WHAT IS THIS?
THE WORST THING POSSIBLE, LOGAN.
MY FAMILY REUNION.
BAMF
AH, HELL.
BAMF

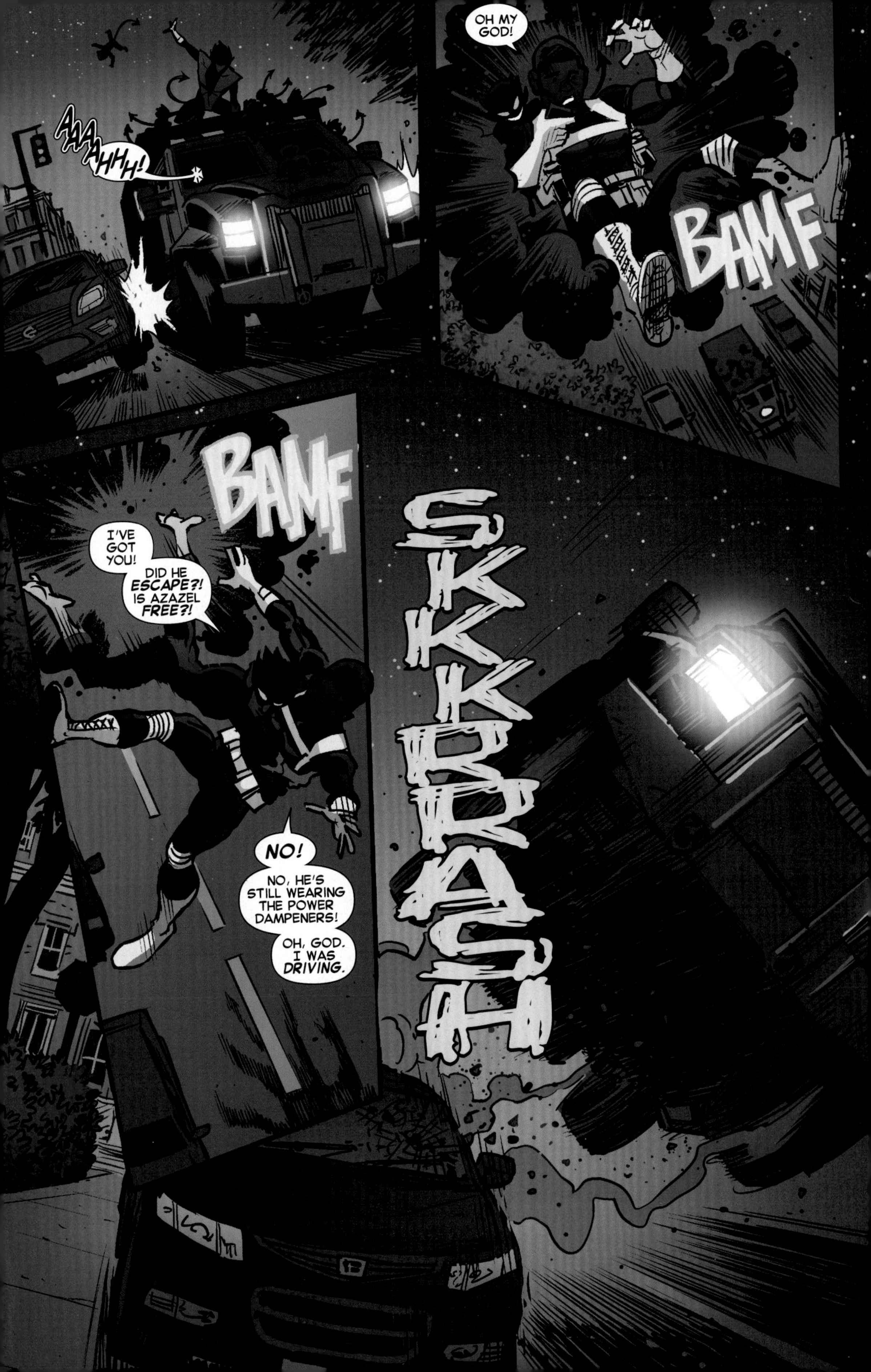
AAAAHHH!
OH MY GOD!
BAMF
BAMF
I'VE GOT YOU!
DID HE *ESCAPE?!* IS AZAZEL *FREE?!*
NO!
NO, HE'S STILL WEARING THE POWER DAMPENERS!
OH, GOD. I WAS *DRIVING.*
SKKRASH

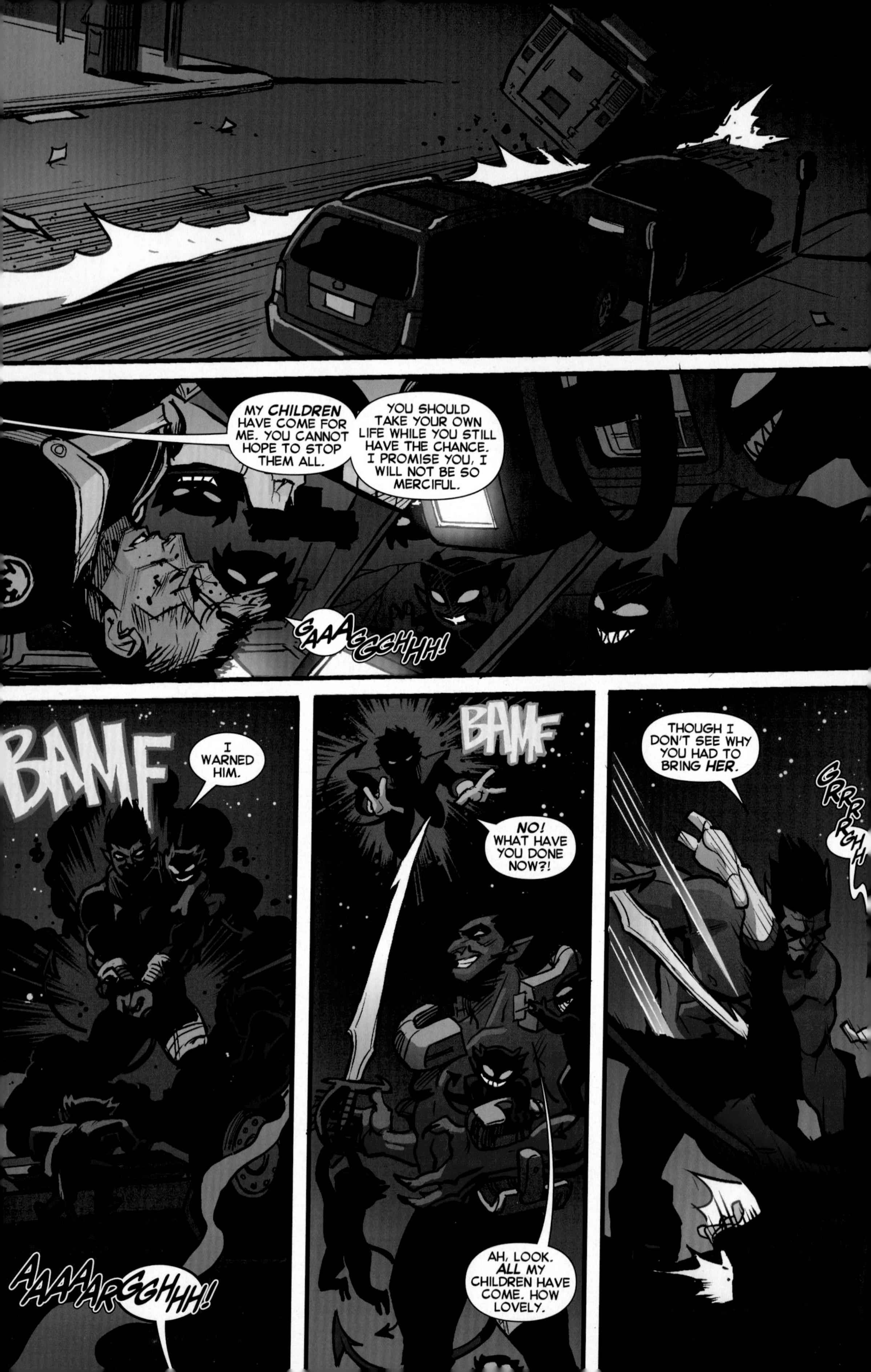
MY CHILDREN HAVE COME FOR ME. YOU CANNOT HOPE TO STOP THEM ALL.
YOU SHOULD TAKE YOUR OWN LIFE WHILE YOU STILL HAVE THE CHANCE. I PROMISE YOU, I WILL NOT BE SO MERCIFUL.
GAAAGGHHH!
BAMF
I WARNED HIM.
AAAAARGGHHH!
BAMF
NO! WHAT HAVE YOU DONE NOW?!
AH, LOOK. ALL MY CHILDREN HAVE COME. HOW LOVELY.
THOUGH I DON'T SEE WHY YOU HAD TO BRING HER.
GRRRRGH

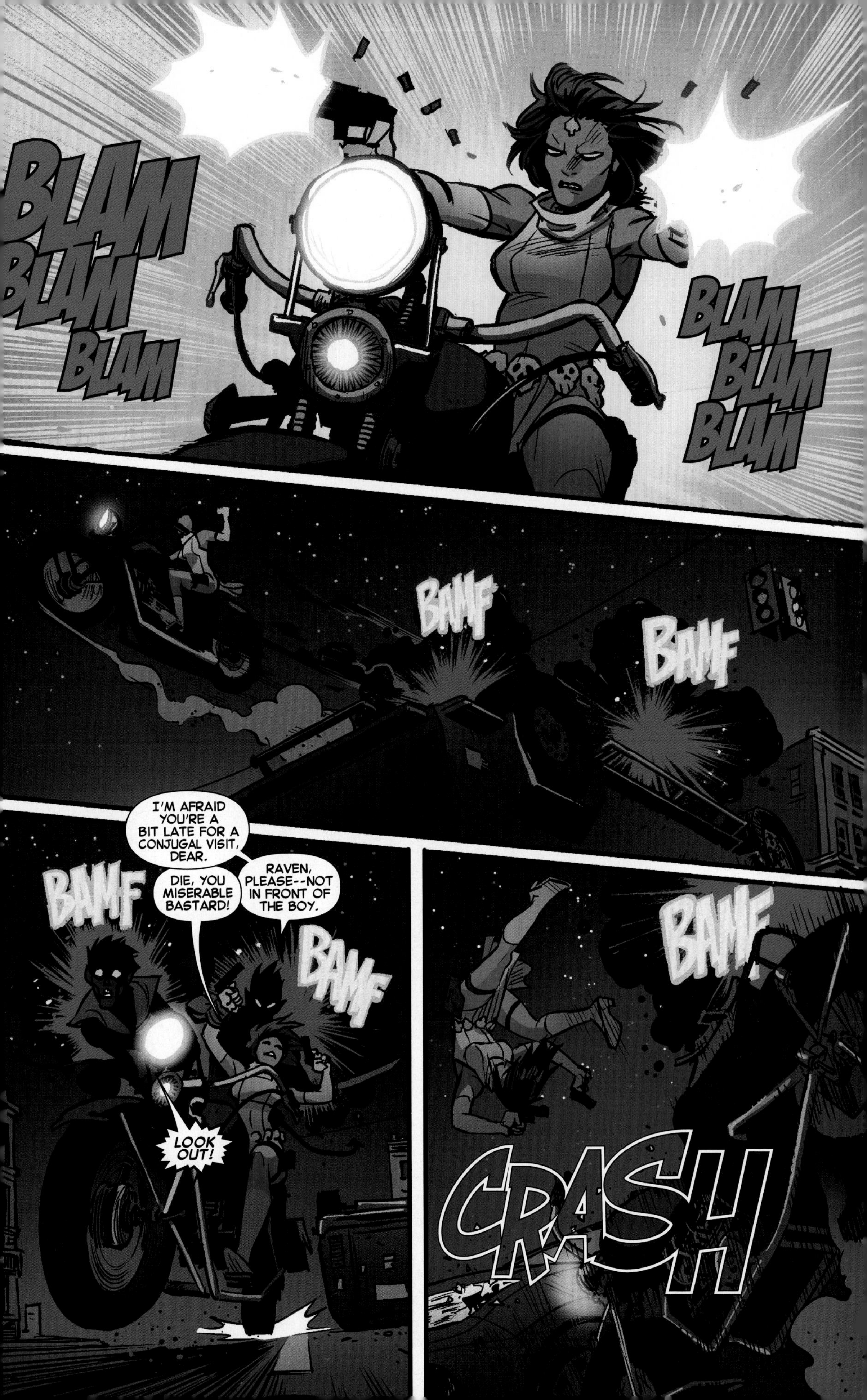
BLAM BLAM BLAM
BLAM BLAM BLAM
BAMF
BAMF
I'M AFRAID YOU'RE A BIT LATE FOR A CONJUGAL VISIT, DEAR.
BAMF
DIE, YOU MISERABLE BASTARD!
RAVEN, PLEASE--NOT IN FRONT OF THE BOY.
BAMF
LOOK OUT!
BAMF
CRASH

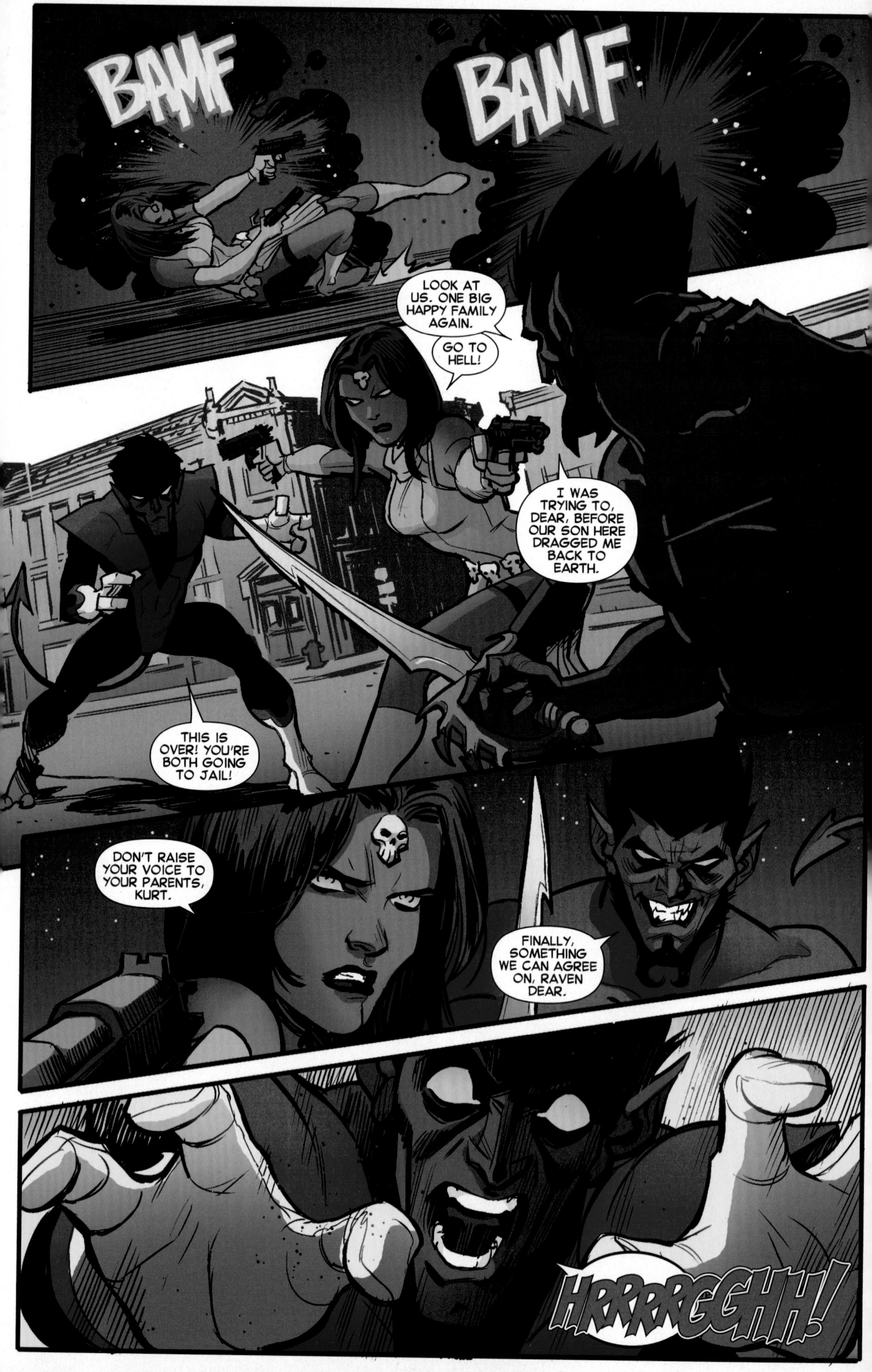
BAMF
BAMF
LOOK AT US. ONE BIG HAPPY FAMILY AGAIN.
GO TO HELL!
I WAS TRYING TO, DEAR, BEFORE OUR SON HERE DRAGGED ME BACK TO EARTH.
THIS IS OVER! YOU'RE BOTH GOING TO JAIL!
DON'T RAISE YOUR VOICE TO YOUR PARENTS, KURT.
FINALLY, SOMETHING WE CAN AGREE ON, RAVEN DEAR.
HRRRRGGHH!

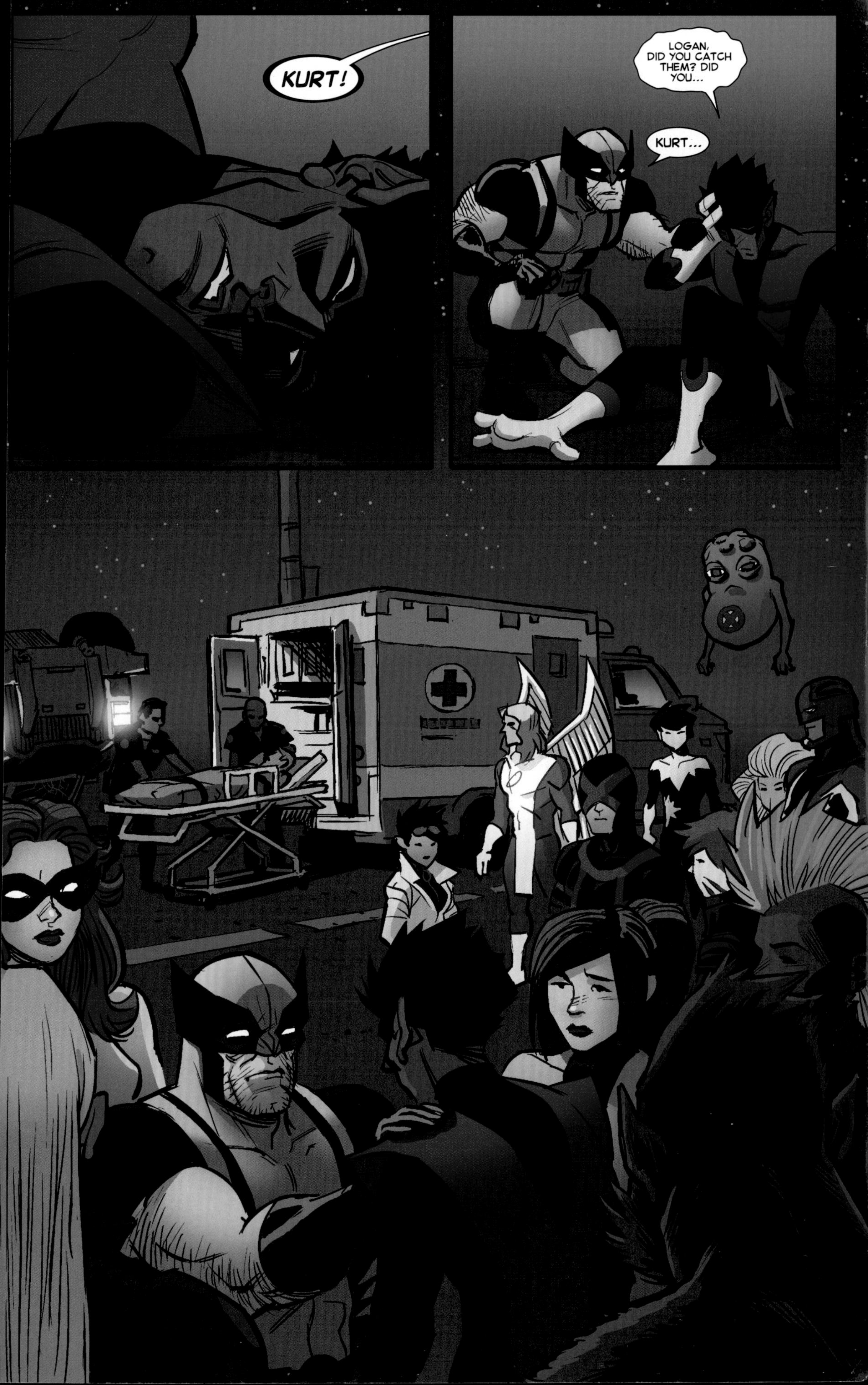
KURT!
LOGAN, DID YOU CATCH THEM? DID YOU...
KURT...

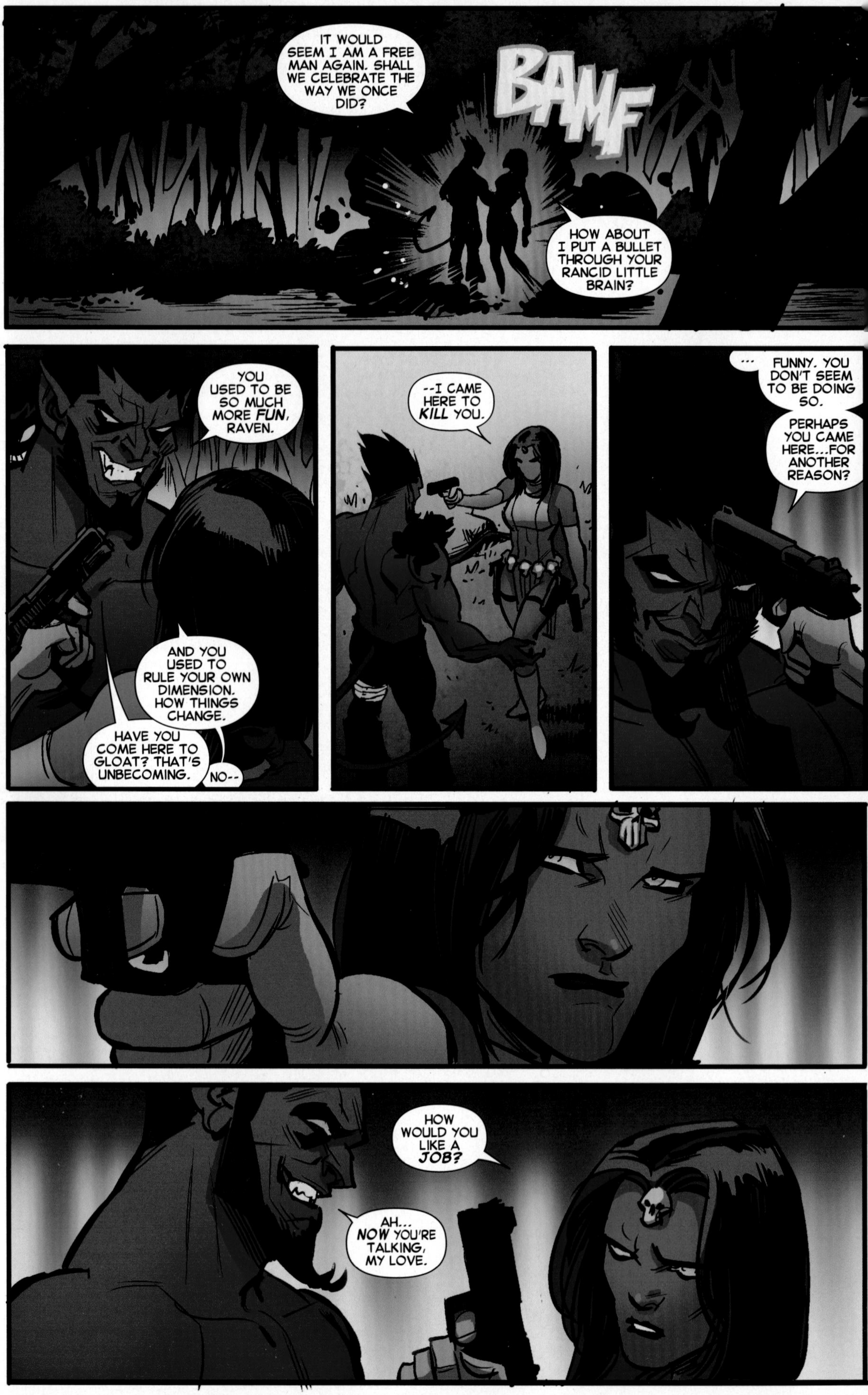
IT WOULD SEEM I AM A FREE MAN AGAIN. SHALL WE CELEBRATE THE WAY WE ONCE DID?
BAMF
HOW ABOUT I PUT A BULLET THROUGH YOUR RANCID LITTLE BRAIN?
YOU USED TO BE SO MUCH MORE FUN, RAVEN.
AND YOU USED TO RULE YOUR OWN DIMENSION. HOW THINGS CHANGE.
HAVE YOU COME HERE TO GLOAT? THAT'S UNBECOMING.
NO--
--I CAME HERE TO KILL YOU.
...
FUNNY. YOU DON'T SEEM TO BE DOING SO.
PERHAPS YOU CAME HERE...FOR ANOTHER REASON?
HOW WOULD YOU LIKE A JOB?
AH... NOW YOU'RE TALKING, MY LOVE.

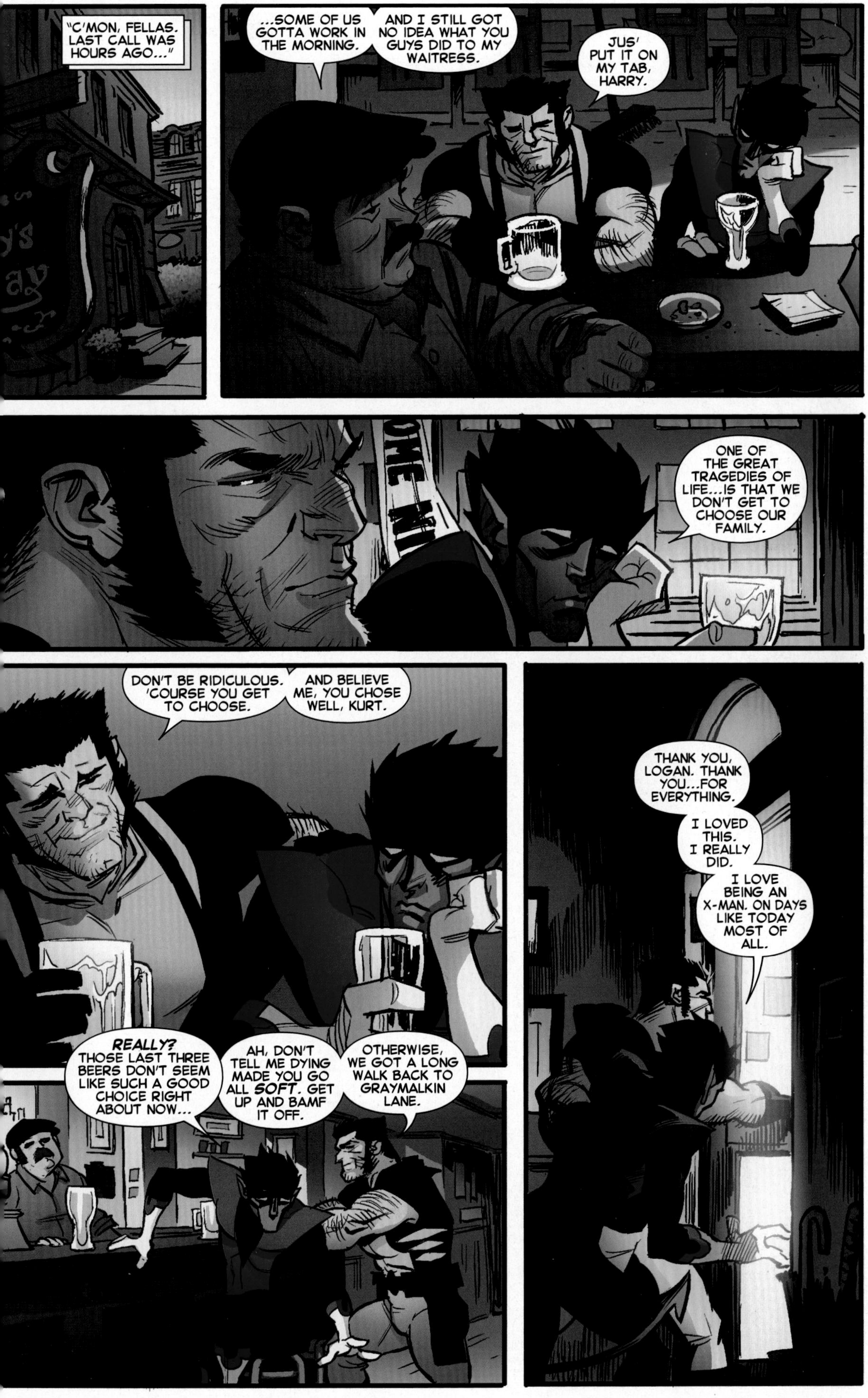
"C'MON, FELLAS. LAST CALL WAS HOURS AGO..."
...SOME OF US GOTTA WORK IN THE MORNING.
AND I STILL GOT NO IDEA WHAT YOU GUYS DID TO MY WAITRESS.
JUS' PUT IT ON MY TAB, HARRY.
ONE OF THE GREAT TRAGEDIES OF LIFE...IS THAT WE DON'T GET TO CHOOSE OUR FAMILY.
DON'T BE RIDICULOUS. 'COURSE YOU GET TO CHOOSE.
AND BELIEVE ME, YOU CHOSE WELL, KURT.
REALLY? THOSE LAST THREE BEERS DON'T SEEM LIKE SUCH A GOOD CHOICE RIGHT ABOUT NOW...
AH, DON'T TELL ME DYING MADE YOU GO ALL SOFT. GET UP AND BAMF IT OFF.
OTHERWISE, WE GOT A LONG WALK BACK TO GRAYMALKIN LANE.
THANK YOU, LOGAN. THANK YOU...FOR EVERYTHING.
I LOVED THIS. I REALLY DID.
I LOVE BEING AN X-MAN. ON DAYS LIKE TODAY MOST OF ALL.

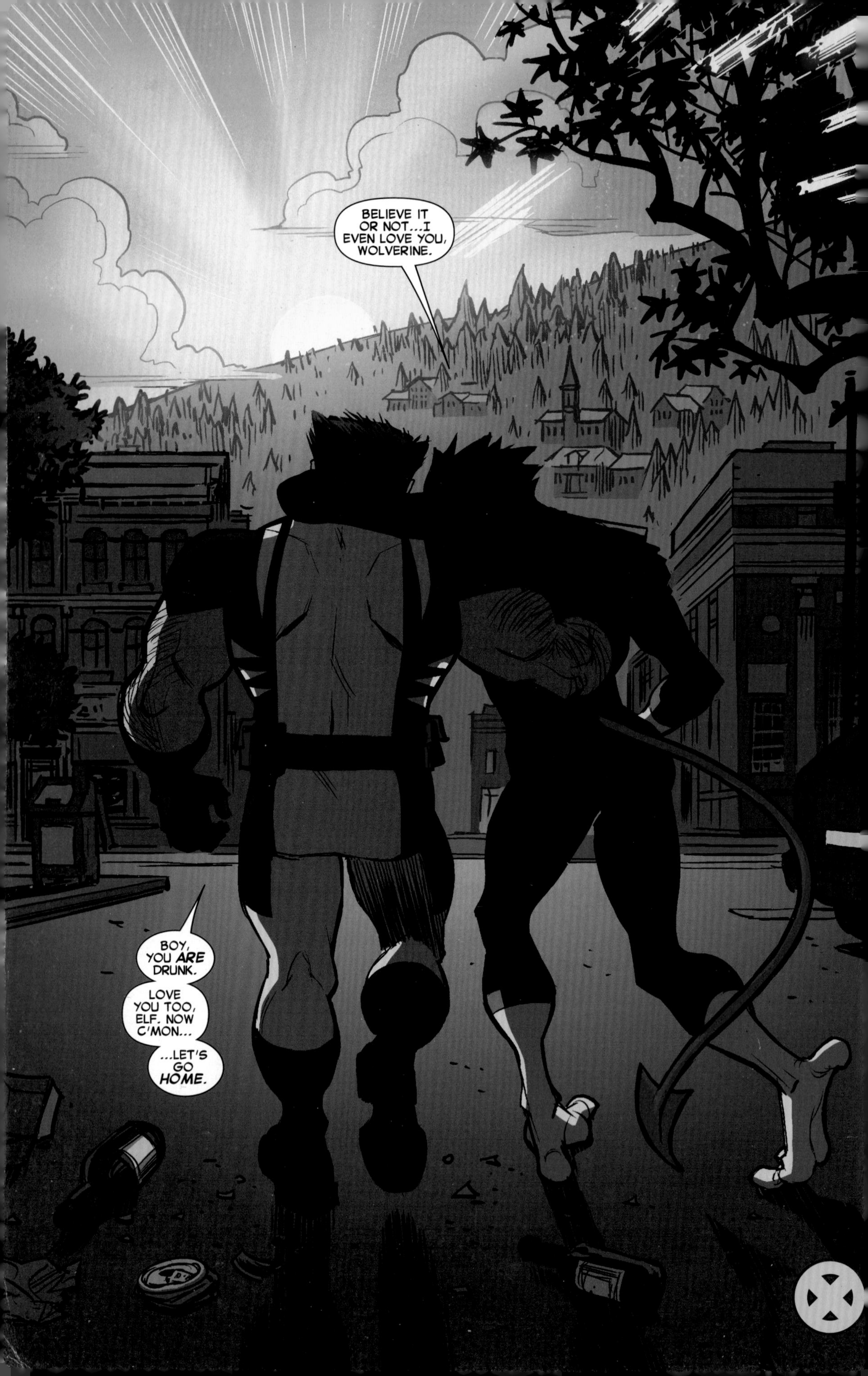
BELIEVE IT OR NOT...I EVEN LOVE YOU, WOLVERINE.
BOY, YOU ARE DRUNK.
LOVE YOU TOO, ELF. NOW C'MON...
...LET'S GO HOME.